Constructing National Security

U.S. Relations with India and China

JARROD HAYES
Georgia Institute of Technology

CAMBRIDGE
UNIVERSITY PRESS

32 Avenue of the Americas, New York, NY 10013-2473, USA

Cambridge University Press is part of the University of Cambridge.

It furthers the University's mission by disseminating knowledge in the pursuit of education, learning, and research at the highest international levels of excellence.

www.cambridge.org
Information on this title: www.cambridge.org/9781107040427

© Jarrod Hayes 2013

This publication is in copyright. Subject to statutory exception and to the provisions of relevant collective licensing agreements, no reproduction of any part may take place without the written permission of Cambridge University Press.

First published 2013

Printed in the United States of America

A catalog record for this publication is available from the British Library.

Library of Congress Cataloging in Publication data
Hayes, Jarrod.
Constructing national security : U.S. relations with India and China / Jarrod Hayes, Georgia Institute of Technology.
 pages   cm
ISBN 978-1-107-04042-7
1. United States – Foreign relations – India.   2. United States – Foreign relations – China.   3. National security – United States.   4. National security – India.   5. National security – China.   I. Title.
E183.8.I4H38 2013
327.73054–dc23   2013007200

ISBN 978-1-107-04042-7 Hardback

Cambridge University Press has no responsibility for the persistence or accuracy of URLs for external or third-party Internet Web sites referred to in this publication and does not guarantee that any content on such Web sites is, or will remain, accurate or appropriate.

*To my wife, family, and friends.
I could not have done it without you.*

Contents

Preface		page ix
	Introduction: Constructing Democratic Security	1
	The Social and Political Nature of Security	2
	Identity as Boundary Condition: Enabling and Constraining Security	4
	Beyond the Democratic Peace: Rising Powers	7
	At Many Crossroads: Relating to International Relations Scholarship	10
	Structure of the Book	11
1	Securitization, Identity, and Security Outcomes	13
	The Copenhagen School and Securitization Theory	14
	Bringing in Identity	23
	Putting the Pieces Together: Identity and the Construction of Democratic Security	31
	Methods: Focal Points and Discourses	39

PART I. DEMOCRACY, SECURITY, AND THE RELATIONSHIP BETWEEN INDIA AND THE UNITED STATES — 47

	The Indo-American Literature	50
	Roadmap and Theoretical Expectations	52
2	Near Miss: The Bangladesh War, India, and the United States in 1971	54
	Historical Overview and Literature	54
	The Case	58
	Conclusions	78
3	Nuclear Games: The United States, India, and the Desecuritization of Nuclear Weapons	79
	Historical Overview and Literature	79
	1974 PNE	81

vii

	The 1998 Nuclear Tests	87
	Desecuritizing Proliferation: 2005 U.S.-India Nuclear Deal	91
	Conclusions	95
	Democratic Identity and Security in Indo-American Relations	96

PART II. THE NONDEMOCRATIC "OTHER": THE SINO-AMERICAN RELATIONSHIP ... 99

    The Sino-American Literature ... 102
    Roadmap and Theoretical Expectations ... 108

4 Near Miss: China and the United States in the 1995–1996 Taiwan Strait Crisis ... 109
    Historical Overview and Literature ... 109
    The Case ... 117
    Public Response ... 137
    Conclusions ... 140

5 Collision Course: The 2001 Hainan Island EP-3 Incident ... 143
    Historical Overview and Literature ... 143
    The Case ... 144
    Conclusions ... 156
    Democratic Identity and Security in Sino-American Relations ... 158

Conclusion: The Social Construction of Security ... 159
    Theoretical and Empirical Contributions ... 161
    Policy Significance ... 165
    Moving Forward ... 167

References ... 169
Index ... 203

Preface

Security is everywhere, and applied to almost everything. The initial impetus for the highway system in the United States was national security. President Dwight Eisenhower's avowed purpose for building the massive transit network was to facilitate the movement of U.S. military forces in the event of a land invasion. Two years later, security was used to justify education policy. The 1958 National Defense Education Act provided, for the first time in American history, large-scale federal support for postsecondary education. The list goes on, from Nixon's War on Drugs[1] to immigration[2] to climate change[3] to AIDS[4] to government deficits.[5] Almost any topic one might think of has probably been included under the rubric of security. In international relations, however, there is a notable exception. As reams of evidence indicate, democracies have been consistently unwilling to label their peers as security threats.[6] The puzzle is obvious: How is it that democracies have avoided constructing each other as threats while so many other subjects have been labeled as such? Indeed, in the United States, the spread of democracy has become a principal basis for ensuring security – as democracy-building efforts in Iraq and Afghanistan and democracy promotion in Libya and Myanmar attest.

This puzzle, the democratic peace in the parlance of International Relations (IR) scholars, provides the genesis for the book that follows. As I argue elsewhere,[7] while innumerable pages have been dedicated to testing – largely through large-N, regression analysis methods – the existence of a zone of peace

---

[1] Dufton 2012.
[2] Kicinger 2004; Wæver et al. 1993.
[3] Barnett 2003; Broder 2009; CNA Corporation 2007.
[4] Elbe 2006.
[5] Sahadi 2012.
[6] Choi 2011; Maoz and Russett 1993; Oneal and Russet 1997; Oneal et al. 2003; Ray 1995a; Russett 1993.
[7] Hayes 2012.

between democracies, relatively little attention has been paid to the dynamics and processes that produce the phenomenon. To put it another way, scholars can claim with significant confidence that the democratic peace exists but cannot say very much about why.[8] As I read more of the democratic peace literature, I was increasingly struck by the extent to which the scholarship has lost sight of the significance of the democratic peace in international relations, focusing increasingly on internal debates over which variables to include in regression equations. The importance of International Relations' failure to come to terms with the forces behind the democratic peace is difficult to overstate. Even before the end of the Cold War, democracy promotion occupied a powerful place in foreign and security policy, although it sometimes existed in tension with the prerogatives of containment. Since the end of the Cold War, U.S. foreign and security policy has explicitly rested on the spread of democracy as an integral element of ensuring U.S. national security, and there is evidence that this reliance has in part been inspired by the scholarship on the democratic peace.[9] On the surface, this relationship represents the achievement of what many social scientists (particularly IR scholars) seek in their work: to influence policy and thus impact the world beyond the halls of academia. Yet there is a danger here. IR scholars have precious little information as to what produces the democratic peace, and this means policy is built on a shaky foundation. Scholars are not able to tell policy makers how democracy leads to peace, and thus leave it up to policy makers to hypothesize what causes the democratic peace and how best to operationalize those mechanisms into policy.

My goal in this book is to provide a coherent theoretical framework for understanding the democratic peace, and in doing so to lay a solid foundation upon which policy makers can build. Specifically, I propose a possible mechanism by which the democratic peace is produced and examine U.S. relations with India and China to determine if and how the mechanism operates. I argue that democratic identity is central to collective understandings of who poses a potential threat in the international system. This identity arises from the practice of democracy and the norms (rule of law, democratic accountability, non-violent conflict resolution) that underpin that practice. Democratic identity in turn shapes the range of possibilities political actors have in terms of presenting external states as threats by making some claims – those involving other democracies – implausible. In making this assertion, I provide one of the first studies to cogently and coherently account for how the democratic peace has come to exist at the societal level.

While the origins of this book lie in the puzzle of the democratic peace, the approach I present speaks to more than the democratic peace. Or perhaps, in

---

[8] Jack S. Levy goes so far as to call the democratic peace the closest thing International Relations scholars have to a natural law (1988).
[9] Presidents Clinton and Bush have referred to the democratic peace in justifications of policy (Bush 2003; Clinton 1994a).

speaking to a phenomenon as large and important as the democratic peace, the study addresses other issues of significance in international relations. Most basically, it argues for the importance of accounting for how shared understandings of the world shape foreign and security policy. These shared understandings create the field on which policy makers operate, making some policy avenues easier and others more difficult. If scholars and policy makers understand that field, they can better account for the foreign and security policies of other states. In short, I argue for a more social, ideational, and contextual study of international security in contrast to the largely material and rational assumptions that tend to dominate the study of IR and security in the United States.

My choice of cases also has timely relevance as the United States and the world contemplate substantial shifts in economic and material (e.g., military capabilities) strength in the foreseeable future as states like India and China develop. In many ways, how this transition will occur is the central international security question confronting scholars, policy makers, and publics. Some IR scholars argue that similar transitions in the past have been the source of major wars, a worrying proposition for the future given the destructive capacities of modern industrialized militaries. Others point to the relationship between the United States and the United Kingdom to argue that transitions need not result in war. In short, the question remains unanswered. By examining U.S. relations with India and China within the context of my identity-based approach, this book provides an alternative perspective on a subject of enduring and timely significance.

While I refer to the approach presented in the following pages as "my" approach, in truth I am only the majority shareholder. I owe a tremendous debt to a small army of people for their advice, support, and guidance. Without these people this book would not exist – or if it did, it would be but a shadow of what is here. Five people stand out at the front of the list. Janelle Knox-Hayes has been my fellow traveler in life and academia. She is an extraordinary wife and partner, helping me refine my ideas, providing motivation to stretch myself intellectually, and offering emotional and editorial support throughout the long process of writing and publishing the book. Patrick James was present at the creation of this project and has been an amazing advisor and mentor, enduring a constant stream of e-mails, phone calls, and paper and chapter drafts over the past seven years. Where both Janelle and Pat had some obligation to endure my impositions, Ted Hopf had none. Yet Ted has been invaluable as I have worked through the book over the last year, reading the manuscript and particularly helping me get the preface and introduction right (or at least better). Indeed, the idea behind the crucial first paragraph of the whole book is Ted's. I have been outrageously lucky to have him as a friend and mentor. Gordon Clark, Janelle's doctoral advisor at Oxford University, has also gone above and beyond any expectation. He pulled on the hidden levers at that amazing institution to provide for me access to one of the world's finest academic libraries while I lived there for two years. Without that access, none of this would have been possible. Gordon also filled in as surrogate advisor, doing a brilliant job of making an outsider in Oxford feel at home. The final member of this party of five is my editor at Cambridge University Press, Robert Dreesen. Robert saw my article in *International Organization* and approached me about the book, already convinced of the merit of the theoretical story I am trying to tell. All who know the pain of trying to sell the merits of a book to (usually) skeptical editors will appreciate just how fortunate I was to get that e-mail from him. From the outset, Robert has been confident in the book and me, and it is entirely because of him that this book has found such an amazing home.

My debts do not stop with those five people. The anonymous manuscript reviewers provided priceless comments and ideas, and I hope I have done justice to their suggestions. Amy Below, Dave Blagden, Paul Brister, Conor Browne, Rosella Cappella, Jason Enia, Jeffrey Fields, Lene Hansen, Carolyn James, Shashank Joshi, Paul Levin, Yitan Li, David McCourt, Harald Müller, John Owen, Jean-Loup Samaan, Karthika Sasikumar, Brent Steele, Kai Thaler, Srdjan Vucetic, Wesley Widmaier, and Pablo Yanguas have all been tremendously encouraging, providing friendship, insights, and more than the occasional confidence boost. My colleagues at the University of Oklahoma and Georgia Tech – particularly Vicki Birchfield, Peter Brecke, Miki Fabry, John Fishel, Mark Frazier, Eric Heinze, Hank Jenkins-Smith, Larry Rubin, Carol Silva, Adam Stulberg, Katja Weber, and Alasdair Young – provided a supportive environment as well as comments on various pieces of the project. One could not wish for better colleagues than these. Emmanuel Adler, Charli Carpenter, Christopher Daase, Michael Doyle, Robert English, Erik Gartzke, Ewan Harrison, Melody Herr, Colin Kahl, David Kinsella, Dan Lynch, Sara Mitchell, Mark Peceny, Brian Rathbun, James Lee Ray, Harvey Starr, David Welch, and Michael C. Williams epitomize all that is great about academia and those who work in it, generously taking time to talk to me about this project, in many cases reading portions and offering feedback. Thanks also go to Fideline Kraft, Jad Knox, Jadine Knox Luz, and Roman Luz for their consistent support and encouragement. I am sure there are others whose names belong here, and that they are omitted speaks to my own poor memory rather than the quality of their contributions. Of course, I alone am responsible for any shortcomings in the book. But without all these colleagues and friends, there would be a lot more of them. I appreciate permission granted by Wiley and Cambridge University Press to use material that previously appeared in journal articles. Specifically, portions of Chapters 1 and 2 appeared in abbreviated form in *International Organization*, and portions of Chapter 3 appeared in *International Studies Quarterly*. I would also like to thank the American Bureau for Medical Advancement in China Foundation for permission to use the image that appears on the cover of the book, John Watt for his assistance in that regard, and Nancy Reis and the University of North Texas Library for providing the image.

Last but not least thanks go to my family: Beverly, Walt, and Toni Thayer and Adam, Jennifer, and Daegan Hayes. My parents, Beverly and Walt, have been steady shoulders to lean on. My brother, Adam, is always good for levity when the weight of scholarly pursuits sets in, and my nephew Daegan reminds me how important it is to understand the issues that fill these pages.

Introduction

Constructing Democratic Security

Security threats, it seems, are everywhere. Almost everything – from immigration to the environment to national debt – has been subsumed under the rubric of security. Yet one of the most remarkable findings in the study of international relations[1] – that democracies do not fight each other – is very much about the absence of security threats. Therein lies one of the most important puzzles confronting scholars of international relations, foreign policy makers, and publics around the world: How does democracy defuse security and in the process create a zone of peace in an international system often characterized by violence? The answers to the puzzle are important because the democratic peace implies a very seductive outcome: a world without war. Far from being a narrow issue, the question of the democratic peace suggests insights on larger issues in international security, ranging from international stability to the role of social and political structures in shaping the behavior of states.

The core of this book is an effort to understand how identity shapes security outcomes in democracies. Specifically, how do external states come to be constructed as existential threats? One of the primary innovations of this book is my argument that that identity acts as both a facilitating and an inhibiting condition, mediating security by making some threat claims believable while rendering others implausible. As one of the most fundamental ties that bind democratic society together, democratic identity performs a potent role in security. It does so by providing securitizing actors with crucial social tools for communicating threat while at the same time making some security claims – specifically with respect to other democracies – extremely difficult. Democratic identity both facilitates and inhibits securitization by empowering and undermining the claim of an existential threat. In the case of an external state that is not a democracy, democratic identity can facilitate the creation of a condition

---

[1] In keeping with convention, I use the lower case when talking about the practice or phenomenon of international relations and the upper case when referring to the academic study.

of security by empowering the claim of an existential threat. In the case of an external democracy, the opposite dynamic occurs. Critically, the democratic identity is vested in the public, and it is the public evaluating the claim of a security threat. The role of the public in security is important in all modern nation-states but it is critically so in democracies, where the political system rests explicitly on the sovereignty of the public and the accountability of political leadership.[2]

By offering a coherent framework to account for the democratic peace, my approach addresses a critical problem in the literature – namely that despite reams of empirical evidence, the scholarship on the democratic peace does not tackle the mechanisms that drive the phenomenon. I offer a more nuanced and more hopeful understanding of the constraining influence of democratic publics than is present in much of the thinking about the democratic peace and international security. The approach I put forward also provides a more general basis for understanding not only when security threats emerge, but also (and perhaps more important) when they do not. Finally, through the case studies of U.S. relations with India and China, my argument addresses the long-standing concern of scholars and policy makers with the relationship between established and rising great powers.

The Social and Political Nature of Security

The idea that identity shapes security processes rests on a claim that security is a social construction and, thus, the product of social and political processes rather than an objective state of nature. As such, my argument parts with the prevailing assumption in International Relations that material factors produce security threats. A state of security does not automatically arise in the presence of specific material factors – like tanks, nuclear weapons, climate change, or immigration. These are physical facts that taken in isolation are devoid of social meaning and consequently devoid of security content. By indicating that a material factor (e.g., nuclear weapons) poses a security threat, a speaker is imparting a security meaning linked to a specific sociopolitical context onto the physical fact.

To use a very simple example to highlight the importance of social and political conditions for establishing security, assume a three-person system. Two individuals on the street are approached by a third carrying a pistol. The first person claims to the second (the audience) that the third actor with the weapon poses an existential threat to the audience's life. Outside of any sociopolitical context, it is impossible to determine how the second person will assess the first's security claim. That is, how well does the threat claim fit

---

[2] Bueno de Mesquita and his coauthors conceptualize the population that selects the political leadership of a state (and to whom major policies must be justified) as the *selectorate* (Bueno de Mesquita et al. 1999, 2004).

with the audience's preexisting understandings of the world?[3] The pistol is the purported source of the existential threat, but on its own the firearm means nothing in terms of security. Without understanding the web of social, cultural, and political conditions that surrounds the pistol, its meaning is unclear. The pistol in the hands of a police officer means something very different than the pistol in the hands of a man wearing a prison jumpsuit. Who is making the security claim? Does the person making the security claim have the credibility to make it? What is the relationship between the person making the security claim and the audience? The nature of the audience matters as well. Is the audience a law-abiding citizen or a gang member? Does that person come from a culture where weapons are prevalent, or where they are rare? The prescribed policy outcomes also rely on the sociopolitical context. What is the appropriate course of action (run away, return the threat, attack, capitulate) for the threat as presented? Even in a simple example, the material factor, in this case the firearm, cannot be understood outside the social, cultural, and political structural web in which it appears.[4]

When it comes to the security relations between states – where the material factors are often far more abstract than in my simple example – sociopolitical factors are orders of magnitude more important. For example, to democratic South Korea, U.S. nuclear weapons mean safety – while to its communist comrades in the north they mean danger. The difference is the sociopolitical context in which security is constructed rather than some change in the physical nature of the nuclear weapons. Changes in the state of security must also be traced to the social context of security, because rarely does the materiality of security change. When Iranian Nobel Laureate Shirin Ebadi notes that democracy is the solution to international concerns over Iran's nuclear program, she is making exactly the same point.[5] Only by changing the social frame of Iran's nuclear program, rather than changing the technology, can the security problem be resolved. Understanding security demands an examination of the social, cultural, and political structures in which the condition of security arises as well as the interaction between those who seek to establish the presence of a security threat and those whom they must convince.

Social and political structures are crucial for understanding how and when the condition of security arises because the claim of security is a political one. Until someone says, "Issue X is a security threat," and the intended audience understands and treats the issue as an existential threat, a state of security does not exist. Take, for example, climate change. Changes in global climate make large storms more frequent and energetic – thus damaging more property and killing more people – but these are natural facts. Until the natural facts are translated into social facts in a specific (security) way – that is, until people

---

[3] Constructivists call this *discursive fit*. See Chapter 1 for a more extensive discussion.
[4] Collingwood and Van der Dussen 1994.
[5] Ebadi 2006.

understand and begin treating climate change as a security threat – climate change is not a security issue. Security is a social and political condition, not an objective reflection of natural facts. Climate change will result in death and destruction, regardless of whether people come to understand it as a threat.[6] The U.S. response to the September 11, 2001 attacks provides a more conventional example. The attacks themselves did not signal a change in the material basis of international security. No new technologies or material capabilities emerged on September 11, although admittedly existing technology was used in a new way. Still, the scope in material terms of that novel use of technology was – relatively speaking – small and easily addressed. So, from a material perspective, the international system on September 12 was the same as it was on September 10. The changes in security witnessed after the September 11 attacks are ideational in their origin. Specifically, what changed was how threat – and by extension the international security order – was understood in the United States.

Identity as Boundary Condition: Enabling and Constraining Security

These examples highlight the point that a collective understanding that a security threat exists results from a political interaction – mediated by social structures – between foreign policy elites and the foreign or security policy audience. Social structures shape what is seen as existentially valuable as well as what can be understood as threatening in the first place. The nature of social systems as interacting social, political, and cultural structures establishes the boundary conditions of security – the collective influence of which is the security space – that both constrains and facilitates the condition of security.

The concept of security space is not another way of saying context matters. Context as a concept encompasses the unique totality of factors that produce a security outcome, including the personalities of the actors and random events as well as the sociopolitical structures in which they operate. The security space concept is an effort to systematically understand the ways social and political structures influence security outcomes. The security space frames the sociopolitical field in which security actors operate. From the standpoint of analyzing international relations, there are two basic levels at which the sociopolitical boundary conditions of security operate: the domestic and the international. While the two cannot be easily separated in reality (indeed, they inform and alter each other as they shape the behavior of states), they are often disaggregated for analytic purposes. While the literature has not systematically explored either level as part of a system of sociopolitical boundary conditions,

---

[6] Lene Hansen points out that the emphasis on speech in this approach to security means it overlooks conditions of insecurity in populations where threats cannot be or are not spoken of – for example, women in repressive societies or as victims of rape in war (2000). To this end, there is a vibrant discussion regarding the normative implications of understanding security as the product of political speech (Aradau 2004; Behnke 2006; Buzan and Wæver 1997; Floyd 2007; McSweeney 1996).

Introduction

far more attention has been paid to the international element. Alexander Wendt's cultures of anarchy as well as much of the subsequent constructivist scholarship focus on international sociopolitical structures, separating out and excluding the domestic sphere from analysis.[7] Far less examined is the role of domestic sociopolitical characteristics in shaping international behavior.[8] Brian Rathbun observes that increased interest in the role of ideational forces in shaping international outcomes is not matched with analysis at the domestic level.[9] Yet the social, cultural, and political connections at the domestic level are far denser and more energetic than they are at the international level. While both international and domestic factors play an important role in constructing international security, the comparative strength of domestic social, cultural, and political systems suggests we should pay more attention to the role of the domestic in shaping state behavior and international systems, not less. Indeed, it may be fruitful to think of the international system or order as (in part) the product of projected domestic social constructions. If this is the case, the structure of the system is generated in significant part by the interactions between these projected social constructions.[10]

Boundary conditions are social constructions, and as such are not hard and fast. They frame spaces where claims of security threat may be easier (facilitation) or more difficult (inhibition) to make. They do not create conditions in which a state of security is impossible or where it is guaranteed. In this way, boundary conditions bear a resemblance to the wave equation of an electron. The wave equation does not clearly delineate where the electron is or is not. Instead, it outlines the spaces where the electron is more or less likely to be present. There are very few if any circumstances where it would be impossible to invoke security. Given the right mix of extraordinary circumstances, the United States and the United Kingdom (or Canada) might treat each other as security threats.

However, while these possibilities exist in the universe of all possible states of security, that does not mean they are meaningful from the standpoint of

---

[7] Wendt 1992.
[8] Hopf 2002.
[9] Rathbun 2004, 4.
[10] The idea that domestic factors matter for international relations is far from novel. Putnam's concept of two-level games indicates an important role for domestic factors (1988). Knopf shows that domestic factors in the form of protest movements can foster cooperation between states, contrary to the usual assumptions of structural theories that posit the sources of cooperation derive exclusively from the international system (1998). Similarly Moravcsik's advocacy for a liberal theory of international relations emphasizes the importance of domestic political coalitions in shaping state preferences (1997). The list could go on. What is important to point out here is that much of this work leaves aside the intersubjective and ideational elements of the domestic context. Rathbun makes this point in his examination of the role of party ideology in shaping European foreign policy toward the Balkans (2004). That is not to say such work is absent, as Rathbun's book shows. Kier highlights the importance of domestic culture for military doctrine (1997). Hopf's 2002 and 2012 books both focus on identity structures as the primary source of Soviet behavior. But these exceptions serve to highlight the rule.

security practice or analysis. Social interaction operates not based on the nearly infinite possible, but instead on the plausible. While the plausible does not provide a basis for prediction, it does provide guidance to scholars and policy makers as to the range of likely scenarios in any given context as well as guidance on how to shape the outcome or understanding of how a given outcome came to pass. The concept of security space also directs the attention of policy makers and scholars not just to security threats, but also to situations where security threats do not emerge. This latter point is often overlooked, but is equally if not more important to understanding conditions of international security. Thus, the concept of security space – by coming to terms with the ways social structures facilitate some courses of action while inhibiting others – has the potential to generate systematic understandings and explanations regarding security constructions and outcomes.

To fulfill the potential to develop systematic understandings of the role of boundary conditions in constructing security spaces requires a collective undertaking, with a variety of scholars contributing to build an understanding of boundary conditions over time. The job is never quite finished because boundary conditions, like all social constructions, change over time. It is in the spirit of building an understanding of boundary conditions that this book operates. I do not seek to explain the social, political, and cultural factors behind the construction of security for all times and places. Instead, I focus on one element of the security space within democracies: the role of democratic identity.

Of course, boundary conditions shape not only what can be made a security issue but also the ways it can revert back to a nonsecurity status – to be desecuritized. Material-based security approaches have difficulty with this concept because what changes are not the material conditions, but rather the social and political understandings of threat. The end of the Cold War is an excellent example. Neither the United States nor the Soviet Union experienced any significant change in their material capacity to inflict harm on the other. Rather, the threat of the other was reconstructed – in this case desecuritized. In this book, the construction of India's nuclear program is another case of desecuritization. There can be little argument that nuclear weapons are generally seen as security threats. Institutions and organizations significantly infringing on sovereignty – the Nonproliferation Treaty, International Atomic Energy Agency (IAEA), Nuclear Suppliers Group – have been established to prevent the spread of nuclear weapons. IAEA reports go to the United Nations Security Council. And yet, as the case shows, India's nuclear weapons are seen by the United States as presenting no security threat. The termination of security rivalries, which are securitized bilateral relations, is yet another example of desecuritization. The issue of desecuritization and the process by which it occurs remains undertheorized and relatively neglected empirically. This book does not remedy this fault, but it does suggest – particularly in the chapter on India's nuclear program – that shifts in political identity can initiate desecuritization.

Identity serves multiple functions in establishing a security space, of which my treatment is but a single facet. Ole Wæver, in his work on societal security with various coauthors, argues that identity itself can serve as the thing to be secured because it is key to maintaining a distinctive social entity.[11] Mitzen's discussion of ontological security also holds that identity can serve as a referent object to satisfy the need of individuals to realize a sense of agency and self.[12] In her treatment, ontological security is generated through routinized interactions with significant others. Mitzen's argument suggests that part of the reason security actors invoke democratic identity in their security arguments is that democratic identity plays an important part of the routine of security interaction between democracies and the rest of the world. Failing to invoke democratic identity would then introduce profound uncertainty on the part of the audience, not as to the behavior of the external other, but as to the nature, place, and "actorness" of the self. By addressing the role of identity as a mediator shaping the security process, my argument provides a complement to these approaches.

Beyond the Democratic Peace: Rising Powers

Through case studies of U.S. relations with India and China, this book also addresses the timely and timeless issue of rising powers. The concept of rising powers – states that through economic development change the hierarchy of power in the international system – speaks directly to one of the central concerns of International Relations, specifically the possibility that the use of military force might accompany shifts in power. If the stream of commentary by policy makers and pundits in the popular media is any indication,[13] the issue is one of contemporary policy significance. The question of conflict associated with rising powers is likely to take on increased urgency as the United States sees its relative military and economic capacity reduced as the so-called BRICS (Brazil, Russia, India, China, South Africa) countries grow in international stature.

Popular concerns over rising powers have corresponding voices among IR scholars. The nuances of the academic discussion are significant, but in simple terms the question goes something like this: Can established dominant powers and rising powers find a way to accommodate each other peacefully? A body of thought in International Relations – power transition theory – holds that major conflicts in the international system are driven by disruptions to the hierarchy of power in the system.[14] That is, peace is maintained in the international

---

[11] Buzan and Wæver 1997; Buzan et al. 1998; Wæver et al. 1993.
[12] Mitzen 2006.
[13] Kagan 2012; Kaplan 2005; Kupchan 2012; Mead 2012; Zakaria 2008.
[14] Houweling and Siccama 1988; W. Kim 1992; Kugler and Lemke 1996; Organski 1968; Organski and Kugler 1980.

system not by the balance of power but instead by a powerful, dominant state that imposes its will to resolve conflicts and maintain stability. As long as the dominant power is unchallenged, the system remains relatively stable and peaceful. When the hierarchy is challenged, war occurs for two possible reasons. One reason is that the dominant state fights the rising power preventatively to avoid being in a weaker, exploitable position later.[15] Alternatively, the rising power initiates conflict at the point of near parity as part of an effort to refashion the international system to its benefit. In either case, power transition theory holds that rising powers, by altering the power hierarchy of the system, are an important and substantial source of conflict. One scholar goes so far as to say, "the fundamental cause of wars among states and changes in international systems is the uneven growth of power among states."[16]

If power transition theory and its closely related, economically oriented cousin hegemonic stability theory (stable international economic systems require a most-powerful state to enforce the rules) are correct, then to understand the future potential of major international conflict there is no better set of relationships to study than those of the United States with India and China.[17] Douglas Lemke and Ronald Tammen summarize the point well: "If China continues to grow in power as it has for the past few decades, it will surpass the United States as the world's dominant power sometime before the middle of this century. Such overtakings among great powers have corresponded with the major wars of the past centuries. These two observations represent the most important strategic calculation of the twenty-first century. They go to the heart of the issue of war and peace, cooperation, or conflict among the great powers."[18]

The intuitive appeal of power transition theory belies an ambiguity at its heart. Not all power transitions are accompanied by wars. While power transition theorists might point to World War I as evidence in support of their central claim, it is hard to overlook examples like the handoff of dominance from the United Kingdom to the United States. Thus, while power transitions may catalyze war, they are neither necessary nor sufficient.[19] Tammen acknowledges power transition theory is probabilistic rather than deterministic.[20] Preventative war is less a particular type of conflict than it is a motivation,[21] which suggests

---

[15] Levy 1987.
[16] Gilpin 1983, 94. There is some dissention within the power transition literature on this point. Some argue it is possible for a peaceful rise to occur if the dominant power works to integrate the rising power into the existing system (Tammen and Kugler 2006).
[17] A conclusion reached by many in the power transition research program. Indeed, Organski foresaw the rise of India and China in his 1958 text in which he originates power transition theory. There he argued that China and India would be the world powers of the twenty-first century (303–7).
[18] Lemke and Tammen 2003, 270.
[19] J. S. Levy 1987.
[20] Tammen 2008.
[21] J. S. Levy 1987.

Introduction

that the significance of rising powers for conflict must be understood in social and political as well as material (or power) terms. A. F. K. Organski, the progenitor of power transition theory, acknowledges that sociological variables like friendship between countries can ameliorate the conflict caused by power transitions.[22] Many point to the importance of the willingness of rising powers to accept the status quo as well as assessments by the dominant power of that willingness as critical to the potential of rising powers to cause conflict.[23]

However, much of the treatment of social and political variables tends to overlook their socially constructed natures, instead assuming them to be objective characteristics. For example, the concept of status quo is central to the idea that rising powers drive conflict. In short, conflict accompanies the power transition either because the dominant power believes the rising power does not accept the status quo (which favors the dominant power) or because the rising power does not accept the status quo and attacks the dominant power as part of an effort to change it. Yet this objective treatment of the status quo variable creates more questions than it resolves. If the dominant power arranges the international system to its benefit, then the implication is that all rising powers will be dissatisfied because the system does not serve their interests.[24] Conversely, it is also not clear why rising powers must be dissatisfied at all, as their rising status means that their power growth rate (however that is defined) significantly exceeds that of the dominant power.[25] This points to the larger problem of the assumptions regarding the factors that shape satisfaction and dissatisfaction that very often underpin the status quo concept and its use by scholars and policy makers.[26]

In the ambiguous treatment of social factors lies a significant problem for much of the discussion surrounding rising powers. If it is the case that power transition is neither necessary nor sufficient as an explanation for conflict, then, like the logic of balance of power, it becomes only part of the larger set of processes scholars must consider if they want to understand the mechanisms that lead to war. Social and political factors need to be more comprehensively accounted for if scholars and policy makers are to understand the implications of rising powers for global conflict. Power transitions take place within a larger sociopolitical security space and are given meaning within that space. Scholars and policy makers must understand how rising states are socially constructed in the security context if they want to understand when rising powers cause conflict – that is, when and under what conditions rising powers are seen as security threats. This is not a point the power transition research program, despite a significant degree of theoretical sophistication, directly addresses.

---

[22] J. S. Levy 1987, 86, fn 10.
[23] Efird et al. 2003.
[24] de Soysa et al. 1997.
[25] de Soysa et al. 1997, 512, fn 2.
[26] Efird et al. 2003, 297.

It is into this breach that my argument steps, providing a basis for understanding why some rising powers may come to be constructed as threats while others are not. The theoretical framework I present here along with the case studies of U.S. security relations with the two most significant rising powers in the international system demonstrate the important role social structures – operating through publics – can play in the ability of great powers to securitize rising ones.

At Many Crossroads: Relating to International Relations Scholarship

As the preceding discussion suggests, the approach I adopt in this book sits at the junction of several different approaches to international relations and international security. By drawing on the Copenhagen School's securitization theory and emphasizing the discursive basis of security as well as the politics of language and interpretation, my approach clearly shares ground with poststructural approaches to security.[27] Even so, my primary focus on so-called traditional security concerns – military-political interactions between states – as well as case studies targeted on U.S. relations with rising powers means my approach shares a certain affinity with security as traditionally understood.[28]

My focus on how domestic political and social structures shape understandings of and behavior in the international system situates this book as part of what Ted Hopf calls *societal constructivism*: "The job of societal constructivists is to find out what is on the slate that decision makers are bringing with them in their interaction with Others. Just as Wendt explores the issue of systemic 'cognitive structures,' we need to pay as much attention to their domestic variants."[29] My approach also fits within the broad conception of critical security studies outlined by Krause and Williams.[30] For Krause and Williams, most if not all approaches – including constructivism, poststructuralism, and feminism – addressing security outside the materialist boundaries of structural realism or neoliberal institutionalism are part of critical security studies. Peoples and Vaughan-Williams put it well when they describe critical security studies as an orientation rather than a precise theoretical label.[31] Specific to this broad understanding of critical security studies is the role of interpretivist epistemologies and ideational factors in shaping security practices and outcomes,[32] points on which I clearly agree.

I do part ways with a narrower definition of critical security studies. Within these pages there is no critique of security as practiced by policy makers or as

---

[27] Buzan and Hansen 2009, 143; Campbell 1998; Peoples and Vaughan-Williams 2010, 62.
[28] Walt 1991.
[29] Hopf 2012, 16.
[30] Krause 1998; Krause and Williams 1997a.
[31] Peoples and Vaughan-Williams 2010.
[32] Krause and Williams 1997b, 49.

Introduction

accepted by publics – in contrast to much of critical theory – particularly the Marxist and post-Marxist variants.[33] I also diverge from the Welsh School's central concern with pursuing a normative agenda of redefining security away from the state and toward individual emancipation and freedom.[34] However, the distance is not as great as it appears at first glance. While I do not explicitly focus on redefining security in individualistic terms, by focusing on security as the product of a political process in which the audience (in democracies, society at large) determines whether an issue becomes one of security I am tacitly sympathetic to Bill McSweeney's contention that security must make sense for individuals if it is to make sense at the international level.[35] At the same time, my identity-based approach accords with Ken Booth's argument that "community is the site of security."[36] Moreover, it seems implausible that the Welsh School's normative agenda can be fulfilled unless scholars understand how states construct the disciplining security the Welsh School rejects. I also share with the Welsh School a skepticism of the claim made by traditional security scholars that conflict is an inherent or natural part of the international system.[37] Conflict takes place by way of the political process of security. It is a process created by polities, not one foisted on them by nature red in tooth and claw. That is in part what is so remarkable about the democratic peace and what is lost in much of the literature on the subject: it reminds academics and policy makers alike that there is nothing inevitable about the use of force.

Structure of the Book

In this introduction, I have provided a general overview of the argument and goal of this book as well as some situation with respect to the International Relations literature. Chapter 1 outlines in greater detail my theoretical approach. Here, I link securitization theory with identity to develop a mechanistic understanding of how the bonds that bind individuals together within democracies both facilitate and inhibit securitizing moves. This chapter wraps up with a brief discussion of research methods. The securitization core of the theoretical framework calls for a focus on the discourse of securitizing actors as well as the acceptance by the audience of the securitizing move, while the identity component requires attention be paid to how the securitizing move is constructed. Given the relative inattention to these issues, the methods used here make a significant contribution to both securitization theory and scholarship on identity.

Chapters 2 through 5 are centrally concerned with case studies of the security relationships between the United States and India/China. Two chapters are

---

[33] Hutchings 2001; R. Jones 2001.
[34] Booth 1991, 2005; R. Jones 1999; Nunes 2012.
[35] McSweeney 1999, 16.
[36] Booth 2007, 268.
[37] Peoples and Vaughan-Williams 2010, 20.

dedicated to each dyad, and brief introductions precede each pair of empirical chapters. These introductions provide general historical background on Indo- and Sino-American relations, discuss the merits of the subsequent cases in the context of the book's central argument, briefly overview the academic literature on relations between the United States and India and China respectively, and summarize theoretical expectations regarding the cases.

Chapters 2 and 3 focus on Indo-American relations. Four focal points – points at which claims of security threats are made or could have been made – comprise the test cases. Chapter 2 concerns the 1971 "near miss" when the United States sent the USS *Enterprise* aircraft carrier to the Bay of Bengal to intimidate India during the Bangladesh War. During those events, President Richard Nixon and National Security Advisor Henry Kissinger clearly saw India as a geopolitical threat to the United States, but recognized that trying to convince the public of their position would be impossible. Chapter 3 focuses on Indo-American nuclear relations. Focal points include India's 1974 "peaceful nuclear explosion" (PNE), the 1998 avowed nuclear weapon test, and the 2005 U.S.-India nuclear energy deal. Throughout Indo-American relations, the Indian nuclear program has never been constructed as a security threat by the United States public, although some have tried. This failure – despite the fact that nuclear weapons have been constructed as security threats – indicates the importance of shared democratic identity for threat construction. The organization of these four cases into chapters is thematic rather than chronological. The 1971 case stands largely alone, while the 1974, 1998, and 2005 nuclear cases comprise a long-running potential security issue between the United States and India.

Chapters 4 and 5 shift from a shared democracy dyad to an autocracy-democracy dyad in the form of Sino-American relations. Two focal points consist of the test cases. The first, comprising Chapter 4, is the 1995–6 Taiwan Strait Crisis when China actively threatened Taiwan during the island's first democratic presidential election – to which the United States eventually responded with the deployment of two aircraft carrier battle groups. Discourse during this period shows a heavy emphasis on the undemocratic nature of China in efforts to construct China as a threat to the United States. Similar patterns are observed in Chapter 5, which concerns the emergency landing (following a midair collision) on Chinese territory of a U.S. military surveillance plane and the subsequent detainment of the plane and its crew by China.

To foreshadow my findings, the role of democratic identity takes center stage in both security relationships. With regard to India, it stayed the Nixon administration's hand when it sought to threaten India during the 1971 Bangladesh War and has desecuritized India's nuclear weapons program. Conversely, in the China cases, the lack of shared democratic identity provides one of the primary means for those who sought to portray China as a threat to make their case. In all these cases, the outcomes demonstrate the importance of identity for shaping international security behavior while reflecting little of the material determinism that dominates traditional approaches to security.

1

Securitization, Identity, and Security Outcomes

In this chapter, I present an identity-based theoretical explanation of security mechanisms within democracies. The goal is not to comprehensively identify all the possible or even plausible security mechanisms in democracies. Rather, I seek to explore what I argue is a particularly important mechanism that shapes how security is socially constructed in democracies. The approach I lay out accounts for the processes that lead to a state of securitization as well as the absence of securitization. One of the by-products of the latter is the finding that democracies do not use force against each other, otherwise known as the democratic peace. Thus, the democratic peace becomes a subset of broader security dynamics rather than a special condition, as it is often treated. The underlying intuition is that threats and security arise out of the human construction of reality. The presence of threat or the state of security are meanings imparted onto a situation or object by social cognition rather than the manifestation of a natural characteristic.

If we understand security and threat as human constructs, then the security process takes place in a specific social, political, and cultural context, and the security policy outcome can only be understood if we account for the ways this sociopolitical fabric shapes the construction of security and the sources of insecurity – threat. That intuition provides the foundation of this book, and this chapter seeks to build a coherent framework for understanding the social construction of security and threat. It does so principally by drawing on two theoretical approaches: securitization theory and social identity theory. It is upon the frame created by these two approaches I then hang a theory regarding the influence of a particular kind of identity (democratic identity) on democratic security outcomes.

To make my case, I first provide an overview of the Copenhagen School as well as the substance and development of securitization theory. In this section I also call for building on securitization theory by emphasizing the importance of the social, political, and cultural context of security. Second, I discuss the social psychological approach known as social identity theory. Third, I synthesize these approaches in combination with my own theorizing on the role of democratic identity into a domestically oriented, mechanistic, constructivist approach to security within democracies as well as discuss the applicability and limitations of the approach. Finally, I outline the methodology and cases I use to assess the validity of my approach.

The Copenhagen School and Securitization Theory

While the Copenhagen School approach has been in development since at least 1987,[1] three texts principally comprise its core – *Identity, Migration, and the New Security Agenda in Europe*; *Security: A New Framework for Analysis*; and *Regions and Powers: The Structure of International Security*.[2] As described in these texts, three central tenets characterize the Copenhagen approach to security: multisectorality, regionalism, and securitization.[3] The Copenhagen approach's sectoral aspect emphasizes the different issue areas – environmental, political, societal, military, and economic – in which security claims are made, marking a break from traditional conceptions of security concerned largely with military threats. The regionalism aspect – termed in *Regions and Powers* as "*regional security complex theory*" – posits that geographic characteristics play an important role in global security dynamics. As a consequence, regions where security issues are interlinked can be identified for analytical purposes. These two tenets are important aspects of the Copenhagen School's coherent approach to security studies, but for reasons that should become evident, they do not play a role in my use of the Copenhagen School. The third core concept, securitization, does, however, play a central role in my theoretical approach.[4]

Buzan, Wæver, and de Wilde argue in *Security: A New Framework for Analysis* that a state of security threat does not exist as an objective "fact" easily recognized by all concerned.[5] Instead, it arises out of an intersubjective, socially constructed security process. At the core of securitization theory is the premise that the act of calling something "security" makes it a security issue. This is the security speech act (called the securitizing move), in which the

---

[1] Jahn et al., 1987.
[2] Buzan and Wæver, 2003; Buzan et al., 1998; Wæver et al., 1993.
[3] While all three texts address all three elements to varying degrees, they also neatly match up in terms of central focus with the three tenets of the Copenhagen School, that is, *Identity* associates with sectoral security, *Security: A New Framework* with securitization, and *Regions and Powers* with regionalism.
[4] As Aradau (2004, 391) notes, while the Copenhagen School has been most successful in the broadening of security based on its sectoral approach, it is securitization that makes the school truly innovative.
[5] Unless otherwise noted, the discussion here of securitization refers to the second chapter of *Security: A New Framework for Analysis*, pages 21–47.

securitizing actor claims a particular actor or issue poses an existential threat to something of value (e.g., individual or collective physical beings, the state, culture, identity). Security is "thus a self-referential practice, because it is in this practice that the issue becomes a security issue – not necessarily because a real existential threat exists but because the issue is presented as such a threat."[6] Because the claim of a security threat concerns the continued survival of an object of value, the immediacy and existential nature of the problem precludes handling through normal political processes, which are often time-consuming and focused on generating workable compromises rather than decisive action. Instead, to address the existential threat the security claim seeks to move the issue into a Schmittian, authoritarian political framework in which deliberation is suspended, power is centralized, and political rights are deemphasized.[7] The securitizing move is an effort to break free of the rules that govern normal political behavior. Although making an issue one of security may facilitate a response, the authoritarian nature of security politics makes the state of security corrosive to democratic societies and generally should be seen in a negative light.

The securitizing move involves three elements: the securitizing actor, a referent object, and the audience. The securitizing actor initiates the securitizing move through the security claim. To make the claim credibly, the securitizing actor must possess sufficient social capital or authority. Typically, the actor occupies a position of appropriate authority (for issues of military security, examples include president, prime minister, foreign or defense secretary) within the sociopolitical context such that his or her security claims would have enough weight to warrant consideration by the relevant audience. The nature of this authority varies by social context, issue, and sector and requires the analyst to understand the ways society empowers certain actors in some situations and not others. For example, the sociopolitical system in the United States empowers the president to make socially credible claims regarding national security, but not most political science professors. This does not mean that presidential securitizing moves are automatically successful, but rather that the president has sufficient authority for the target audience (Congress, the public) to pay attention to the securitizing move.

The focus of the securitizing move is the referent object; the subject – nation-state, group identity, economic system – the securitizing actor claims faces an existential threat. As with the securitizing actor, the nature of the referent object varies by sociopolitical context. The referent object cannot be anything. Instead, it must be an object that is existentially valued. That is, the

---

[6] Buzan et al., 1998, 24.
[7] Aradau, 2004. *Schmittian* here refers to the work by German political philosopher Carl Schmitt, whose work formed the philosophical foundation for Nazi control of Germany in the 1930s. Schmitt's work focused on the efficiency of power centralization (dictatorship) and the unification of the state through the identification of a threatening "other" (Schmitt, 1928, 2007).

audience perceives the referent object as a thing of value whose survival needs to be guaranteed. A mundane example might be the existential valuation most societies place on the continued survival of the nation-state. Conversely, a given small business in a free market economy is not existentially valued (beyond the owners of the business) because the operating framework of the free market values the vulnerability of economic actors. Thus, although possibly valuable, small businesses do not enjoy society-wide existential valuation and as a result make for poor referent objects.

The final element – audience – plays a critical role in determining the success of a securitizing move. Whereas the securitizing actor initiates the security claim, it is always done with respect to a target audience, a group who must accept the existential valuation of the referent object as well as the claim of an existential threat to that object. As with the other elements of securitization, the composition of the audience depends on the sociopolitical context. Securitizing moves regarding the national identity of Thailand find little traction in France. The audience for a national security securitizing move in totalitarian, theocratic, and democratic polities varies tremendously. In principle, although I address statewide audiences, nothing precludes the audience from being an ethnic group, tribe, or village. If the audience accepts the existential valuation of the referent object and the claim of an existential threat, then securitization is successful and the issue moves out of normal politics into the realm of security. If the audience rejects either component, the securitizing move fails and the issue remains within normal politics.[8] To this end, securitizing actors need to use language the audience can identify with and understand to communicate the threat assessment. The U.S. invasion of Iraq in 2003 serves as a concrete way to illustrate the securitization dynamic. Preceding the invasion, President George Bush argued that Americans might fall victim to Iraq's weapons of mass destruction either directly or by proxy through terrorist organizations. Here, the securitizing actor is George Bush and the referent object is the physical safety of Americans, which was threatened by Iraq's possession of weapons of mass destruction. The audience, the U.S. public, agreed with the assessment and accepted the movement of the issue out of normal politics (resulting in the use of military force).

There are some gaps and tensions in securitization theory as outlined by Buzan, Wæver, and de Wilde. Although the authors indicate security as a process, the reliance on speech act theory suggests securitization arises out of a singular act. Yet few outcomes in politics, where securitization is firmly lodged, occur as the result of a single claim or act. Politics and human interactions are dynamic; they are an interlinked process rather than a chain of singular

---

[8] Buzan and colleagues are not clear whether this rejection must be proactive or if it can be passive. I suggest that it can be both. That is, the audience may actively reject the security claim (perhaps evidenced by a decrease in the social capital of the securitizing actor) or may passively reject the security move by ignoring it (e.g., the issue fails to gain traction in political parlance).

events.[9] Thus, securitization as outlined by the Copenhagen School is, in effect, ahistorical. I mean this in two ways. First, securitization theory underemphasizes the effort over time to build a security case. It is unrealistic to expect that the securitizing move exists in isolation to politics preceding it, or apart from subsequent or external events. The following example draws out the point. Over a span of months in 2002 and 2003, President George Bush progressively built a security case against Iraq. Evidence was marshaled, security claims were repeated, and the repetition reinforced and imbued those claims with credibility. Iraq was securitized as the result of a securitization process rather than a single securitizing act. Second, securitization provides little theoretical grounding for understanding new issues that arise in the context of institutionalized or latent securitizations. For example, India's development of a nuclear weapon took place in the context of the latent securitization of nuclear proliferation. How is this new issue influenced by its historical security context? This point raises the issue of broader social, political, and cultural context. Although the Copenhagen School recognizes the importance of sociopolitical context for understanding why and how securitizing moves emerge and succeed, the approach pays limited attention to the issue. The school does note that "external facilitating conditions" play an important role in the securitizing move,[10] but limits discussion to the social capital of the securitizing actor and the nature of claimed threat – tanks are generally held as threatening, bunny rabbits are not.

It is this issue of external facilitating conditions with which I am centrally concerned. Scholars have, with varying degrees of explicitness, begun to address the issue. Balzacq argues that securitization as outlined by the Copenhagen School originators does not provide adequate leverage for examining real-world security acts.[11] The focus on the formal structure of the security speech act suggests a natural law-type, unchanging, permanent practice, which stands in stark contrast to the generally social constructivist approach of the Copenhagen School. To remedy this, Balzacq shifts the formulation of securitization from speech act to strategic practice, emphasizing three aspects: the audience-centered nature of effective securitization, the context dependence of securitization, and the importance of power (principally, the differential between securitizer and audience) in the securitization act. Stritzel also emphasizes the importance of the securitization process rather than the speech act as a singular event and the "broader discursive contexts from which both the securitizing actor and the performative force of the articulated speech act/text gain their power."[12] Like Balzacq, Stritzel reformulates securitization into a

[9] Stritzel, 2007. I have also benefited on this point from discussions with Michael C. Williams.
[10] External facilitating conditions contrast with the internal facilitating conditions, which primarily focus on the rhetorical structure of the securitizing move. This structure consists of an existential threat, a referent object, and the means by which the threat will be resolved.
[11] Balzacq 2005.
[12] Stritzel 2007, 360.

tripartite analytical framework focusing on the performative force of the threat claim/texts, the social and discursive context, and the positional power of the securitizing actors. Alker argues, like Balzacq and Stritzel, that to understand securitization the sociohistorical and institutional contexts as well as the identities and values engaged by political speech must be accounted for.[13] Claims regarding securitization and desecuritization should be done in the context of a "rich historical understanding" of the societies in question.[14] McDonald likewise argues, "the question of why particular representations resonate with relevant constituencies is under-theorized in this framework [securitization theory]."[15] Indeed, McDonald goes so far as to claim that the role of facilitating conditions is so undertheorized as to remain outside securitization theory. Alan Collins, in exploring the relationship between security discourses arising over decisions regarding instructional language in Malaysia, highlights governmental strength as an important factor driving securitization.[16] Ralf Emmers points to institutional norms within the Association of Southeast Asian Nations (ASEAN) – for example, consensus – as well as institutional inertia to explain why securitizing moves have not produced common security responses to transnational crime in Southeast Asia.[17] Richard Higgott traces the securitization of economic globalization within the United States to the preponderance (unipolarity) of American economic and military strength in the global system.[18] Laustsen and Wæver implicitly point to the role of religion in conditioning securitizing moves when they discuss the ways religion is used as a referent object for securitizing moves.[19] Viatcheslav Morozov highlights the role romantic nationalism plays in shaping the security and foreign policy discourses in Russia.[20] Juha Vuori, drawing on Austin, points out that speech acts like securitization are performed according to historically, socially, and culturally contingent conditions.[21] Despite this body of work, the literature on security and securitization theory has not comprehensively addressed the ways external facilitating conditions enable, constrain, and shape securitizing moves and outcomes. This book builds on these efforts to expand securitization theory into a more complete theory of security.

Taking greater account of the sociopolitical structures shaping securitizing moves leads to important conclusions about the nature of security across polities and societies. The collection of social and political structures that shape security outcomes creates a security space in which analysts can expect to find

[13] Alker 2006.
[14] Alker 2006, 76.
[15] McDonald 2008, 564.
[16] Collins 2005.
[17] Emmers 2003.
[18] Higgott 2004.
[19] Laustsen and Wæver 2000.
[20] Morozov 2002.
[21] Vuori 2008, 73.

contestation over security. The security space is social, political, intersubjective, and discursive. It takes form through the practice of socially embedded actors and how they discursively construct that practice. In predominantly Muslim states, securitizing moves predicated on threats to Christian identity are not likely to succeed. In developing states with minimal Internet access, efforts to securitize the Internet (e.g., exposure to alien norms) will not likely find traction. Although these moves are not impossible, they are unlikely to succeed. As such, Islamic religious identity or Internet access establish a boundary condition for securitization, demarcating the subset of securitizing moves plausible within the state-society system from the universe of all possible securitizing moves. Security owes much to the sociopolitical forces that give the securitizing move its power. We might, then, think about the boundary conditions of security – a set of meta-stable social and political structures that define a security space in which some securitizing moves are less likely to succeed while others are more likely to succeed.

The concept of the security space is not another way that context matters. Context as a concept encompasses the totality of factors that produce a security outcome, from random or unpredictable events like the self-immolation of Mohamed Bouazizia – the Tunisian fruit seller whose death helped spark a wave of unrest in the Middle East in 2010 – to the personalities of policy makers to the sociopolitical structures defining society. The idea of security space is an effort to systematically understand the ways social and political structures influence security outcomes. Yet as the term *security space* suggests, agency does not disappear from the equation. Actors still make decisions in the security space whether to attempt securitization or not. The structures of the boundary conditions do not dictate the decision. They only shape the contours of what actors understand as plausible and what is not. Actors, in observing the boundaries of the security space, reify them. The routinization of observing the boundaries of the security space makes them more politically potent, to the point that not observing them may present a threat to the ontological security of the state – creating uncertainty as to the nature, place, and "actorness" of the self.[22]

Boundary conditions shape securitizing moves in at least two ways. First, they determine what is existentially valuable and what is not. Objects/ideas/practices that are not existentially valued do not provide a basis for securitization because the loss of the referent object is not significant enough to justify extraordinary measures. Take petroleum as an example. Oil as a physical substance inheres no aspect of security. The security aspects of oil arise from the value given it by society. In low-energy-density societies such as rural Sudan, oil provides a much more limited basis of securitization than it does in high-energy-density societies such as suburban America. Second, boundary conditions determine the plausibility claim of an existential threat. For

---

[22] Mitzen 2006.

example, in the United States efforts to securitize climate change have largely failed. Why? Surely the referent object, be it the economy (large-scale economic damage) or personal welfare (rising waterlines, food shortages, etc.), is existentially valuable to Americans. The problem lies in the sociocultural fabric of the United States, in which religion (God will preserve) and skepticism of science and authority combine to reduce the credibility of the existential nature of the threat (climate change is real, but will not have the claimed effect) or to discredit the purported threat altogether (climate change is not real).

Boundary conditions and the security space they define are not permanent fixtures, but instead temporally dependent conditions that enable securitizing moves. For example, Lene Hansen and Helen Nissenbaum argue that cyber security has been successfully securitized and indeed comprises a unique sector in security studies.[23] The very concept of cyber security, and the reasons and rationales underlying securitization, would be alien without the social, economic, and political changes of the past thirty years. Thus, we cannot understand cyber security as the result of a securitization process without understanding the evolution of the social, economic, and political fabric of society and the ways technology has penetrated society and in turn been given meaning. However, constructivists have argued that social processes can take on social strength through repetition, thus becoming sedimented or habituated.[24] Thus, scholars can talk about stable patterns in securitization wherein sociopolitical boundary conditions significantly influence securitizing moves over long periods of time. Indeed, the more securitizing moves observe the contours of the security space, the more securitization reinforces the security space in a feedback cycle like that described in structuration theory, wherein social structures (identities, social groups, systems of governance, etc.) shape the behavior of actors and actors in turn recreate the structures through their behavior.[25] The security space created is to some degree unique to each sociopolitical system, and yet these systems may share enough commonalities with other systems to create shared international security spaces (or orders) with converging understandings of threat.

The argument in this book is that democracy is one of these attributes that is both unique and common. There can be little doubt that American democracy differs from democracy as practiced in Germany or France. Yet all three states are still democracies and meaningful similarities contribute to a shared security space. Democracy in the form of democratic identity is a particularly important boundary condition because it links the domestic system (where social structures are strong) with the international system (where social structures are weak). Democracy is at its core a system of resolving political disputes. Because politics transcends the domestic-international boundary, democratic

---

[23] Hansen and Nissenbaum 2009.
[24] Hopf 2010; Wendt 1999.
[25] Giddens 1984.

identity as a mediator of the security space transcends that boundary as well, linking states in the international system together through shared domestic practices such as observing the rule of law and nonviolent conflict resolution. In this way, constructing another recognized democracy as a threat holds the potential to implicitly undermine the basis of domestic governance. This is not the case with identities such as nationalism, which are by definition exclusive to a single nation. There is no linkage between the domestic system and the international system for these identities, and the security spaces they help to construct are thus exclusive.

The concept of a sociopolitical security space is a large one, and as such a wide range of factors may play a role in the construction of security including everything from economics to conceptions of honor.[26] The argument in this book is that political identity plays an important role, but as I discuss in subsequent sections, this role is neither deterministic nor exclusive. Determining the factors that shape the boundary conditions of the space can be made deductively, as I do subsequently, or inductively.[27] In either case, the concept does not require that analysts abandon the precept that there is an intersubjectively established reality that can be observed and studied. Systematically accounting for boundary conditions and their strength offers the possibility of anticipating in a rough way securitizing moves that are unlikely. Similarly, understanding issues that societies are likely to see as existentially important or that have already been securitized gives scholars a means for understanding the social tools with which securitizing moves might be successfully executed. Neither, however, does it preclude the application of more critical approaches to security. Charting the security space gives scholars concerned with emancipation a basis for understanding how the state – or agents acting on its behalf – controls security discourses and practices. In turn, knowing how the security space is constructed and controlled gives critical security studies scholars concerned with emancipation the means with which to challenge repressive practices. Security discourses are laden with power relations (the positional power of the securitizing actor and the power centralizing nature of successful securitization), and nothing about the study of security as a sociopolitical construction means that security is a normative good. If what states make of security depends at least in part on the sociopolitical foundations of the state, and if security lies at the heart of the international system, these premises suggest there is not one international system but instead multiple interacting international systems arising from differing constructions.

It is possible to think about the security space both in terms of Copenhagen School–style sectors – economic, environmental, military, political, societal – and holistically in terms of the actors' (state, tribe, intergovernmental organization) general security disposition(s). The security space is probabilistic rather

[26] Lebow 2010; Widmaier 2005.
[27] Hopf 2002.

than deterministic. Unlike the boundary conditions of physics, social boundary conditions of the security space are not hard and fast. Instead, they represent gradations of increasing social difficulty. The further one pushes, the harder (but not impossible) the task becomes. Acute unforeseen events may push securitizing actors and/or their audiences beyond the boundaries of the previous security space, or may allow entrepreneurial securitizing actors the opportunity to reshape the security space (possibly by arguing that past approaches have failed). Changes over time can also alter the security space as societies (either domestic or international) shift in their conceptions of the world. Two hundred years ago, threats to slavery could have legitimately served as a basis for a securitizing move in some places. Fortunately, today the same cannot be said. Security spaces change over time as the sociopolitical forces that define the boundary conditions change. Thus, if scholars want to understand the conditions of security in the past (usually in pursuit of the causes of war), it is imperative to understand how the security space was defined previously. Arguments about security over time must confront this temporal issue directly and at least argue why the posited causal forces have remained a consistent element of the security space.

I recognize the applicability of securitization theory as an analytical tool is by no means universally accepted. Some within the critical security community argue that securitization, because it addresses a political process, reifies and privileges the undemocratic security dynamic through the process of analysis. Combined with the relative neglect within the theory of the desecuritization process, critics argue that Copenhagen School securitization actually serves as an advocate for authoritarian-like, Schmittian security at the expense of democratic processes and politics.[28] It is obviously beyond the scope of this book to answer these critiques conclusively. The debate over securitization theory is an important and healthy one. Rather than engage in this debate, however, I sidestep it by utilizing securitization as a practical tool for analyzing security and "tracing incidents of securitization and desecuritization."[29] Likewise, Hayward Alker notes, "for analytical, comparative purposes, one neither needs to articulate a well-developed normative position nor has to endorse or condemn ... the political worthiness of the political processes one is seeking to analyze."[30] I do not dispute that the securitizing move, successful or not, can and often is sociologically damaging and represents a failure of normal politics to address the issue, but these concerns do not impact securitization theory as an analytical tool. Indeed, using securitization theory as an analytical tool for uncovering how security issues are constructed and shedding light on the security process would be the first step toward a meaningful normative or ethical approach

---

[28] Aradau 2004.
[29] Taureck 2006, 55.
[30] Alker 2006, 75.

toward security studies. In doing so, the analyst also draws attention to the constructed nature of security claims, the opposite of reification.

Bringing in Identity

Although securitization theory provides powerful analytical tools for examining how the state of security comes to exist, it is not designed to be a complete theory of security. As I discussed earlier, securitization theory does not seek to explain when, where, or under what circumstances we might expect securitization to occur – what I call the *security space*. The security space has the potential to incorporate a wide range of elements, certainly too many for one book to address. Instead, I focus here on the role of political social identity in shaping the security space. Why identity? Ted Hopf points to the importance of social cognitive structures – of which identity is one of the most important – as the basis for the ordering and patterning of social life, giving rise to practices as well as meaning to action.[31] Without these structures, every situation would be unique as participants negotiated the significance and ground rules of interaction from scratch. In his seminal text on nationalism, Anderson starts with a puzzle: What compels people to die for others they have never met?[32] The answer is the "imagined community" of the nation, a shared identity that binds society together under the state. The power of the national imagined community suggests that we cannot understand security without understanding the impact of identity. This point is supported by Rodney Hall's work on national collective identity.[33] Hall finds the relationship between state and society has evolved over time. Where once state legitimacy rested on dynastic succession, by the late nineteenth century the state had evolved from the territorial state to the nation-state, dependent on support from the collectively imagined national self. The imagined national self is universal, not the property of a particular type of state. Thus, even in authoritarian states where the relationship between state and society is more hierarchical than it is in democracies, identity plays a critical role in fixing state-society relations. As my central focus is on the state-society relationship in the context of securitization as a political act, the role of political identity must be front and central.

What do International Relations scholars mean when they talk about identity? Before the sociological or constructivist turn in International Relations,[34] identity played little role in understanding or explaining the behavior of states. Since that turn occurred, of course, identity has increasingly played an important explanatory role. Typically, as Hall and Hopf lament,[35] constructivism

---

[31] Hopf 2002, 23.
[32] Anderson 1991.
[33] Hall 1999.
[34] Checkel 1998.
[35] Hall 1999; Hopf 2012.

operates at the systemic level, focused on the identity of the state,[36] and it is through a state-centric perspective that identity is usually invoked.[37] Alexander Wendt's important article on identity locates it at the systemic level and the roles states play in the international system.[38] In his 1998 article on the promise of constructivism, Hopf refers to the identity of the state when talking about U.S. involvement in Vietnam: "U.S. military intervention in Vietnam was consistent with a number of U.S. identities: great power, imperialist, enemy, ally, and so on."[39] Likewise, the literature on security communities and the role identity plays in their construction focuses on the systemic level.[40] Similarly, David Rousseau's exemplary work on the role of shared identity in threat perception largely focuses on state identity, albeit the way this identity influences policy makers.[41] Wesley Widmaier similarly locates the influence of identity – in Widmaier's case liberal versus social democratic economic identities – as state centered but operating through decision makers.[42]

Although there are exceptions to my characterization of the literature as state-centric – Hopf's excellent analysis of Russian identity, Hall's argument regarding domestic reconceptualizations of the national state, Thomas Berger and Robert Herman's chapters in Peter Katzenstein's seminal edited volume as well as Berger's book-length treatment of cultural antimilitarism in Japan and Germany, Katzenstein's treatment of Japanese national security, and Lars-Erik Cederman and Christopher Daase's call for the incorporation of corporate identity – these exceptions highlight the prevailing approaches to identity.[43] That the state should be the primary focus of the literature should not come as a surprise. In the history of the study of international relations, scholars have traditionally focused on states as coherent actors capable of making decisions and taking action. Despite complaints about the willingness of neorealist and neoliberal institutionalist scholars to anthropomorphize the state at the expense of internal characteristics and behaviors, constructivism as influenced by Wendt has generally followed in those footsteps, although not without dissent.[44] Although I do not contest the analytic value of the prevailing trend of treating the state as person, I contend that this approach leaves much of the world unexamined. States may at times behave as though they are coherent

[36] Adler 1997; Hopf 1998; Katzenstein 1996; Onuf 1989; Risse-Kappen 1995; Wendt 1992.
[37] My point here is not to say that systemic-level identity investigations are unimportant. Identity systems do not operate in isolation. Social identity constructed by states at the international level influences corporate identity at the sub-state level, and the reverse is also true. I only seek to highlight the relative neglect of domestic-level identity dynamics.
[38] Wendt 1994.
[39] Hopf 1998, 178.
[40] Adler and Barnett 1998; Williams 1998.
[41] Rousseau 2006.
[42] Widmaier 2005.
[43] T. U. Berger 1996, 1998; Cederman and Daase 2003; Hall 1999; Herman 1996; Hopf 2002; Katzenstein and Okawara 1993.
[44] Lomas 2005; Wight 2004.

actors, but often they are not. Moreover, understanding international relations only through systemic-level analysis strips much of the politics that takes place in the world out of the picture. Particularly in democracies, which are some of the most powerful actors in the international system, the exclusion of the domestic factors that shape international behavior results in incomplete understandings. Domestic factors matter for authoritarian states like China as well, as the protests over the 1999 bombing of China's embassy in Belgrade show.[45] On this point, I agree with Colin Wight's contention that although the state has actor-like qualities, treating states as persons means denying agency to humans. In short, what is missing from much of the literature is an understanding of how domestic identity dynamics factor into shaping international behavior and the security system.

To account for the role of identity beyond the state (traditional IR) or the individual (political psychology) in shaping the security space requires an approach that addresses the role of identity in society. To this end, incorporating findings from social psychology, specifically what Michael Hogg calls the *social identity approach* (SIA),[46] can make a significant contribution. What Hogg refers to as the social identity approach incorporates both social identity theory and its closely related sibling, social categorization theory.[47] Many scholars refer to *social identity theory* or SIT as the generic term encompassing both theories, although this is technically incorrect. Surprisingly, given its dominant position in social psychology and strong experimental validation, the social identity approach remains underutilized in the study of international relations. Initially developed by Henri Tajfel and John Turner, the social identity approach focuses on how identity derived from group membership shapes the social behavior of individuals.[48] More specifically, it is concerned with how group membership shapes the behavior of individuals toward fellow members of the group (ingroup) as well as toward members of other groups (outgroup). Originally, the approach focused on the role ingroup-outgroup dynamics play in driving social conflict, and the most influential uses of the approach in IR have been along similar lines.[49] Over time, scholarship has expanded to explore the reason and rationale of group membership as well as how membership shapes intergroup dynamics and personal behavior. Indeed, it has become one of the primary theoretical vehicles for understanding social cognition.[50]

Within the social identity approach, three elements drive group membership and social behavior: self-categorization; ingroup affect; and ingroup ties,[51] or what Tajfel originally describes as "knowledge of his membership of a social

[45] Gries 2001.
[46] Hogg 2006.
[47] Tajfel and Turner 1979; Turner et al. 1987.
[48] For comprehensive literature reviews, see R. Brown 2000; Hogg 2006.
[49] Gries 2005; Mercer 1995.
[50] Hogg 2006; Hogg et al. 2004.
[51] Cameron 2004.

group together with the value and emotional significance attached to that membership."[52] *Self-categorization* refers to the process by which individuals partition the world into ingroups and outgroups.[53] Cognitively, these groups are represented by context-specific prototypes or identities. The identity of a worker as a Christian does not activate and is not relevant in the context of a professional association, whereas the worker's identity as an accountant may be very relevant. Once activated, these prototypes define the group, prescribing the attitudes, norms, feelings, and behaviors of ingroup and intergroup relations. The process of applying these prototypes is called *depersonalization* – people are conceptually flattened, shifting from being viewed as unique and multifaceted to being viewed as exemplars of the relevant prototype.[54] The basis of perception in the social context shifts in accordance with self-categorization: "Social categorization of the self ... actually transform[s] self-conception and assimilate[s] all aspects of one's attitudes, feelings, and behaviors to the ingroup prototype; it changes what people think, feel, and do."[55] Self-categorization tells actors who they are, how they are expected to think/act/believe, and what to expect from others inside the group as well as from members of outgroups.

Self-categorization tells actors who they are, but does not alone account for why they associate in groups in the first place. To account for the glue that holds groups together, the social identity approach turns to ingroup affect and ingroup ties. *Ingroup affect* refers to the emotional attachment members of the ingroup have with respect to each other. *Ingroup ties* refers to the utility individuals derive from group membership (e.g., access to resources). While material-based ingroup ties clearly play an important role in binding groups together, according to the social identity approach, much of the fuel for ingroup-outgroup distinction lies in emotional processes, specifically the pursuit of positive distinctiveness.[56] Groups offer individuals both a source of identity (thus locating the self in the social environment) and self-esteem. People want to feel good about themselves, and in social circumstances that means ensuring their group excels over alternative groups. This need to excel pushes ingroup members to preferentially advantage their fellow group members over outgroup members. Some argue this need for superiority drives conflict dynamics between the ingroup and the outgroup. In their foundational 1979 article, Tajfel and Turner argue that conflict arises when subordinate groups reject the status quo (or subordination) and seek a more positive self-image. This pursuit of a positive self-image brings the subordinate group into conflict with the dominant group, which maintains positive self-image through its dominant

---

[52] Tajfel 1978, 63.
[53] Abrams and Hogg 1990; Hogg 2003; McGarty 1999; Oakes 1996; Tajfel et al. 1971.
[54] *Depersonalization* – the shift in perception away from individuality to prototypicality – should not be confused with *dehumanization*.
[55] Hogg 2001, 187.
[56] Crocker and Luhtanen 1990.

position. This dynamic led Jonathan Mercer to conclude that the social identity approach provides robust support for structural realist predictions about the inevitability of conflict in the international system.[57]

Over time, scholars of social identity have refined their understanding of the forces that bind groups together. In doing so, the self-esteem hypothesis and follow-on interpretation regarding the inevitability of conflict have both been contested. Hogg notes that self-esteem as a motivator for group behavior has only mixed experimental validation.[58] Others have challenged the claim that the ingroup's desire for positive self-image results in conflict.[59] Groups can use a variety of coping mechanisms to enable positive distinctiveness without resorting to conflict. Peter Gries identifies four modalities: changing the dimension of comparison, changing the meaning of the value being compared, changing the target of comparison, and self-deception.[60] In each case, the ingroup-outgroup comparison is creatively reconstructed to avoid damage to positive distinctiveness. Hogg and others also propose an additional motivation – uncertainty reduction – as a possible explanation for group behavior.[61] In essence, actors classify themselves and others into groups as a means of clarifying behavior expectations and scripts for the self in a given social context and overcoming uncertainty over the potential behavior of others. Uncertainty reduction then would not necessarily produce conflict.

In considering the role of social identity as part of an effort to understand security space, corporate identity cannot be overlooked. If social identity prescribes the behavior and expectations of the self and other, then corporate identity defines the boundaries of the self and other. Thus, corporate identity is an integral element of self-categorization. When analysts talk about the West, social identity refers to the norms, ideas, and behavioral expectations that adhere to members of the West. Corporate identity, on the other hand, defines who is included in the West. Is Japan part of the West? Is Poland? These are questions of corporate identity. Cederman and Daase, in their call for endogenizing corporate identity through a sociational approach, highlight the contingent nature of identity.[62] In deploying an identity, actors use categorization to create the group: "New actors can thus be born or disappear 'overnight' without accompanying change in the cultural 'raw material,' which is typically quite stable. What matters, rather, are 'imagined communities' ... based on politically relevant categories rather than all cultural traits."[63] Thus, citing Barth (1969), Cederman and Daase highlight that the relevant features used to demarcate identity are not those that objectively differentiate groups, but instead those

---

[57] Mercer 1995.
[58] Hogg 2001.
[59] Brewer 1999.
[60] Gries 2005.
[61] Hogg 2000; Hogg and Abrams 1993; Reid and Hogg 2005.
[62] Cederman and Daase 2003.
[63] Cederman and Daase 2003, 13.

the group members regard as significant. If this is the case, political actors will contest corporate identity far more than social identity. Because the behavioral expectations that inform social identity are relatively stable, and because contesting social identity means contesting the audience's view of itself, challenging the content of social identity is not likely to get political actors very far. The boundaries of the group, however, are potentially far more malleable because members of the ingroup can and do exit, but also because excluding or including others in the ingroup does not necessarily require a reassessment of the self. Thus, challenging corporate identity is likely to prove far more politically expeditious than challenging social identity.

There are limits, however, to the malleability of categorization, either of the self or the other. While identities are context dependent, they are grounded in the knowledge as well as the cultural and normative raw material of the society. In the United States, a hypothetical effort to frame the United States as a nondemocracy to generate sympathy for the actions of China during the Tiananmen Square repression of 1989 would not be successful. Likewise, efforts to frame China as a democracy during that same period would fail. Thus, while the act of categorization makes the group, the range of possible categorizations for a given sociocultural context is limited. Just as I argue there is a security space that constrains the range of probable securitizing moves, there is a sociocultural space that limits the range and use of categorizations. In his work on Cascading Activation, Robert Entman emphasizes the importance of "cultural congruence," how well the interpretation (framing) of an event or issue by political leaders and the media matches up with political culture.[64] The quality of the match between interpretation and political culture plays a critical role in the success of framing, and forecloses some framing options altogether. The same can be said for categorization. Efforts at categorization must observe cultural congruence.

This issue of cultural congruence as critical to facilitating and constraining categorizations might be more generally termed *discursive fit*.[65] The central intuition of discursive fit is that how the world is understood through language or discourses – that is, categorization – does not float free. Instead, discourses-as-representations-of-the-world are nested within specific social contexts. In any given context, social structures resonate with and empower some discourses while resisting and disempowering others. Throughout his work on the role of identity in shaping Soviet and Russian foreign policy, Hopf has emphasized the importance of the linkage between identity and discourse. He argued at the outset of his 2002 book pioneering societal constructivism that identities are linked with specific discourses and the predominance of certain identities empowers associated discourses: "Every individual in society has many identities. Each identity has associated with it a collection of

---

[64] Entman 2003, 2004.
[65] The act of categorization is, after all, a discursive claim as to what the Other is.

discursive practices, including a language with vocabulary, written or verbal, and characteristic physical behaviors, such as gestures, dress, customs, and habits ... Every society is bounded by a social cognitive structure within which some discursive formations dominate and compete."[66] Similarly, Harald Müller notes that compliance with international regimes is predicated on political discourses, which are in turn grounded in domestic political structures.[67] Moreover, Müller argues that critical to successful regimes is the integration of compliance issues into domestic discourses. Regime survival is most threatened when compliance remains constrained to small foreign policy cadres, a point suggestive of the argument I make in this book.

Hopf and Müller are relatively unique, however, in their explicit focus on discourse. Much of the work on cultural congruence only implicitly addresses discourse, instead focusing on how domestic structures mediate the acceptance of international norms. Jeffrey Checkel argues that domestic norms have an important impact on whether and how international norms resonate.[68] That is, the success of international norms discourses depends to a significant extent on the degree to which they fit with domestic societal structures. Where the match is good, the discourses are effective in shaping behavior. Where fit is poor, however, domestic identity can impede international norms from changing behavioral outcomes. Andrew Cortell and James Davis likewise suggest that international rule adoption is shaped by the "domestic salience of the international rule or norm," which is "largely derive[d] from the legitimacy accorded it in the domestic political context."[69] One of the most important factors that conditions the impact of international norms is the "cultural match" between the norm and widely held domestic or national understandings, beliefs, or obligations.[70] Gary Goertz and Paul Diehl put the situation thus: "The unique national experience of each country will make its propensity to follow [a] norm different."[71] In a similar vein, David Strang and John Meyer point out that cultural parallels facilitate the diffusion of social practices: "The cultural understanding that social entities belong to a common social category constructs a tie between them ... where actors are seen as falling into the same category, diffusion should be rapid."[72]

Despite the importance of what Cortell and Davis call *domestic salience* – a concept broadly similar to discursive fit or cultural congruence – they note that scholarship on the subject is not well developed and call for greater attention to be paid to how norms affect particular states and foreign policy decisions.[73]

---

[66] Hopf 2002, 1.
[67] Müller 1993, 386.
[68] Checkel 1999.
[69] Cortell and Davis, Jr. 1996, 454, 56; 2000.
[70] Cortell and Davis, Jr. 2000, 73.
[71] Goertz and Diehl 1992, 653.
[72] Strang and Meyer 1993, 490.
[73] Cortell and Davis, Jr. 2000, 67.

I would carry this point further and argue that the degree to which social structures like identity shape how issues are constructed through discourses remains significantly underdeveloped. Much of the literature on norms assumes the discursive priors that transmit norms from one society to another. Failing to account for the discursive foundations of norms means that scholars studying international relations are missing the crucial mechanism driving the transfer of norms as well as the resulting behavior change. The significance of discourses is such that Hopf argues, "Discourses themselves are institutions. A discourse of the nation daily defines who is inside, and who is outside, the national community. This discourse operates like an institution insofar as it daily guides, implicitly and explicitly, each actor's sense of herself as a member of that community, or as an outsider looking in."[74] A newly developing approach in political science known as *discursive institutionalism* promises greater sustained attention to the relationship between social structures and discourses as the primary means of understanding.[75] Although my central focus is not discursive fit per se, it does play an important role in my approach. Without the idea of discursive fit, the basis for understanding democratic discourses (i.e., categorizations) as markers of the influence of democratic identity is undermined. Likewise, the concept of a security space arising from social and political structures loses its analytical resonance. In focusing explicitly on discourses and their relationship with security policy outcomes, this book contributes to a rapidly developing understanding of the interaction of discourses and social structures. By doing so, it also addresses the spirit of Cortell and Davis's call.

To that end, the social identity approach has the potential to improve scholarship on discursive fit/cultural congruence/domestic salience by providing important baselines for understanding how identity shapes the security space in which discourses operate. For emotional and cognitive reasons, actors associate in groups, and those groups have powerful effects on how members see themselves and relevant others in the world. Yet this finding does not translate in a clear way into international relations. On its own, SIA is agnostic on the effects of particular identities. Do political identities have the same impact as religious identities? As economic identities? Interpretations of SIA such as Mercer's miss the larger picture. SIA gives strong reason to believe identities play an important role in shaping how we interact with the world, and provides reasons we cohere into identity groups in the first place. But identities have content – the identity prototype – and that content matters for how those identities influence discourses and international behavior. Thus, to understand the impact of identity, we have to link identity content with the basic ingroup-outgroup dynamics explained by the social identity approach. Additionally, while SIA enjoys impressive laboratory validation, the control of the laboratory is not the same as the chaos and the dynamism of the world

---

[74] Hopf 2012, 23.
[75] Schmidt 2008, 2010.

beyond the laboratory walls. In the rough and tumble of daily events, how do actors self-categorize and how do they accept the categorizations of others? That is, how do groups establish their boundaries or corporate identities?

Putting the Pieces Together: Identity and the Construction of Democratic Security

In my discussion of securitization theory, I emphasized the importance of the sociopolitical space securitization operates within and the ways this space can facilitate or inhibit securitizing moves. I conceptualize these forces as boundary conditions constituting a security space that establishes the range of plausible securitizing moves from within the universe of all securitizing moves. The social identity approach has powerful potential to help scholars understand important forces that define the security space. In this section, I use these foundational elements to make an argument about the role of democratic identity in shaping the political and military security space of democracies. Why democracy? There is strong evidence in the International Relations literature that something about democracy systematically affects security outcomes for democratic states, producing a zone of peace between democracies in the midst of a conflictual international system.[76] Thus, explaining the influence of democratic political identity has the potential to illuminate important interstate forces that generate security regularities in the international system. Democratic states are also some of the most powerful states in the international system, lending increased importance to any effort to understand the construction of their security spaces.

Building on the social identity approach, the argument I make here is a deductive one constructed on theorizing about the nature of society under democratic governance.[77] In particular, I argue that stable democracies require the presence of a democratic social identity shared across the public. This is a group identity, specifying the nature of social reality within democracy. The norms that inform democratic identity include nonviolent conflict resolution, rule of law, compromise, and transparency.[78] These norms inform democratic identity, which, in conjunction with the democratic political structure to which they are tied, generate a framework for defining the self and the other and expectations of political behavior. They also function as a critical linkage in the imagined political community that recreates democracy every day. The basic ordering principles as listed here are at least in part generated from the bottom up. If a large enough group within the democracy actively chooses to abide by

---

[76] Babst 1972; Choi 2011; Danilovic and Clare 2007; Ember et al. 1992; J. S. Levy 1988; Maoz and Abdolali 1989; Mitchell 2002; Mousseau and Shi 1999; Oneal et al. 2003; Reuveny and Li 2003; Rummel 1975; Russett and Oneal 2001; Small and Singer 1976.
[77] For an inductive approach to identity, see Hopf 2002.
[78] Dixon and Senese 2002; Maoz and Russett 1993; Owen 1994, 1997; Russett 1993.

a different set of norms, to use physical violence to achieve political interests for example, the democracy falls apart. Action can make the actor,[79] and the practice of democracy makes the democratic actor. Because of this active participation in the ideology of democracy – as opposed to the passive reception of more hierarchical social orders – I expect democratic identity to play an important part in threat perception and construction by the public. Public participation in the democratic system also contains elements of habit and practice.[80] Citizens buy into the democratic program every day they habitually practice the societal expectations of the democratic system. This habitual aspect should strengthen democratic identity.

For such an identity to function, there has to be flexibility in the other delimiters of political identity. The criteria establishing the boundaries between the self and the other (corporate identity of democracy) overwhelmingly rely on the markers and practice of democracy. Differences in religion, cultural practices, economic perspective, gender, and race all have to be tolerated if a democracy is to succeed. The grounds for recognition and respect in a democracy must be open.[81] Were they not, the democracy would tear itself apart. A democracy can only operate if the population willingly participates in the program. If most people chose to identify (politically) with their religion at the expense of their democratic identity, the state would become a theocracy. Democratic governance fundamentally rests on the priority in the political sphere of democratic identity among the citizenry.

Democracy as identity has both social and corporate identity elements. Corporately, democratic identity is about who is considered part of the democratic community. Socially, democratic identity informs role and behavioral expectations. Thus, there are questions of who "we" are and what "we" are expected to do. Both elements inform interests. The social identity approach indicates that the placement of self and other has important ramifications for the self's interests in any interaction because the roles the self and other take on are commensurate with their social identities.

Democracy, as a social identity, distinguishes between members of the self and the other. If a state is to be democratic, then democratic identity must be a significant factor in the imagined community that binds the society together under the state. Policies involving negotiation and reconciliation – democratic political behavior – are justified by appealing to democratic norms and social identity. Leaders emphasize that the external state warrants these approaches (as determined by social identity) as a trustworthy member of the democratic community (as determined by corporate identity), that these behaviors are expected in return, and that the situation can be approached without significant concerns over violence. Policies involving aggression and violence – nondemocratic

---

[79] Meyer et al. 1987.
[80] Hopf 2010.
[81] Williams 2001.

political behavior – are justified by demonstrating that the target state is beyond reason or trust, that such behavior could result in violence against the home state (an existential threat). Political leaders achieve this aim by emphasizing the undemocratic identity (again a question of corporate identity) and the external state's unwillingness to reliably operate by democratic norms (an element of social identity). The nondemocratic state poses an existential threat because it is dissimilar from the democratic self, defined in part by the exclusion of violence from conflict resolution within the ingroup. Thus, democratic social identity— by prescribing behavior boundaries—reduces uncertainty about future action. Contestation over shared democracy is contestation over democratic "actorness." The story is very much about how the lines of democracy as a class of actor are drawn (corporate identity) and the ways democracy shapes expectations of behavior of the self and other (social identity).

At this point, it is fair to ask why democratic identity occupies a privileged position in threat construction. In part, it is because democratic identity provides the basic operating instructions for the political sphere within democracies, including the resolution of political conflicts of interest. Democratic identity is also a participatory identity, recreated through the active participation of the public. It is identity resting on positive action rather than identity through negative action (which we might expect in more nonparticipatory political systems, where identity emphasizes noninvolvement in the political sphere). Democratic identity plays a fundamental role in establishing political behavior expectations of the self and the other in a way other identities in the political context do not. Here, the critical element is the operating context, cultural congruence, and the role they have in the contestation over self-categorization. In a religious dispute, one's political identity is likely to be far less salient than religious self-categorization.

Security is a political act,[82] and thus political identity as the foundational set of norms and expectations regarding the conduct of politics should play a pivotal role in categorization and assessment of threat. Given the hypothesized strength of democratic political identity as a participatory identity, I argue that it plays a central role in political and military sector securitization. Moreover, the justifications for securitizing acts in democracies are bound to include identity-related arguments, since questions of war and peace are existential issues in democracies.

A final reason to argue for the importance of democratic identity is the large audience securitizing actors in democracies face. I address this point in greater detail shortly. Briefly, to be successful, securitizing actors in democracies must appeal to the factors that have the widest appeal – the greatest cultural and political congruence among the largest number of people. Democratic identity is one such identity. To reiterate, democratic identity is not all-powerful. Other identities may come into play in the construction of security through the securitizing move. The argument here is only that democratic identity plays a

[82] As is war (Von Clausewitz 1976, 87).

particularly central and important role in democratic security construction. Moreover, democratic identity is not deterministic. The social reality of the democratic identity does not dictate that we must like our fellow democrats or that democracies *should* make war against nondemocracies. In the case of shared democracy, however, it does make the claim of an existential threat, a central element of the securitizing move, extremely difficult.

The securitization dynamic is not unique to democracies. What is unique to democracies is the primary audience. In their selectorate model of war, Bruce Bueno de Mesquita and his coauthors point out that leaders of democracies must deal with larger support coalitions than leaders of authoritarian states.[83] Thus, owing to the structural nature of democracy, securitizing actors in democracies must deal with a large, varied audience. In a democracy, the public plays a critical role in security policy. It is inherent to the nature of democratic governance: leaders are accountable to the public for their policy decisions. Regardless of democracy size, this audience is very large, with a wide variety of assessments regarding the national interest. In this case, democratic securitizers are forced to construct the security claim using language that appeals to a diverse audience and that taps into existing threat construction frameworks.

Securitizers rarely, if ever, have the time to construct a threat assessment framework from the ground up. Instead, they rely on existing frameworks that serve as assessment platforms by which people evaluate who can be trusted and who cannot, and what types of behaviors and reactions to expect from a given counterparty under particular conditions. Because securitizers in democracies face large audiences, they are forced to appeal to basic ties that bind the imagined community together. Consequently, in cases of national security, the dominant political identity (democratic) of the public and the attendant set of norms provide some of the most potent bases for grounding a securitizing move with respect to external states. This is a different dynamic than in authoritarian states, where we would expect the primary audience to be concentrated in the policy-making elite. In democracies, we would expect contestation over securitizing moves to occur within the elite, but the primary audience (and adjudicator) of this contestation is the public. The role of the public as securitization audience is one of the critically defining elements of democracy over other types of governance.

Combining the work on the individual level with securitization produces a more complete picture of democratic security mechanisms. Democratic norms and identity shape the security policy of democratic political leaders in two ways. First, leaders have internalized the democratic norms and identity, shaping their personal perception of threat. Second, democratic political structures bind leaders to the democratic norms and identity of the electorate. Leaders in autocracies face a very different identity and norms environment. Political structure, identity, and norms are far more personalistic, indicated by small

---

[83] Bueno de Mesquita et al. 1999, 2004.

selectorates and hierarchical political structures.[84] The governing identities and the interests of the state are grounded in the particulars of the ruling group. Consequently, the language of securitization will appeal to the identity and norms of the ruling group rather than the national citizenry. There are obviouslya wide range of states in between these two ideal types, and those states will have different security spaces depending on the relative importance of private versus public audience. China, for example, is an authoritarian state, but one in which security policy must at least in part be publically legitimized. It is possible to make general statements about audience type (democracies: public; autocracies: private), but the analyst must determine the particulars of the audience in each sociopolitical context. Even in democracies, private rather than public audiences sometimes determine security policy, as in the case of covert action.[85]

None of this is to say that relations between democracies are always cordial.[86] Often they may not be. Day-to-day relations between states are built on policies and interactions that never rise to the level of security and may escape public attention. At these subpublic levels of policy, a multitude of factors come into play, none of which are addressed here. Because these policy matters do not rise to the level of security, the framework proposed here does not speak to them. The mechanism proposed here only deals with issues visible to the public, where leaders attempt to securitize or desecuritize the matter. It is not a comprehensive theory of democratic foreign policy, if such a thing were even possible.

Melding securitization theory with social identity offers an analytical avenue for studying the role of norms and identity in the formation of security policy in democratic states. It seats the locus of action at the domestic level, where security is constructed and where the sociopolitical fabric is most dense. The social identity approach provides a theoretical and empirical basis for looking to the role of identity in securitization. The ingroup-outgroup dynamic has been clearly linked to conflict, even if it does not necessarily lead to conflict. The social group plays a critical role in establishing the parameters of social reality. If we are to understand international conflict (very much a social behavior), we must account for social groups. In this context, the social identity approach prompts us to focus on the process of self-categorization, a communicative action that establishes the boundaries of corporate identity, in the process establishing the boundaries of social behavior and perception.

Combining securitization with the social identity approach provides a structured way of looking at the security process, focusing on the communicative action of leaders and their audiences. We should expect conflict to be preceded by securitizing moves that, while communicating the presence of an existential

[84] diZerega 1995.
[85] Forsythe 1992; James and Mitchell 1995; John 2002.
[86] Wesley Widmaier's study of U.S.-India relations beautifully illustrates this (2005).

threat to a referent object, also ground the claim of an existential threat in social identity and seek to establish the ingroup-outgroup categorization (boundaries of corporate identity). Opponents of the securitizing move should challenge the self-categorization as one possible political approach, thus making identity in the securitizing move a site of political contestation. This approach also ties norms and structure together in explanation. To securitize successfully, leaders must use the language of security; they must appeal to certain norms and identities to communicate the idea of a threat and that the object threatened is valuable. The nature of the audience (general public, small group of oligarchs, military officers), as well as the norms and identity language the audience responds to, are linked to the political structure. Securitizers in autocracies face a very different audience, requiring a very different language of securitization, than those in democracies. I expect that political leaders use the language of democratic identity and norms to signal possible threats or the lack thereof to their securitizing audience.

It is important to point out that the argument presented here is not purely structural. To make such an argument would deny the political agency that lies at the heart of securitization theory. Nor does the approach of this chapter conflict with work by scholars focusing on the agency of individuals.[87] I seek to identify the social boundary conditions that shape securitizing moves, increasing or decreasing the odds of successful securitization. Thus, the approach does not posit that individuals act as automatons at the mercy of sociopolitical boundary conditions. These conditions certainly make some securitizing moves easier and others more difficult, but they are not immutable. In line with the burgeoning literature on discursive institutionalism,[88] committed political actors with sufficient credibility, power, or authority could alter the sociopolitical context in which they operate.

Moreover, sociopolitical boundary conditions do not require actors act in specific ways. The presence of democratic identity does not necessarily mean democratic leaders must or should see authoritarian states as existential threats (e.g., the long-standing alliance between the United States and Saudi Arabia). Instead, boundary conditions provide broad frameworks for securitization. The fact that Saudi Arabia is not a democracy, combined with the presence of democratic identity in the United States, provides a sociopolitical basis for securitization should political actors seek to make that claim. In relying on democratic identity (as opposed to some other identity) to do so, however, political actors reinforce the sociopolitical structures within which they operate. Through the process of structuration, the use by political actors of rhetorical tools defined by a particular set of boundary conditions lends strength to those sociopolitical structures, increasing their legitimacy and making them more relevant for future securitizing moves. By discursively abiding by democratic identity in securitizing moves, political actors increasethe relevance of democratic identity

[87] Owen 1994; Schafer and Walker 2006; Widmaier 2005.
[88] Schmidt 2008, 2010.

in future securitizing moves. In some ways, this process might be conceived of as a long-term form of rhetorical entrapment.[89] Thus, the approach here is more structural than individual-level explanations, without being purely structural. In this way, it reflects the balance between agency and structure that characterizes constructivism.

The approach I have outlined produces a range of benefits. Because the proposed framework redirects analytical and theoretic focus to the political dynamics within the state, it stands apart from approaches that focus on the state in the system, individual policy makers, and abstracted rationalist models of domestic politics. The theory outlined here also seeks to account for the role of structure and norms in security outcomes to address the gaps that arise out of the literature's tendency to analytically disaggregate them. Rather than privileging either norms or structure as much of the literature on international relations tends to do, my approach points to both as playing a critical role in security outcomes. Democratic political structure conditions the nature of the audience and the obligations of the securitizing actor to address the security move to that audience. Identity and norms condition the content of the securitizing message. All this is in addition to the co-constitutive linkage constructivism claims between political agents and structure.[90]

The approach also redirects attention to the domestic context, where social and political processes are far denser than they are at the systemic level, and addresses the critique that explanations based on domestic variables are reductionist. For example, Patrick James and Glenn Mitchell argue that the beliefs of the populace are not necessarily reflected in the state.[91] The securitization framework provides a linkage between the public and the state. On major issues in the public eye, securitization affords a means for understanding if the linkage between public belief and state action is a fallacy or reality. Linking securitization and social identity also gives IR scholars a means to engage empirically with a subject (identity) that has presented significant challenges.

For securitization theory my approach begins to thicken securitization's analytical power by highlighting a set of tools – identity – political actors can use to make securitization claims and by enhancing the reach of securitization theory on societal dynamics. It also contributes to understandings regarding ways social context can act as boundary conditions, simultaneously enabling and constraining securitizing moves. In doing so it answers Holger Stritzel's call for greater effort to understand the role and significance of broader social context for the securitizing move.[92] While the Copenhagen School acknowledges there are constraints on securitizing moves, the approach here adds greater specificity. It also applies securitization theory in an empirical context and in

---

[89] Schimmelfennig 2001.
[90] Adler 1997; Hopf 1998.
[91] James and Mitchell 1995.
[92] Stritzel 2007.

the process develops a methodology for the use of securitization theory. Finally, it helps build greater specificity regarding how securitization processes function, and to what effect.

For the social identity approach the framework presents a possible avenue for incorporating SIA into IR and aids in establishing external validity. While SIA has been rigorously tested in experiments, its validity beyond controlled settings remains an open question.[93] Because social identity does not speak directly to international relations, applying the approach's theoretical toolbox faces a number of questions, notably at what level of analysis should it apply and how the approach applies outside the experimental setting, particularly in the context of dynamic, complicated, and chaotic social situations like those that characterize IR. Employing the social identity approach as I do here also begins to address a critical weakness Hopf and others point out, namely that scholarship in the SIA tradition has neglected the social element to focus almost entirely on the psychological element.[94] Thus, in theorizing about how identity content impacts social psychological behavior, my approach helps to balance the scales.

For democratic security, the approach reintegrates the finding of a democratic peace back into a broader discussion of the processes of security within democracy, and in turn into the general discussion on international security. The democratic peace is thus a subset of a set of security processes that occur across states in the system. By focusing on the conditions that facilitate and inhibit securitization, the framework also addresses the willingness of democratic states to use force as often, if not more, than other types of states. The approach also satisfies Charles Lipson's and Harald Müller and Jonas Wolff's call for dyadic mechanisms for a dyadic, interactive phenomenon.[95] While the focus here is on the internal dynamic of the state, this dynamic cannot occur without a counterparty, and the nature of the counterparty as well as the dynamics of corporate identity have a direct impact on the internal security dynamic of a democracy. By its very nature, securitization theory forces us to consider a dyadic, dynamic phenomenon with a dyadic, dynamic mechanism.

Finally, the framework I have proposed also accounts for the apparent problem of the covert use of force by democracies against other democracies.[96] In these cases, policy makers sought to keep intervention from the public eye, suggesting they believed a securitizing move would be unsuccessful. Individuals can be motivated by a variety of interests, and many may have nothing to do with national interest calculations (e.g., personal political calculations or ideological

---

[93] Hymans 2002.
[94] Hopf 2002, 2, and others.
[95] Lipson 2003; Müller and Wolff 2006. Lipson makes the following point: "The democratic peace is fundamentally an interactive phenomenon. It is not about why one democracy or another is peaceful. It is about why two democracies seldom fight each other" (2003, 4).
[96] Forsythe 1992; James and Mitchell 1995.

Securitization, Identity, and Security Outcomes

particularities). When the structure of democracy allows leeway in the state security apparatus, exemplified by executive control over classified or secret policy implementation instruments (e.g., CIA covert operations teams), for the executive to take security policy measures without the securitization dynamic typical of democracies, we should expect that covert uses of force may depart from what my approach anticipates. This is particularly in cases when the leadership of the executive branch has not internalized the norms of democracy or when, as in the Cold War, an alternative identity assumes a higher security profile.[97] These situations do not necessarily undermine the democratic peace because they take place outside the mechanisms that generate democratic peace. If the framework I have proposed here does indeed play a significant role in generating the democratic peace, restricting the ability of executives to autonomously use force should reduce or eliminate interdemocratic use of force.

The approach I outline here produces expectations of democratic political behavior. If the external state is a democracy then political leaders will be unable to securitize it, and will often not even try. This does not mean some political actors will not make the attempt. To do so, political leaders will attempt to reconstruct the external democracy in nondemocratic terms. To counter these claims, political leaders who seek to keep the external democracy from being securitized will emphasize shared democratic identity. Contestation should revolve around the construction of the external state because political actors are seeking to tap into the democratic prototype and the conceptions of security embodied therein. The same dynamic takes place with respect to nondemocratic external states. Those seeking to securitize the external state will emphasize that state's nondemocratic characteristics and identity, while those who seek to defuse the securitizing move will emphasize the external state's democratic characteristics. After a brief comment on methods, the discussion turns to the first set of case studies: the security relationship between India and the United States.

Methods: Focal Points and Discourses

In this book, I focus on the importance of understanding the causal mechanisms that translate social forces like identity into international security reality through case studies.[98] My emphasis on causal mechanisms derives from the scholarship on scientific realism and Mario Bunge's systemism philosophy, although scientific realists and Bunge see mechanisms in different (but, in my

---

[97] Interesting, in these cases the securitization dynamic in a democracy comes to resemble that of an autocracy. Particularly in the case of an upper echelon decision-making environment dominated by political appointees, the language of securitization may reflect the ideological commitments of this presumably ideologically homogenous group.

[98] I am not the first to note the importance of mechanisms in the social sciences. In recent years a number of scholars have called for a renewed focus on mechanisms in the social sciences and international relations, in particular Checkel 2006; Tilly 2001.

opinion, compatible) ways.[99] Scientific realists have questioned the Humean, deductive-nomological model of science.[100] These questions have given rise to a model of science focused on processes and mechanisms: "The real goal of science is neither the explanation of events nor the explanation of patterns, though this idea catches some of the truth of the matter. Rather, it has as its goal an understanding of the fundamental processes of nature."[101] Explanation, then, "requires that there is a 'real connection,' a generative nexus that produced or brought about the event (or pattern) to be explained."[102] Accordingly, correlation *on its own* cannot serve as explanation (much less understanding) because it does not allow the analyst access to the mechanisms at play: what causes what *and how*. The methodology behind the effort to uncover mechanisms supports this contention: "Explanation takes the form of a narrative that identifies the critical social mechanisms and links them sequentially with the contingent but causally pertinent acts of persons."[103]

Bunge likewise emphasizes the importance of mechanisms in systemism, his philosophy of social science.[104] Bunge argues that the study of the social sciences is the study of social systems and thus requires a systemist approach over traditional approaches that compartmentalize social studies into holistic or individualistic boxes. Both holism – typified by structural realism[105] – and individualism – rational choice theories, for example – miss critical pieces of the explanatory puzzle located at the alternative level in the social system.[106] The central focus of the systemist approach is human systems, for example, the interaction between individuals and society. Explanation should link rather than separate the structural and individual levels. Systemism is in part an attempt by Bunge to restore the importance of mechanisms in understanding and explanation.[107]

In his 2000 paper, Bunge provides the example of the relationship between economic development and population dynamics.[108] It is well known that there

---

[99] Bhaskar 1975; Bunge 1996, 2000, 2004; Harré and Madden 1975; Manicas 2006.
[100] Others introduced scientific realism to IR theory – particularly Wendt 1999, Dessler 1989, and Hollis and Smith 1990. Indeed, ontologically my conceptualization of boundary conditions of security shares much with Dessler's proposed transformational model of international relations. However, in contrast to my epistemologically oriented discussion, these works focus largely on scientific realism's ontological implications. For example, Wendt's use is as a means of distinguishing his variant of constructivism from hermeneutical, post-positivist approaches.
[101] Manicas 2006, 14.
[102] Manicas 2006, 20.
[103] Manicas 2006, 5.
[104] Bunge 1996, 2000, 2004.
[105] James 2002.
[106] A *system* is defined as a "complex object whose parts or components are held together by bonds of some kind" (Bunge 2004, 188). According to the systemist perspective, "everything in the universe is, was, or will be a system or a component of one" (Bunge 2004, 190).
[107] Bunge defines a *mechanism* as "a process (or sequence of states, or pathway) in a concrete system, natural or social" (2004, 186).
[108] Bunge 2000, 150.

is a relationship between developed economic status and aging in the population. From the holist perspective (macro level), the linkage is clear: economic growth drives population stagnation. Unfortunately, why this might be remains a mystery. The underlying motivating dynamic is missing. On the individualist (micro) level, old age security drives a decline in fertility as parents no longer need numerous children to ensure their survival as they age. Problematically, what brings about old age security is exogenous to the linkage between age security and fertility rates. Systemism brings both levels of explanation together for a more satisfying and meaningful model. Economic growth facilitates old age security, driving down fertility and resulting in population stagnation. The causal mechanism depends on linking individual level dynamics (micro level) to structural level phenomena (macro level).

Leaving aside epistemological discussions, two issues take center stage: data and case selection. Regarding case selection, several points stand out. First, the value of focusing on the United States is worth noting. Over the past fifty years, it has been one of, if not the most, internationally engaged democracies in the world.[109] As a consequence, the level of interaction between the United States and far-flung democracies where cultural similarities are minimal is much higher than it would be with smaller, more parochially concerned democracies, particularly those of Europe. This enables the examination of relationships that are not significantly shaped by shared regional history (as would be the case with inter-European relations) or by shared culture. In effect, the expansiveness of U.S. global engagement provides an opportunity to better focus on political identity. Moreover, the United States does not have an extensive background as a colonial power that might shape internal and external perceptions. There are of course, drawbacks to focusing on the United States, foremost among them the possibility that exceptionalism in the U.S. security process or some aspect thereof reduces or eliminates the generalizability of the results. Since the goal here is to explore a possible mechanism driving security construction rather than to develop a general model of security, the issue of generalization is not overly problematic. Finding that the mechanism has empirical support in the U.S. context opens up further research possibilities in other states. The focus on causal-process or mechanistic observations, despite the small number of cases, in this study is also recognized as a valid path to causal inference.[110] The weaknesses of the methods here simply create new possibilities for future research. No study can answer all possible critiques, particularly in terms of methods. As such, any research design requires trade-off in terms of strengths and weaknesses vis-à-vis alternative designs.[111] The best social scientists can do is recognize the strengths and weaknesses of any given approach.

---

[109] Some have argued that "[t]oday's world revolves around Washington DC" (Choi and James 2005, 2).
[110] Brady et al. 2004, 12.
[111] Collier et al. 2004, 48.

Second, the focus on security over war creates a particular set of case selection issues. War, the traditional focus of the study of international security, is a discrete event. Securitizing moves are less obvious, particularly if a research design seeks to avoid overdetermined outcomes. To resolve these problems, I have chosen to utilize a focal points approach derived in part from James Mahoney and Gary Goertz's Possibility Principle.[112] Cases are built around events or circumstances that could provide an external basis for a securitizing move. These focal point situations provide temporal framing, an important consideration because the initial stages of securitizing moves can be difficult to identify. Focal points also aid in addressing the "nonevent" problem confronting all of social science.[113] The focal point approach also meshes well with the application of securitization theory to security constructions in democracies. Because securitization theory focuses on the relationship between securitizers and their audience, potential security issues must be important enough to garner the attention of the audience. This is exceptionally important in democracies, where the audience is large and disparate, and where many daily issues and situations go unnoticed. Focal points provide a means for identifying situations or issues that intrude on the public consciousness.

In U.S. relations with India and China, I have identified six focal points as a basis for analyzing securitizing moves. In the section on Indo-American relations, Chapter 2 concerns the Bangladesh War, when India opposed Pakistan – an ostensive ally of the United States – in support of Bangladesh's succession. Chapter 3 addresses a collection of three focal points related to India's nuclear program: the 1974 "peaceful nuclear explosion" (PNE), the 1998 nuclear weapons tests, and the 2005 U.S.-India nuclear technology trade deal. In both chapters, securitizing moves were clearly possible. The Bangladesh War saw the dismemberment of a country participating in the U.S. system of containment. The focal points in Chapter 3 all concern nuclear weapons and technology proliferation, an issue where securitization has clearly occurred. In the section on Sino-American relations, Chapter 4 addresses the 1995–6 Taiwan Straits Crisis, when China threatened Taiwan, a U.S. ally of sorts also undergoing democratization. Chapter 5 takes up the 2001 EP-3 (or Hainan Island) incident, when Chinese authorities held U.S. military personnel and equipment for over a week.

Third, the U.S.-India and U.S.-China dyads are extremely useful from a case selection standpoint. The United States is purportedly the global hegemon.[114] India and China are the two largest countries in the world by population

---

[112] Mahoney and Goertz 2004.
[113] The issue is particularly acute in the democratic peace literature. Because there are very limited, if any, cases of interdemocratic war, it is difficult to explain in a rigorous theoretical and empirical way why an event did not occur without having positive cases to contrast against the negative. This is referred to as the "'dog that didn't bark'" problem (Doyle and Roden 1993, 23; Ray 1995a, 41).
[114] Schweller and Pu 2011.

with rapidly modernizing economies (the tenth and second largest economies, respectively, in 2010 according to the World Bank), and as my discussion of rising powers in the introduction suggests, these are the two countries seen as most likely to challenge the balance of material power. Thus, U.S. relations with these two countries are likely to be the most important for international relations in the twenty-first century, lending the cases an intrinsic value surpassing their methodological instrumental value. Of course, instrumentally India and China bring significant methodological benefits. With respect to U.S.-India relations, both countries are firmly democratic while sharing limited cultural similarities. Moreover, the relationship represents a difficult one for the theoretical approach I have adopted. The United States and India have long suffered a difficult relationship, with relations blowing hot and cold over the span of the Cold War. For much of the Cold War India was associated with the Soviet Union. The Indian economic philosophy accordingly was far more socialist than that of the United States.[115] India was and remains the chief rival to Pakistan, a long-standing, albeit on and off, ally of the United States. These characteristics have traditionally set U.S. and Indian geopolitical and geostrategic interests in opposition. The United States and India have not traditionally had strong economic links, eliminating a potentially confounding factor. Additionally, the India case is unique among major democracies because it stayed outside the expansive network of U.S. alliances formed to contain the Soviet Union during the Cold War. Thus, other than shared democracy, there is nothing in the relationship between the United States and India to constrain securitizing moves. China provides an important variation as a clear nondemocratic state contrasting against democratic India, allowing for the possibility that the securitizing move made by U.S. political leaders will differ in comparison with moves made with respect to India. In contrast to India, economic ties between the United States and China are particularly strong, at least since Deng Xiaoping initiated economic reforms in the 1980s. This point on economic ties is important because the expectations of neoliberal approaches to international security would suggest that these relationships would work at cross purposes of the securitization processes my approach anticipates, again reducing conflating factors.

Within the cases, the securitization core of my theoretical arguments implies a focus on the ways security discourses construct India and China. The empirical focus rests on the claims and arguments made by those with sufficient political capital, elected political leaders, to make a securitizing move.[116] A structured analysis is made of the securitizing moves, with a particular emphasis on the

---

[115] Widmaier 2005.

[116] Chilton, in his excellent monograph on language and politics, argues that politics and speech are fundamentally linked (not the least because both are uniquely human) and that "politics is very largely the use of language" (2004, 14). Thus, accepting that security is the result of a political act, it makes sense for us to examine the language of security.

role of identity. Looking carefully at the securitization discourses made by U.S. decision makers should reveal patterns of identification and the relationship between this identification and U.S. policy. This means focusing on the public argument transmitted by executive and congressional political leaders directly to the public and through the media. In the United States, the primary political figure in terms of foreign policy formation is the president. Consequently, presidential and executive branch discourse, embodied in official texts, press releases, speeches, press conferences, and interviews, figures centrally in the subsequent analysis. Although Congress does not have a strong formal role in foreign and security policy, it does serve as a politically important forum for discussion where counterarguments can be voiced with significant political weight. Here again, texts of arguments made by congressional leaders – media reports, interviews, and speeches – play an important role, as does the Congressional Record. Finally, securitization is successful only if the audience accepts the securitization argument. Although this acceptance is difficult to measure, public opinion polling does offer an important empirical proxy.

In generating the sample of texts examined in the empirical chapters, I turned to a range of resources. For public statements made through the media by both executive and legislative branch actors, I relied on the digital archives of the *New York Times* and to a lesser degree the *Washington Post*. The *New York Times* comes as close as the United States has to a newspaper of record, and has traditionally had far greater international coverage than other newspapers. Texts were identified through keyword searches, typically over a timeframe preceding the apex of the crisis by twelve months and following it by three months – although there is significant variability to the timeframe depending on the nature of the events. For congressional statements, I read the Congressional Record for a similar timeframe or did a keyword search where the Record has been digitized. The Presidential Papers publications provided a comprehensive record of public presidential speeches. For newer cases, I read through online press archives of the White House, Department of State, and Department of Defense. Where available, I drew on the documents included in the Foreign Relations of the United States (FRUS) series published by the Department of State. To do so, I consulted every document in the relevant volumes, although in the case of the Bangladesh War the archivists at the State Department gave the crisis its own volume. The availability of previously classified documents in the FRUS series for some of the cases, specifically those situated in the 1970s, creates some unevenness to the cases. For those cases for which there is FRUS coverage, the data are much richer and better able to access the political calculations of political leaders as well as the effects of public social structures like identity. For the more recent cases, the declassification process has yet to take place, and these cases consequently rely far more on public statements. I recognize this inconsistency, but there is little to be done for it. Data constraints are something all social scientists must confront, and my study is no different. A possible solution would be to look at cases only from a specific period to homogenize the type of data available, but that approach would constrain the study's ability to comment on behavior over time, the greater problem in my opinion. In all, I have sought to recover as much as possible of what was in the public discourse for the cases. An important caveat here is that I did not include in my data visual and audio media. In many cases, particularly the older ones, the media is unrecoverable. Even in more recent cases, the sheer volume of visual and audio makes it nearly impossible to review it or store it. Some audiovisual data are captured in the texts, often when political actors gave televised speeches and press conferences.

While securitization theory suggests the approach I have outlined here, there is support for it within the broader constructivist literature. Colin Kahl argues that constructivist analysis requires an interpretive epistemology "that seeks to explore the meanings, understandings, and interpretations of the relevant actors, the processes involved in generating these intersubjective meanings, and the behavioral patterns that result."[117] Of the three methods of interpretation Kahl outlines, my approach uses two: it analyzes "explicit statements made in public and private sources for what they do and do not say about the notions of national identity and the degree of affinity between states" and analyzes the symbolic use of democratic identity.[118] Ted Hopf's work on the role of identity in foreign policy formation in 1955 Soviet Union and 1999 Russia also takes an approach similar to that presented here, although he adopts a distinctively inductive method.[119] The approach I adopt is also similar to Paul Chilton's analysis of Enoch Powell's 'Rivers of Blood' speech.[120] Chilton focuses on legitimizing communication within the speech, a strong parallel to the implicit effort within the securitizing move to legitimate the removal of an issue from normal politics. Finally, Ronald Krebs and Patrick Jackson argue that scholars should focus on what actors say, in what contexts, and to what audiences, a prescription very much in line with the approach taken here.[121]

---

[117] Kahl 1999, 132.
[118] Kahl 1999, 136–7.
[119] Hopf 2002.
[120] Chilton 2004, 111–16.
[121] Krebs and Jackson 2007.

PART I

DEMOCRACY, SECURITY, AND THE RELATIONSHIP BETWEEN INDIA AND THE UNITED STATES

In Part I, the chapters focus on two significant aspects of the relationship between the world's largest democracies: (1) the 1971 "near miss" when the Nixon administration sent an aircraft carrier battle group to the Bay of Bengal to intimidate India; and (2) U.S. policy toward India's nuclear program. The choice of U.S.-India relations arises from the critical and difficult nature of the relationship for my framework. The criticality of the relationship arises from the unique geopolitical status of both states. India is the world's largest democracy. With over a billion people and rapid economic development, India exemplifies the future of democracy: non-European and in the developing world. India is also one of the few examples of stable democracy in a developing state. With the sole exception of Indira Gandhi's state of emergency from 1975 to 1977, India has enjoyed uninterrupted democracy. The stability of India's democracy in the face of major development challenges is an astounding feat, particularly compared with other developing states like Turkey and many of the democracies in South America where until relatively recently military interference in the government was common. The United States is the world's wealthiest and most militarily powerful democracy, and by most measures the oldest. If shared democratic identity is to play a meaningful role in structuring international security, there are no two more important countries between which for it to operate. India also represents a key relationship for the United States. India's economic growth makes it a significant world player, a proto-great power. As a great power itself, the United States has a keen interest in what India does. Nascent great power status aside, India also sits in one of the most explosive regions in the world. Not only does South Asia bear witness to the nuclear-powered rivalry between India and Pakistan, it is also a central theater in global efforts to contain the influence of militant Islamic ideology. The Indo-American relationship is critical for world peace.

A range of factors in Indo-American relations holds the potential to confound application of the framework I present in this book. The two countries have significant cultural differences, particularly when compared to the common cultural background shared between the United States and Europe. Misunderstandings and cultural barriers have been a regular aspect of relations between the two states.[1] One author has characterized the relations between the two countries as one of "[m]oral indignation and mutual incomprehension, even at times a sense of betrayal."[2] For example, throughout the Indian droughts of 1965 and 1966 President Lyndon Johnson kept U.S. food aid desperately needed by India to prevent wide-scale starvation on a tight tether, releasing only enough aid to keep India from the brink of famine. His motivation, according to a number of staffers and policy makers, was to push India to focus on desperately needed – and largely neglected – agricultural reforms. The Indian government, led by Indira Gandhi, did not interpret Johnson's policy in a similar light. Angry and alienated, Gandhi released several statements, particularly with respect to Vietnam, that were broadly in agreement with the Soviet position.[3] The cultural differences coupled with India's geostrategic nonalignment make the Indo-American relationship a difficult one for my approach. That said, the turbulent history and lack of cultural similarity are useful from a research design perspective: they isolate the democracy variable.

From a strategic perspective, the U.S.-India case is also a difficult one for my framework. Indeed, looked at through the framework of realism, the case of Indo-American relations presents one of the strongest possibilities for war between democracies. India, particularly during the Cold War, often strategically defined its position contrary to the West through Indian advocacy for and participation in the Non-Aligned Movement. Relations between the United States and India throughout much of the Cold War were strained, as India was perceived as actively undermining U.S. containment policy.[4] India, seen as a friend to the Soviet Union for much of the Cold War, was by extension unfriendly to the United States – although this perception has varied with time and the political party of the sitting president.[5] Pakistan, a longtime U.S. ally, has been India's archrival since the separation of the two states in 1947. Indian security policy directly opposes long-standing American security policy and interests. It was the first state outside the permanent members of the United Nations Security Council to openly develop and test a nuclear device – the 1974 "peaceful nuclear explosion" (PNE). India also remains firmly outside the Non-Proliferation Treaty and the attendant International Atomic Energy Agency (IAEA) nuclear safeguards. On both counts, India's security

---

[1] Kux 1994.
[2] Hathaway 2002.
[3] Ahlberg 2007; Kux 1994, 243–60; Sathasivam 2005, 78–9.
[4] Kapur and Ganguly 2007.
[5] Widmaier 2005.

policy stands in direct contravention to U.S. policy and efforts directed toward preventing the proliferation of nuclear weapons. While defenders of India claim the Indian nonproliferation record surpasses that of other nuclear states, including the United States,[6] India's nuclear work at the very least accelerated the Pakistani nuclear program, which in the end was highly detrimental to nonproliferation efforts.

Part I focuses on how U.S. leaders have attempted to construct the U.S.-India security relationship. The two subsequent chapters address four focal points where potential security issues between the United States and India have been critical. These are the 1971 Bangladesh War (Chapter 2), the 1974 peaceful nuclear explosion, the 1998 nuclear tests, and the 2005–6 nuclear technology deal (Chapter 3). These cases represent the most coherent, promising points of investigation in the U.S.-India relationship. All of them are highly visible incidents, requiring political leaders in the United States to securitize or desecuritize the issue or situation in public. Three of the cases involve nuclear weapons or nuclear policy – a well-recognized security issue both within the Indo-American relationship and in security studies more generally.[7] The fourth, Richard Nixon's deployment of the *Enterprise* carrier group into the Bay of Bengal during the 1971 Bangladesh War, constitutes the only time the United States has in any significant way suggested the use of force against India. Indeed, the events of 1971 constitute one of the so-called near misses of the democratic peace.[8] These cases present excellent opportunities to examine how security issues with respect to India are securitized and whether the democratic identity of the American public plays a role.

Neoliberal institutional models that focus on institutions and economic interdependence have surprisingly little to say about the Indo-American relationship. Few authors reference the impact of economic interdependence, and those who do are generally dismissive.[9] Other than the United Nations, the United States and India do not share membership in any significant multilateral institutions. Bilaterally, as discussed earlier, India has actively sought to keep itself out of the U.S. sphere of influence, up until recently avoiding significant ties to the United States as much as possible. Economic ties between the United States and India have historically been and remain relatively weak. Popular debates in the United States about outsourcing aside, U.S.-India trade figures are underwhelming given the size of the two countries. According to the Organisation for Economic Co-operation and Development (OECD), U.S. total commodity imports from India in 1989 (the earliest year available) totaled just over 3.5 billion USD. That placed India at twenty-fifth on the list of U.S. import trading partners, below Australia, Brazil, Canada, China, France, Germany,

---

[6] Ollapally and Ramanna 1995.
[7] Bertsch et al. 1999; Gallucci 1994; Kux 2002; Noorani 1981; Sagan and Waltz 2003.
[8] Ray 1995b; Widmaier 2005.
[9] Sagar 2004; Timberg 1998.

Hong Kong, Indonesia, Italy, Japan, Malaysia, Mexico, the Netherlands, Nigeria, Saudi Arabia, Singapore, South Korea, Spain, Sweden, Switzerland, Taiwan, Thailand, the United Kingdom, and Venezuela. U.S. 1989 exports to India were 2.4 billion USD, ranking India twenty-fourth in terms of export value. By 2000, U.S. imports from India added up to 11.3 billion USD, placing India at twenty-first on the import list, little moved from its position ten years previous. U.S. exports to India fared even worse, accounting for only 3.6 billion USD, putting India thirty-first from the top in terms of export value. Total trade with India amounted to less than one percent (.73%) of total U.S. trade. Trade connections only began to increase significantly after 2003. By 2010, the latest data available from the OECD, U.S. imports from India were 30 billion USD (fourteenth place) and exports were 19 billion USD (seventeenth place), totaling 1.5 percent of U.S. trade.[10] Given the relatively small trade figures and the relative lack of growth characterizing the Indo-U.S. trade relationship, economic interdependence does not seem to be a strong tie to bind the United States and India together.

The Indo-American Literature

The strained relations between the United States and India is a major theme in the literature on Indo-American ties. The title of Dennis Kux's history of Indo-American relations, *India and the United States: Estranged Democracies*,[11] largely summarizes the academic discourse. Authors have asked: "Can the U.S. and India be Real Friends?"; argued that détente between the United States and India "Won't Happen"; and explored the nuclear tensions between the two states.[12] More hopeful works also reflect the predominant tension theme. Recently authors have claimed that India and America are "Estranged No More"; that the relationship between the United States and India has witnessed a "Remarkable Turnaround"; and that Indians and Americans are engaged in a relationship-transforming "Courtship."[13] Within these works, the tendency is to focus on the determinants of the relationship at the systemic or at the decision-making level, almost exclusively from an explicitly or implicitly rationalist perspective. With the rare exception – Wesley Widmaier's 2005 article on the 1971 crisis – the literature on U.S.-India relations largely overlooks the potential for constructivist contributions.

Indeed, the literature is remarkably atheoretical in nature. Much of it is descriptive, as to be expected given the predominantly diplomatic historical approach. However, there are distinct theoretical undercurrents. At the systemic

---

[10] OECD (2010) SITC Revision 3 (online database) (http://www.oecd-ilibrary.org/content/data/data-00054-en)
[11] Kux 1994.
[12] Chadda 1986; Ollapally and Ramanna 1995; Singh 1983.
[13] Adhikari 2004; Hathaway 2002; Kapur and Ganguly 2007; Kux 2002.

level, neorealist, rationalist, power-oriented explanations (implicit and explicit) of U.S. foreign policy dominate. A consistent theme in historical treatments of Indo-American relations is the application of the logic of great power competition to South Asia. The dynamic of power politics weaves its way throughout Kux's oft-cited history of U.S.-India relations. More explicitly, McMahon argues that the strategic lens of the Cold War fundamentally defined relations between the United States and India. For McMahon, the inapplicability of this lens explains much of the tension between the two states.[14] Chadda rejects the possibility of a U.S.-India détente because geopolitical forces push the United States into the Pakistani camp.[15] Banerjee's innovative application of dependency theory to explain the U.S. tilt toward Pakistan in 1971 ultimately appeals to geopolitics to explain why U.S. policy makers felt the need to defend the power elite in Pakistan.[16] The theme continues into the post–Cold War literature, with the emphasis shifting to the ways the end of the Cold War altered the systemic pressures on the United States and India. For the United States, geopolitics need no longer be seen through the filter of Soviet containment. Instead, China has become the principal geopolitical target. Some authors explain improving U.S.-India relations as an attempt by the United States to balance against the rise of China.[17] Scholars explaining the Indian approach toward the United States also rely on power politics arguments, arguing that Indian need for support against potential Chinese threats leads policy makers to the United States.[18]

Work on the individual level has tended to focus on the strategically motivated decisions of political leaders largely operating outside the constraints of the domestic context. Kux's meticulous history of the relationship between India and the United States focuses predominantly on the diplomatic exchanges and the role of leaders and key policy makers in fashioning the relationship.[19] Kux's account also emphasizes the importance of systemic-level geopolitical logic for policy makers. There are exceptions, of course. One of the most notable of these exceptions was Lyndon B. Johnson's efforts to encourage Indian agricultural self-sufficiency, which significantly damaged relations between the two states. Likewise, Strobe Talbott's diplomatic history of the events surrounding the 1998 nuclear tests focuses largely on the interpersonal interactions of leaders and the way these interactions shaped policy. While there is some note of domestic political context – Talbott mentions the efforts of Senator Jesse Helms to block the passage into law of the Comprehensive Test Ban Treaty – the domestic dynamic does not figure significantly in Talbott's narrative.[20]

[14] McMahon 1994.
[15] Chadda 1986.
[16] Banerjee 1987.
[17] Guihong 2005; Rajamony 2002.
[18] Jha 1994; Kapur and Ganguly 2007.
[19] Kux 1994.
[20] Talbott 2004.

While the role of domestic politics is not absent in the literature, neither is it of significance. Some authors note the role of domestic forces, but only tangentially. Hathaway does discuss the role of domestic forces, but limits his scope to the influence of the Indian American community and eventually concludes that domestic concerns are marginal and that U.S. policy with respect to India will be made on the basis of (unexamined) national interest.[21] Similarly, Rubinoff argues that Indian expatriates in the United States have played a key role in influencing policy and perception in both the United States and India.[22] There is an important gap in the literature regarding the role of norms and identity in structuring the U.S.-India relationship. To some degree, this lacuna is understandable; the U.S.-India relationship *appears* to be dominated by geopolitical strategic concerns. The predominance of systemic pressures makes the U.S.-India case a difficult one for constructivism. Yet constructivist approaches have the potential to speak in important ways to Indo-American relations. For example, why has the United States refrained from using force against a rising challenger in the system despite sometimes significant conflicts of interest? This puzzle is particularly acute given the relative weak economic ties between the United States and India that neoliberal institutionalists would point to as generators of cooperation. Another puzzle in Indo-American relations relates to the curiously muted response by the United States to India's nuclear program. Indian nuclear weapons development takes place in contravention of international institutions – for example, the Non-Proliferation Treaty and the Nuclear Suppliers Group – in which the United States has invested deeply and that have played a key role in regulating the spread of nuclear weapons. From a neorealist theoretical perspective, the development of nuclear weapons by a rising power and an antagonist to a long-standing U.S. ally both in the Cold War and the War on Terror should be cause for alarm. From a neoliberal institutional perspective, the international legal frameworks binding the United States into a nonproliferation agenda should push the United States to oppose the Indian nuclear program. Yet the United States has remained remarkably unconcerned about India's nuclear program for over three decades. A constructivist approach offers the potential to provide insight on both of these puzzles, in the process speaking to dynamics that underpin the broader U.S.-India relationship.

Roadmap and Theoretical Expectations

The chapters are organized similarly. In each, I begin with an issue overview and a review of relevant literature. I then move on to the case or cases themselves, analyzing the security constructions of political leaders in the United States with particular attention to how shared democratic identity structures the security arguments. In the chapter on the 1971 Bangladesh War, I end with an empirical

---

[21] Hathaway 2002.
[22] Rubinoff 2005.

Democracy, Security, and the Relationship

and analytical summary. This summary is also present in the second chapter on U.S. construction of India's nuclear program, but is followed by an effort to situate all the cases within a theoretical reading of Indo-American relations as exceptions to or aspects of the general pattern of relations. The chapter wraps up by tying the cases back to the general theoretical framework.

It bears repeating that the objective of these chapters is not to explain the formation of U.S. foreign policy with respect to India. Instead, the aim is to examine how U.S. policy makers attempt to construct their security policy vis-à-vis the American public. My claim is that the democratic identity that binds the imagined community together acts as a constraint of the security and foreign policy options available to leaders. At the psychological level, leaders may construct threats and formulate security policy using very different rationales than what they present in public, as indeed the evidence presented in Chapter 2 suggests. My analytical framework leads to the following expectations. When attempting to securitize a fellow democracy, U.S. policy makers are expected to deemphasize the external state's democratic characteristics and identity while emphasizing any nondemocratic aspects. When attempting to desecuritize an issue or external state that had been previously securitized or would normally be expected to be securitized, policy makers are expected to emphasize the democratic characteristics and identity of the external state. With respect to the 1971 crisis, when Nixon and Kissinger clearly militarized action against India, their public discourse should reflect efforts to portray India as undemocratic to justify their policy position. Those who opposed the policy are expected to emphasize India's democratic characteristics in an effort to undermine the existential threat argument. These dynamics are expected to play out with respect to the 1974 PNE, 1998 nuclear tests, and 2005 nuclear deal cases. As securitization theory indicates, the success of these efforts can be measured by audience support for the policy. If securitization is successful, the public accepts the existential threat argument as well as the identification of the threat and the policy prescription.

2

Near Miss

The Bangladesh War, India, and the United States in 1971

Historical Overview and Literature

When India was granted independence by the British in 1947, the former crown jewel of the British Empire split into two separate states: secular, predominantly Hindu India and the religiously oriented Muslim state of Pakistan. While India enjoyed territorial continuity, Pakistan did not. The bulk of the Pakistani state lay to the northwest of India and was dominated by the Punjabi ethnic group. To the east of India, near Burma (Myanmar), lay East Pakistan, with an almost completely Bengali population and no physical connection to West Pakistan. In 1970, the first democratic election in Pakistan's history gave a parliamentary majority to the Awami League, an East Pakistan party that favored autonomy for East Pakistan. West Pakistani leaders, who dominated the outgoing government, were generally unhappy with the election results and a political impasse emerged. Negotiations stalled over how much autonomy Bengali East Pakistan should enjoy. In March 1971, following demonstrations in East Pakistan, the military moved to reassert control. President Yahya Khan outlawed the Awami League and ordered the military to arrest Awami leaders and disarm Bengali military personnel. The crackdown was brutal, with particular attention paid to East Pakistan's Bengali Hindu population. The military action in East Pakistan pushed million of refugees into India, placing significant strains on the state and federal governments. Indian Prime Minister Indira Gandhi denounced the Pakistani action and provided covert assistance to Bengali members of the Pakistani army who had escaped detention. Indian and East Pakistani political leaders also began a concerted campaign to raise public awareness of the situation and mobilize public opinion against Pakistan. In the meantime, the Indian military began to draw up plans for a military response in the winter.[1]

---

[1] Kux 1994, 289–92; National Security Council 1971; Sathasivam 2005, 9–10, 82; Sisson and Rose 1990.

Near Miss: The Bangladesh War, India, and the United States

The American response was muted. While the consul general in Dhaka urged condemnation of West Pakistan based on a policy (and national interest) centered on human rights, he was unaware of Nixon and Kissinger's efforts, funneled through Pakistan, to establish formal contact with China.[2] On July 15, 1971, Nixon announced Kissinger's mission to Beijing and his own forthcoming trip. In sharp contrast to U.S. efforts in 1962 when Kennedy extended aid to India during the short Sino-Indian war of that year, Kissinger made it clear that should China move against India in the context of an Indo-Pakistani war, the United States would do nothing to assist India. Shortly afterward, on August 9, Indira Gandhi announced the signing of a friendship treaty between New Delhi and Moscow. Thus the geopolitical stage was set.[3]

By November 1971, the situation in East Pakistan reached a tipping point. Bangladeshi guerrilla fighters were increasing their attacks on Pakistani military forces in East Pakistan, often with Indian artillery support. In the United States, policy against India had hardened. By that point, Nixon had chosen to tilt U.S. policy in favor of Pakistan, and Kissinger was pushing the foreign policy apparatus hard to implement the tilt.[4] In early December, after attacking Indian airfields, Pakistan declared war on India. The Indian response was immediate, moving against Pakistani forces in East Pakistan while mounting sufficient operations in the west to prevent the arrival of reinforcements. Pakistani and U.S. leaders thought China would come to Pakistan's aid, but were mistaken. While the Chinese verbally supported Pakistan, no military support was forthcoming. Within two weeks, the fighting in East Pakistan – soon to be Bangladesh – was over as ninety-three thousand soldiers surrendered to Indian forces. While few in government agreed with them, Nixon and Kissinger grew concerned that India would continue the war effort and attack West Pakistan. Despite assurances from both the Indian government and the Soviets that such an attack was not in the offing, Nixon ordered the USS *Enterprise* carrier group to the Bay of Bengal.[5] The move "deeply angered" Indian leaders, set back U.S.-India relations for decades, and strengthened the hand of those within India who wanted to move forward on nuclear testing.[6]

One of the benefits of this case for my analytical agenda lies in the difficulties alternative approaches have explaining events. Structural realist balance of power predictions are indeterminate.[7] The secession of overwhelmingly poor East Pakistan would not meaningfully change the regional or global balance of

---

[2] Blood 1971b.
[3] Kux 1994, 292, 94–5.
[4] Kux 1994, 302.
[5] Kux 1994, 305.
[6] Kux 1994, 307.
[7] Waltz 1979. Waltz claims that neorealism does not apply to foreign policy, although Elman points out that Waltz himself uses neorealism in foreign policy analysis (Elman 1996, 10). Additionally, as Hopf (2002) argues in his concluding chapter, Waltz draws on foreign policy choices as evidence for his systemic theory.

power. Even assuming that secession did change the balance of power, structural realism does not explain the secretive, milquetoast U.S. response where a more robust response would be called for. Shifting to balance of threat does not resolve the problem of underdetermination.[8] Reframing the balancing/bandwagoning impetus from power to threat does not help us understand why India might be construed as a threat, much less why the United States would choose to oppose India rather than acquiesce to India's actions as a means of gaining influence over Indian foreign policy making. Admittedly, India had recently signed a friendship treaty with the Soviets, but this on its own does not mandate a balancing response. Under neorealism, alliances enjoy no permanence in the anarchic system, so the alliance with Pakistan for its own sake cannot be explanatory. Variants of structural liberalism (neoliberalism) do not fare better. Emphasizing economic interdependence and international institutions as moderators of conflict, neoliberalism has little to say on patterns of behavior in the absence of these factors.[9] In 1971, India and the United States shared no appreciable institutional ties outside the United Nations and negligible economic interdependence.[10]

The case also provides significant benefits for understanding U.S. relations with India. The Bangladesh War set the tone for Indo-American relations for decades and is one of the few instances scholars have identified where overt shows of force have occured between democracies. Strikingly, despite the importance of the case, the events of 1971 have received little attention in the academic literature.[11] Of the literature that does exist, diplomatic history is by far the dominant approach.[12] Diplomatic history treatments predictably focus on Nixon and Kissinger as the principal forces that drove the confrontation between the United States and India, with an emphasis on Nixon and Kissinger's strong tendency to view the world through a realpolitik geopolitical lens. While these approaches are valuable, and rich with historical context, they underexamine the relationship between Nixon and Kissinger and the broader political system, including the public. In undervaluing that relationship, the diplomatic historical approaches are unable to identify forces that might operate in the Indo-American relationship beyond 1971. For example, Van Hollen

---

[8] Walt 1987.
[9] Keohane 1984; Keohane and Martin 1995.
[10] Assuming trade as a proxy for economic interdependence, the UN COMTRADE database (United Nations 2010) puts U.S. annual exports to India in 1971 at 648 million USD (~1.5 percent of total exports) and imports at 329 million USD (~0.7 percent of total imports).
[11] Van Hollen 1980. Although this may be an extension of a generalized lack of interest by academics in U.S. foreign policy toward India (Sathasivam 2005, vii). In part, the lack of scholarly interest may arise from India's relatively slow economic growth in the decades after independence, making the Indian story one more of unrealized potential than international presence. Another possible explanation is its participation, indeed spearheading, of the Non-Aligned Movement, effectively removing it from the international dynamic – the Cold War – that dominated the study on international relations in the United States until the early 1990s.
[12] Haendel 1977; Kux 1994; T. Thornton 1992; Van Hollen 1980.

contends that Nixon and Kissinger were isolated from the public as well as the rest of the foreign policy-making architecture, suggesting that the events of 1971 were the unique product of Nixon and Kissinger's personal thought processes. While it is undoubtedly the case that individual-level characteristics of Nixon and Kissinger had a tremendous impact, it is untenable to hold that social factors did not play an important, indeed, as I argue, critical role. For a quick example of the importance of the public for foreign policy making in the Nixon White House, one need look no further than 1970 as the administration tried to come to terms with a natural disaster in the region – a monsoon that killed as many as five hundred thousand East Pakistanis:

KISSINGER: I have two problems about the Pakistanis. I called the Pakistan ambassador. He is satisfied. I asked about sending a delegation. They are probably not eager to have a delegation.

HALDERMAN: We don't care. It's to avoid the negative. We have to look humanitarian.

...

HALDERMAN: What good can they do with wheat.[sic] We are treating it as a bureaucratic thing.

KISSINGER: That's not true. We have sent three cables a day.

HALDERMAN: Does anyone in Iowa care about three cables a day to the Pakistanis? They watch thousands of people die and we should be doing something.[13]

Leaving aside the political context, Widmaier finds in his analysis of 1971 U.S. policy that broader social constructions of democracy influenced Nixon and Kissinger's approach. Specifically, Widmaier argues that leaders in liberal democracies, with their emphasis on individualism and the free function of the market, may view the stress on equity in social democracies as undemocratic, a constraint on individual freedom for the sake of some arbitrary public interest. Alternatively, leaders in social democracies may view the emphasis on economic and individual competition in liberal democracies as an indicator of the willingness of liberal democracies to engage in systemic competition. Thus, influenced by these social constructions of democracy, Nixon and Kissinger were predisposed as liberal (free market) democrats to be antagonistic toward social democratic India.[14] Widmaier's study suggests that even at the individual level, analysts cannot ignore how societal-level constructions shape policy.[15]

---

[13] United States Office of the President 1970b.
[14] Widmaier 2005.
[15] There is an apparent tension between the argument proposed by Widmaier and that which I put forward. Widmaier holds that liberal and social democratic identities create conditions of cooperation and conflict between democracies. In part, this highlights the importance of political parties in interdemocratic relations. Widmaier notes that when Democrats are in power U.S.-India relations are smoother than when Republicans are in power. This argument would appear to conflict with my claim that shared democracy, regardless of flavor, impedes securitization. The tension is easily resolved, however. First, Widmaier's argument largely deals with day-to-day relations, which my argument does not address. Other than the 1971 case, Widmaier presents no evidence for the social-liberal distinction as a basis for securitization, and in the 1971 case

My treatment of the case addresses many of the problems in the literature. The treatment clearly seeks to identify a factor that shapes U.S.-India relations over time and how that factor shaped one of the most contentious events in their shared history. Not only will this enrich understandings of how and why the events of 1971 played out, but it is also a critical point for understanding how the United States will engage with and accommodate India's changing place in the international system. The case also challenges the idea that Nixon and Kissinger acted uninfluenced by the public and other branches of government. In fact, Nixon and Kissinger display an acute awareness of Congress and the public, even if they did not appreciate either. This finding suggests that 1971, and U.S. foreign policy in general, cannot be understood by focusing on policy makers alone.

The Case

There is no ambiguity as to the position of Nixon and Kissinger, as the primary foreign policy formulators, on the events in East Pakistan. Both supported the military government of Yahya against the democratically elected Awami League (and as a consequence East Pakistan more generally, where the Awami League received 75 percent of the vote) and democratic India. While other major powers condemned West Pakistan, Nixon and Kissinger pushed a U.S. policy tilting toward Pakistan.[16] Despite the fact that Yahya's government was actively and severely repressing East Pakistan, and that India was also a victim with millions of refugees straining its infrastructure and resources, Nixon and Kissinger marked India as the principal threat, not Pakistan:

NIXON: The Indians need – what they need really is a –
KISSINGER: They're such bastards.

---

much of the effect was concentrated by the particularities of Nixon and Kissinger. Finally, in the case that follows there is no evidence that the liberal-social distinction played out in public. This is not to say that Widmaier's observation is irrelevant – quite the contrary. Widmaier's point is that democracy is what democracies make of it, and that point serves as a valuable antidote to the tendency to reify democracy. As I note previously, corporate and, to a lesser degree, social identity are not fixed. The liberal versus social divide could conceivably become the basis for redefinition of corporate democratic identity, subsequently serving as a basis for securitization.

[16] United States Department of State 1971l. In a CIA briefing on the events and prospects for the future of Pakistan, the analysts noted that, with the exception of China, "none of the major powers have shown any support for the central [West Pakistan] government's efforts in Bengal." The Soviets in particular had likely concluded that "the odds favor a separatist solution or at least that Islamabad has little chance of imposing its will on East Bengal in any lasting and effective way" (United States Central Intelligence Agency 1971). On the tilt, Kissinger colorfully told the Washington Special Actions Group: "I've been catching unshirted hell every half-hour from the President who says we're not tough enough. He believes State is pressing us to be tough and I'm resisting. He really doesn't believe we're carrying out his wishes. He wants to tilt toward Pakistan, and he believes that every briefing or statement is going the other way" (United States Department of State 1971l).

NIXON: A mass famine. But they aren't going to get that. We're going to feed them – a new kind of wheat. But if they're not going to have a famine the last thing they need is another war. Let the goddamn Indians fight a war [unclear].
KISSINGER: They are the most aggressive goddamn people around there.
NIXON: The Indians?
KISSINGER: Yeah.
NIXON: Sure.[17]

Remarkably, the threat assessment made by Nixon and Kissinger, made on May 26, came at a time when India and Pakistan were not directly engaged in military action against each other and not long after India had been deluged by refugees. While there was evidence that India was helping train Bengali resistance fighters, the level of Indian assistance at that point was limited.[18] In November of that year, the animosity toward Indira Gandhi and the general perception of threat by Kissinger and Nixon hardened:

NIXON: This is just the point when she is a bitch.
KISSINGER: Well, the Indians are bastards anyway. They are starting a war there. It's – to them East Pakistan is no longer the issue. Now, I found it very interesting how she carried on to you yesterday about West Pakistan ... You very subtly – I mean, she will not be able to go home and say that the United States didn't give her a warm reception and therefore, in despair, she's got to go to war.[19]

The threat posed by India in the eyes of Nixon and Kissinger was twofold. First, India posed an indirect threat to containment. Indian support for Bangladesh was expected to enable the rise of an independent state. The poverty and lack of natural resources in Bangladesh would in turn result in a state ripe for communist infiltration. The second threat was more direct. Nixon in particular saw the ultimate Indian aim as the destruction of Pakistan, an ally to the United States and a component of containment policy.[20] In November, Kissinger warned Nixon that India in his opinion had become a Soviet client:

KISSINGER: Except for Vietnam, I'd give her [Indira Gandhi] five minutes of the Tito talk because it will go right back to the Russians as well as to the Vietnamese.
NIXON: Will it?
KISSINGER: Oh, yeah. They have the closest diplomatic ties now with Russia. They leak everything right back to them.[21]

By December, Kissinger became more explicit in linking India to the Soviets in his threat assessment:

---

[17] United States Department of State 1971j.
[18] United States Department of State 1971m.
[19] United States Department of State 1971e.
[20] United States Department of State 1971i.
[21] United States Department of State 1971e.

[W]hat we may be witnessing is a situation where a country equipped and supported by the Soviets may be turning half of Pakistan into an impotent state and the other half into a vassal.[22]

At one point, Kissinger went so far as to call the crisis "our Rhineland," a reference to Hitler's militarization of German Rhineland at the outset of World War II.[23] This powerful imagery indicates how strongly Kissinger and Nixon came to see the Indian threat.

As policy makers, Nixon and Kissinger seemed unbound by democratic norms and identity.[24] They supported efforts by U.S. Ambassador to Pakistan Joseph Farland to transfer State Department officials who brought the events in East Pakistan to governmental and public attention.[25] Neither Nixon nor Kissinger seemed to have any qualms about the efforts of President Yahya to role back democratic reforms – reforms generated because of internal political pressure – and abuse the citizenry in East Pakistan.[26] Meeting with the Pakistani president in late 1970, Nixon commented he hoped Pakistan would "keep a strong Presidency as in France," and did not contest Yahya's claim that Pakistan was unfit for parliamentary democracy. Later, after the repression of East Pakistan had begun in earnest, Nixon and Kissinger showed no concern for the loss of life in East Pakistan or the damage to the fledgling democracy in Pakistan:

KISSINGER: There's *nothing of any great consequence*, Mr. President. Apparently Yahya has got control of East Pakistan.
NIXON: Good. There're sometimes the use of power is...
KISSINGER: The use of power against seeming odds pays off. 'Cause all the experts were saying that thirty thousand people can't get control of 75 million.
NIXON: Well, maybe things have changed. But hell, when you look over the history of nations, thirty thousand well-disciplined people can take 75 million any time. Look what the Spanish did when they came in and took the Incas and all the rest. Look what the British did when they took India ... But anyway I wish him [Yahya] well.[27] (emphasis added)

The violation of human rights on a massive scale – a cable from Dacca dated March 30, 1971 described the situation as "selective genocide"[28] – the failure to respect rule of law, and most certainly the complete lack of nonviolent

---

[22] Gwertzman 1972.
[23] United States Department of State 1971h.
[24] This would not surprise anyone a few years later as Nixon's role in the Watergate scandal, particularly his efforts during the subsequent cover-up became apparent. Nixon's efforts to obstruct the investigation into the Watergate Hotel break-in clearly demonstrate a fundamental disregard by the president for the rule of law and normal political process.
[25] United States Department of State 1971c. Including the U.S. consul general in Dacca, Archer Blood; the head of the United States Information Service in the region; as well as the head of U.S. AID for Pakistan, Eric Griffel.
[26] Hughes 1969; Khan 1999, 274–5.
[27] United States Department of State 1971n.
[28] Blood 1971a.

conflict resolution seemed irrelevant to Nixon and Kissinger in their evaluation of the situation. In fact, the nondemocratic aspects of Yahya's behavior, the projection of force to suppress the democratic will of the East Pakistanis, seemed to impress them the most. As evidence mounted of military atrocities in East Pakistan, Nixon and Kissinger remained unmoved. In a Senior Review Group meeting, Kissinger commented after being told of significant casualties at a university that "They [the British] didn't dominate 400 million Indians all those years by being gentle."[29]

Outside the Nixon-Kissinger decision-making space, Nixon's construction of India was radically different. He regularly referred to India's democratic government. Nixon emphasized the importance of Indian democracy in a private meeting with Foreign Minister Dinesh Singh, arguing that if India, as a parliamentary democracy, "does not make the grade, the example for the rest of the world will be profound."[30] Reiterating this point during a visit to India in a meeting with Prime Minister Indira Gandhi and top U.S. and Indian aides, Nixon went further, arguing that "[i]t is essential that India succeed."[31] Within the administration, Nixon also focused on Indian democracy, telling the U.S. ambassador to India, Kenneth Keating – who at the time was pushing Nixon and Kissinger to pull funds from the Pakistani foreign aid package and transfer them to India to help that country deal with the massive influx of refugees – that:

I know that country is trying to make it (unclear) basically with some semblance of democracy – private enterprise, call it whatever you want. And I know that looming over from the north are the Chinese (unclear). It's, therefore, very much in our interest to see that India, we want them to succeed. Because there are 550 million people, we want them to do well.[32]

In August 1971, despite the strong perception of threat evinced by Kissinger and Nixon, Nixon refused to make a public securitizing move. During a news conference, Nixon's only comments on the East Pakistan crisis were to emphasize the amount of aid donated by the United States (70 million USD) to aid India in dealing with the massive number of refugees generated by Yahya's military action. No mention was made of Nixon's belief that India sought to dismantle Pakistan or that India posed a direct or indirect threat to U.S. interests.[33]

By the end of September, however, Nixon and Kissinger were moving to securitize India while justifying their failure to securitize Pakistan, albeit within government circles. In a conversation with British Foreign Secretary Sir Alec Douglas-Home and British Ambassador to the U.S. George Baring, Earl of Cromer, Nixon and Kissinger explicitly pointed to India as the primary reason

[29] United States Department of State 1971k.
[30] Saunders 1969a.
[31] Saunders 1969b.
[32] United States Department of State 1971b.
[33] *New York Times* 1971e; Nixon 1971a.

the crisis had not been resolved. Kissinger claimed India had "totally thwarted it [meeting between Bengali resistance and Yahya]. They made it impossible for these people to deal with us; they're forcing them to check everything with them, they are padding demands, which are totally incapable of fulfillment." In a prelude to arguments made later in public, Kissinger was attempting to justify the U.S. government's anti-Indian approach by targeting India as the primary responsible party in the crisis. The increasingly dire security situation in East Pakistan could and should be laid at the feet of India. At the same time, Nixon repeatedly defended President Yahya, leader of a Pakistani government responsible for thousands of deaths and millions of refugees, as a "decent man."[34]

The growing effort by Nixon and Kissinger to securitize India within the halls of government in September was not reflected in their public discourse. To the American public, Nixon and Kissinger maintained a façade of neutrality. In October, in a statement on relief aid to south Asia, Nixon once again focused on relief efforts rather than security concerns and specifically mentioned India as a primary recipient of emergency aid.[35] In greeting Prime Minister Gandhi during her November 1971 visit to the United States, Nixon immediately brought attention to India's democratic system:

Our distinguished guest here today has the unique distinction, through the parliamentary system of India, that more people have voted for her leadership than for any leader in the whole history of the world. Madam Prime Minister, we welcome you because you represent the world's largest free nation, the world's largest democracy. We welcome you also for another reason ... India and the United States are bound together by a higher morality [than treaties], a more profound morality that does not need legal document to make it live. I speak of the common devotion that the people of India and the people of the United States have to the cause of freedom, to the cause of representative government ... to the cause of peace.[36]

Presaging later arguments by his administration, Nixon used the language of shared democracy to mask the pro-Pakistan position of the U.S. government. By appealing to Indian democracy, Nixon was communicating to his audience, through the press, as well as to Indira Gandhi, that arguments claiming the United States had chosen Pakistan over India were false. By highlighting democracy, Nixon was diffusing the pro-Pakistan critique by demonstrating that he recognized India as a fellow democracy and would therefore not support the Pakistani military dictatorship at India's expense. The democracy rhetoric also served as an effort to mask Nixon's failure to address the ongoing and deepening crisis in East Pakistan, or the massive burden imposed on India by the resulting refugee outflow – issues certainly at the forefront of India's concerns

---

[34] United States Department of State 1971g.
[35] Nixon 1971c.
[36] Nixon 1971b; Welles 1971b. In using this language to undermine the claims of his political opponents, Nixon laid a rhetorical trap for himself, making it more difficult for him to execute a securitizing move when he decided to deploy military assets (Schimmelfennig 2001).

Near Miss: The Bangladesh War, India, and the United States

at the time. The principal reason Nixon used the rhetoric of democracy is he expected it to resonate with his audience, the American public.[37]

By the time the war started in earnest in December 1971, Nixon and Kissinger had deeply securitized India. Kissinger actively disseminated his belief to other government officials that India was aggressing against Pakistan and that the Soviet Union was pulling the geopolitical strings. Kissinger had also begun to use a heavily security- (and gender) laden term with respect to the situation: *rape*. Before the war started, Kissinger was concerned Pakistan would "get raped" if the crisis was brought before the UN, to which Secretary of State Rogers replied: "They will if the fighting doesn't stop."[38] Kissinger extended the rape image in a discussion with Secretary of the Treasury John Connally:

The thing that concerns the President and me is this; here we have Indian-Soviet collusion, raping a friend of ours ... Thirdly, if the Soviets get away with this in the Subcontinent, we have seen the dress rehearsal for a Middle Eastern war.[39]

As for restraining India:

No matter what we do, we can't do as much for them [India] as the Soviets have already done on the thing that interests them [India] which is to rape Pakistan.[40]

By the time India and Pakistan engaged in direct military confrontation, Kissinger and Nixon used the rape metaphor regularly to describe their fears for (West) Pakistan.[41] The rape language conveys the impression that innocent, vulnerable Pakistan was in danger of assault by the aggressive, menacing nexus of the Soviet Union and India. This posed a threat not only to Pakistan; in the logic of containment, if the Soviet Union, through its Indian proxy, was successful in destroying Pakistan, it would be emboldened to strike at far more geopolitically and economically precious territory in the Middle East. On December 8, 1971, Nixon and Kissinger acted to move U.S. policy outside the realm of normal politics. In a phone conversation with Pakistan Ambassador to the United States Raza, Kissinger told him to tell the U.S. State Department that Pakistan wished to invoke its "mutual security treaty" with the United States.[42]

---

[37] On a more speculative level, Nixon may have also sought to undermine Gandhi's (assumed) agenda by using the language of shared democracy to defuse a securitizing move by Gandhi toward the United States.
[38] United States Department of State 1971p.
[39] United States Department of State 1971q.
[40] United States Department of State 1971q.
[41] Three times in the span of an hour-long conversation. While Nixon did not use the word, he clearly agreed with the assessment.
[42] United States Department of State 1971r. There was in fact no mutual security treaty. According to the State Department: "No mutual security treaty has ever been concluded between the United States and Pakistan. The references to such a treaty and unqualified

Nixon and Kissinger, in their effort to justify their securitization of India, attempted to deemphasize Indian democratic identity and to reframe India as undemocratic. In a December discussion planning their public relations strategy, Nixon strongly emphasized that India was defying the will of the global peoples and ignoring the will of the United Nations, determined through democratic voting:

> The general tone is that in view of India's refusal to accept the terms of the General Assembly resolution passed by the overwhelming majority of 104–10 calling for an immediate ceasefire, the withdrawal of armed forces, the United States has now decided again to take this grave issue to the Security Council ... All right. Add one sentence. "If India defies," put it this way, "If India should defy the overwhelming weight, defies, should continue to defy the overwhelming weight of world opinion as expressed by a blankety blank vote in the UN General Assembly."[43]

By focusing on India's refusal to heed world opinion and the will of the UN, established through a democratic voting process, Nixon sought to target the core pillar of American public support for India: shared democratic identity. Nixon also sought to reframe India's identity, casting it not as a democracy, but as part of the communist system accepted as posing an existential threat to the United States:

NIXON: Now, "Pakistan has accepted. India has refused. India, supported the Soviet Union" –
KISSINGER: That was the next question I wanted to put to you.
NIXON: "India, supported by the Soviet Union, has refused" – now we are going.
KISSINGER: Supported only by the Soviet Union.
NIXON: Supported only by the Soviet Union. Well, some other Communist countries.
KISSINGER: Supported by the Soviet Union.

---

references to an assurance offered to Pakistan by the Kennedy administration indicate that Nixon and Kissinger were ill-informed about the nature and extent of a U.S. commitment to take military action to assist Pakistan in the event of an attack by India. Kissinger's reference to a mutual security treaty during this conversation is an apparent reference to the Agreement of Cooperation signed by the United States and Pakistan on March 5, 1959, in the context of Pakistan's membership in the Baghdad Pact. The agreement (10 UST 317) obligates the United States to take appropriate action 'as may be mutually agreed upon' to defend Pakistan against aggression. The agreement cites the Joint Resolution to Promote Peace and Stability in the Middle East of March 9, 1957. (PL-7, 85th Congress) The Joint Resolution contemplated, among other things, the use of armed forces to assist nations against aggression by 'any country controlled by international communism' so long as such use of force was consonant with the treaty obligations and the Constitution of the United States" (United States Department of State Office of the Historian 2008). Kissinger would later argue with Secretary of State Rogers over the matter as Rogers insisted the Kennedy agreement in no way committed the United States to use military force to aid Pakistan (United States Department of State 1971o).

[43] United States Department of State 1971f.

NIXON: Supported by the Soviet Union. Can we say other Communist countries? Use the word Communist for a change. And, well that throws in the Chinese and the Romanians. All right, supported by, at any rate, supported by the Soviet Union.[44]

By linking India with the Soviet Union, Nixon sought to remove India from the community of democracies.

Even in early December, the Nixon administration moved to securitize India in an almost passive aggressive manner. For example, the Nixon administration moved quickly to cut off all military export licenses to India. Only forty-eight hours separated the Nixon administration's announcement that no new export licenses would be granted to India and the announcement that all existing licenses would be canceled as well.[45] This stands in stark contrast to the hesitant manner with which U.S. military export licenses were handled with respect to Pakistan, a point made by the Indian ambassador to the United States.[46] From the vantage point of the public, the speed of Nixon's decision to cut India's licenses meant he perceived India as a primary threat, but the administration was reluctant to clearly stake the claim. Charles Bray, the State Department spokesman, indicated that the suspension was due to "continuing Indian incursions into Pakistan," implying that India, not Pakistan, bore responsibility for the crisis. Additionally, unidentified U.S. officials began to suggest that India was untrustworthy. Responding to Indian reports that Pakistani air forces had struck at airfields near India's border with West Pakistan, they stated: "It's hard to believe Indian reports about those Pakistan air attacks."[47] The Nixon administration was quietly building its case for securitizing India.

The administration's rhetoric attempting to securitize India became more explicit on December 4, when a State Department official blamed India for the crisis:

India bears the major responsibility for the broader hostilities [between Pakistan and India]. We believe that *since the beginning of the crisis* Indian policy, in a systematic way, has led to the *perpetuation of the crisis*, a *deepening of the crisis*, and that India bears the major responsibility for the broader hostilities that have ensued.[48] (emphasis added)

Secretary of State Rogers made the final connection for the American public, claiming that the crisis "posed a threat to international peace and security." The public argument was set: India posed a threat to U.S. interests because the crisis it had perpetuated and deepened posed a threat to international security. While

---

[44] United States Department of State 1971f.
[45] T. Smith 1971; Welles 1971c.
[46] Welles 1971c. It is true that licenses to Pakistan were eliminated earlier than they were for India, but the Nixon administration did so under strong pressure from Congress and the public and did not move quickly to implement the policy, waiting several months after the start of military operations in East Pakistan.
[47] Welles 1971c. In fact, the Indian reports were accurate (Kux 1994).
[48] Welles 1971d.

the administration did not directly address India's democratic nature despite Nixon's recognition that democracy lay at the heart of American public support for India, it did highlight undemocratic behavior. The United States had not even received "minimal" cooperation from India. India had also refused the good offices of the secretary general of the United Nations and "refused U.S. requests to urge the guerrillas not to attack United Nations ships and trucks carrying relief supplies."[49]

Less than a week after the Nixon administration initially announced the cutoff of military aid to India, the *New York Times* reported economic aid would be cut as well, a move Nixon had refused to make against Pakistan.[50] In announcing the cut, a dramatic act against a country as poor as India, the State Department labeled India the "main aggressor."[51] Now India was not just to blame for perpetuating and deepening the crisis; it was actively and openly using force. The Nixon administration was slowly building the securitizing move.

Starting on December 14, in line with the planning sessions between Nixon and Kissinger, the administration began to recast India's identity as that of a "client" to the communist USSR. The *New York Times* reported "senior state department officials" were "puzzled" by Soviet "willingness to forsake possible dramatic improvements in relations with the United States" by continuing to back India.[52] The implication is that the Soviet Union had sunk deep roots into India and India's government, otherwise the Soviets would be willing to reduce tensions with the United States. What else could explain their apparently irrational behavior? Moreover, the improvement in relations was described as *dramatic*; by inference, the Soviet stake in India must be truly significant to forego such a boon. A day later, the *New York Times* reported the Nixon administration was considering canceling a summit with Soviet leaders if they did not pressure India to cease hostilities, further linking India and the Soviet Union by suggesting Moscow played a significant role – appropriate to a Soviet patron-client relationship – in Indian decision making.[53] In a postbellum attempt to justify Nixon's policy, well-known syndicated columnist Joseph Alsop – citing Henry Kissinger – again attempted to restructure Indian identity in terms of its association with the Soviet Union and to highlight the threat posed by India. According to Alsop, Kissinger indicated there was "'a strong possibility' that India would become a 'vast new Soviet strategic base area.'"[54]

---

[49] Welles 1971d.
[50] Interesting, the Nixon administration presented the same argument used in calls to cut economic aid to Pakistan, namely that the continuance of aid would facilitate military operations by allowing the target state to transfer funds from the civilian to the military budget.
[51] Gwertzman 1971c.
[52] Gwertzman 1971a.
[53] Naughton 1971.
[54] Welles 1972.

The shift in Nixon's reference to Indian democracy is remarkable. While Nixon and Kissinger maintained a façade of neutrality, Indian democracy figured heavily in their rhetoric about India. As the crisis deepened, particularly in December when the Nixon administration was making a concerned effort to securitize India, no reference was made to Indian democracy at all. In effect, the rhetoric of democracy served to diffuse arguments by critics that the Nixon administration had in fact securitized India and was acting in line with that assessment. A background briefing given by Henry Kissinger exemplifies this dynamic. In response to strong criticism, particularly from members of Congress, that the Nixon administration was anti-Indian, the White House (Kissinger) responded by pointing to Indian democracy:

> There have been some comments that the Administration is anti-Indian. This is totally inaccurate. India is a great country. It is the most populous free country. It is governed by democratic procedures. Americans through all administrations in the postwar period have felt a commitment to the progress and development of India, and the American people have contributed to this to the extent of $10 billion. Therefore, when we have differed with India in recent weeks, we do so with great sadness and great disappointment.[55]

There are two critical points here. The first lies in the accusation that the administration was anti-Indian. For such a critique to carry weight, it must reflect the perception by large portions of the electorate (since the critique was made for political purposes) that India, despite administration efforts to convince the public to the contrary, was not a threat. Had the administration succeeded in securitizing India, the anti-India critique in fact would not be a critique, but a commendation. Second, when forced to defend itself against claims that it was anti-India, the administration attempted to defuse the critique by appealing to what was perceived to give rise to the strength of the critique. That is, the administration appealed to shared democracy – by pointing to Indian democracy – in an effort to confront the anti-India argument on ideological grounds. How could an administration that recognizes Indian democracy be anti-Indian? The administration then continued to argue that India was behaving undemocratically, in this case by claiming that concessions wrung out of President Yahya before the onset of the war were ignored by India. Playing to public belief about the nature of democratic identity, the administration claimed to have "withheld assigning blame [after fighting started in November, but before the onset of formal war] because it was reluctant to believe that India had come to a naked recourse to force."[56]

The Nixon administration was not alone it its effort to securitize India. Although support in Congress was weak, some did take up the cause. In the

---

[55] Gwertzman 1971d; *New York Times* 1972. At the time the source was identified only as a White House official. Later, Senator Barry Goldwater (R-AZ) identified the source as Henry Kissinger (Gwertzman 1971b).
[56] Gwertzman 1971d.

House of Representatives, Representative Bradford Morse (R-MA) made a clear effort to link India to the "clear and present danger to international peace" that war between India and Pakistan would engender. Claiming that the floor of the House was not an appropriate location to review the details of how Pakistan sought to use force to "reimpose its authority over its rebellious eastern province," Morse focused on India as the primary agent in a situation that, if it evolved into war, was the "greatest threat to world peace since World War II."[57] Tellingly, Morse made no reference to Indian democracy or to the victory of the Awami League in democratic polls that initiated the crisis.[58]

After the war, Nixon returned to highlighting Indian democracy in his public statements. In his 1972 *Third Annual Report to Congress on United States Foreign Policy*, Nixon described India as:

[A] great country, a free and democratic nation, in whose future as a model of progress for the developing world the United States has invested its hopes and resources.[59]

Apparently, after months of refusing to characterize India as a democracy, Nixon had returned to language symbolic of his frustration with the public's unwillingness to perceive aggressive democratic states as threats. Nixon also attempted to draw the distinction Kissinger attempted earlier by differentiating between India and Indian action. Nixon again referred to India's democracy before stating that:

It makes no sense to assume, however, that a country's democratic political system ... requires our automatic agreement with every aspect of its foreign policy. We disagreed with specific Indian actions in November and December, and we said so.[60]

Nixon's message is clear. As fellow democracies, India and the United States may disagree at the level of policy, but these disagreements do not mark a more fundamental disagreement that would enable the United States to securitize India. The Bangladesh crisis was one such situation where the Nixon administration simply disagreed with a few "specific Indian actions." Nixon's public position stands in stark contrast with his private securitization of India. Behind closed doors, Nixon and Kissinger constructed India as a significant security threat and they attempted to do so, albeit tentatively, in public. They failed to do so, and reverted to language that would minimize the negative political consequences of their policy. Nowhere does Nixon, despite the revelations of the Anderson Papers, discuss the tilt toward Pakistan or the deployment of the *Enterprise* task group. Public democratic identity, it seems, forced Nixon to disavow policy he played a central role in formulating.

---

[57] Representative Morse (R-MA) 1971.
[58] The Awami League was the main East Pakistan political party, controlling all but two (167 of 169) of the East Pakistan seats in the Pakistan National Assembly and dominating the East Pakistan provincial assembly.
[59] Nixon 1972, 296.
[60] Nixon 1972, 303.

Despite their efforts to securitize India, policy makers in the Nixon administration displayed an acute awareness of the difficulties facing any effort to convince the public. In many cases, the problem of selling administration policy to the public revolved around the difficulty in convincing Americans that a fellow democracy could be a threat to the United States.

There are indications that before the crisis policy makers were aware the public did not perceive democracies as threats and did perceive nondemocracies as threats.[61] In discussions with President Yahya in 1969 (after the imposition of martial law), Secretary of State Rogers indicated that, while the administration was sympathetic to the Pakistani position, the imposition of martial law "presented problems for some in the U.S."[62] Later that year during the Nixon visit to India, Kissinger also acknowledged "the strong feeling of many Americans for India," linking this feeling with his opinion that "American liberals had oversold Indian democracy."[63] Interesting, the problem for Kissinger was the overemphasis on Indian democracy by political opponents of the Nixon administration, engendering a favorable perception within the public that hindered the ability of the Nixon administration to act, ostensibly, according to U.S. interests. Nixon, in broaching the idea that Pakistan might serve as an intermediary between the United State and China, mentioned "a psychosis in this country about India."[64] While Nixon did not explain why such a "psychosis" exists, it seems reasonable to conclude that India's democratic identity played a significant role. Similarly, Nixon complained in November 1971 to the Pakistani foreign minister that public opinion was strongly in favor of India:

> I have indeed. Let me say that the President [Yahya] is a good friend to me. He is a good friend to Kissinger. I – let me be quite candid with you. As I told your former ambassador, and as the President knows, there's a huge public relations campaign here. Many of our friends in the other party, and including, I must say, some of the nuts in our own party – soft heads–have jumped on it, have completely bought the Indian line. And India has a very great propaganda line. And if you read our press, I mean, you get the whole impression that India's completely right.[65]

---

[61] According to a dispatch from the U.S. Embassy in Pakistan, when Admiral Syed Mohammad Ahsan (the deputy martial law administrator in Pakistan) paid a visit to Undersecretary of State Elliot Richardson, the "Under secretary said US view of problems sometimes result of reaction, or even over-reaction, to earlier lessons. Experience with Hitler and Mussolini have left unfavorable image authoritarian regimes. He believed US understood fact that sometimes military regimes are necessary and constructive; but how to judge when constructive, and having judged, how to communicate judgment, is difficult. Public and Congressional opinion this subject must be taken into account, e.g., Reuss Amendment which limits foreign military sales when sales would have affect of arming military dictators who are denying social progress to their own people" (United States Embassy to Pakistan 1969). Richardson seems to indicate that while U.S. political leaders were willing to deal with and even encourage military regimes, the American public was far less accommodating.

[62] United States Embassy to Iran 1969.
[63] Saunders 1969c.
[64] United States Office of the President 1970a.
[65] United States Department of State 1971d.

Again, while Nixon does not indicate why he believes the public strongly favors India, the fact that Republicans fell in with the consensus seems to indicate that public support was both broad and deep.[66]

In conversation with Kissinger and Attorney General John Mitchell, Nixon highlighted the impact of democratic identity on threat perception:

[Y]ou see this is where *The New York Times* and the rest are wrong, where they said that if aggression is engaged in by a democracy it's all right. But where it's engaged in by a dictatorship, it's wrong ... then they say but India is a democratic country, and Pakistan is a totalitarian country, a dictatorship, and therefore India – we shouldn't be on the side of a dictatorship but on the side of the democratic country.[67]

In discussions regarding moving an aircraft carrier into the Bay of Bengal, Kissinger expressed some concern regarding public backlash:

KISSINGER: Secondly, we should move the helicopter ship. I'm not so much in favor of moving the carrier. We'd have to do a helicopter ship and some escorts into the Bay of Bengal. And claim that they're for evacuation. Thirdly, on the Jordanian –

NIXON: [unclear]

KISSINGER: Well, it shows we are – not on the Indians but on the Russians –

NIXON: Why the carrier?

KISSINGER: Well because I think once the news of that hits *there'll be so many people screaming we're [there] for intervention*. And then we have to explain what we will never do.

NIXON: [unclear] we did – you know that we did the whole damn Turkey thing [unclear] for the purposes of being able to evacuate Americans. You remember?

KISSINGER: Yeah, but in –

NIXON: Can't play this game here. Is that correct?

KISSINGER: I would be reluctant – you know you should [unclear – consider?] both courses. From the Chinese angle I'd like to move the carrier. *From the public opinion angle, what the press and television would do to us if an American carrier showed up there I* –

NIXON: What, why – can't the carrier be there for the purpose of evacuation?

KISSINGER: Yeah, but against whom are we going to use the planes? Against whom are we going to use the planes? Are we going to shoot our way in?

NIXON: So what do we move? Move a little helicopter ship in there? What good does that do? And why do it?

KISSINGER: Well it's a token that something else will come afterward. Gets our presence established there.[68] (emphasis added)

---

[66] Nixon does mention Indian propaganda, but does not elaborate. On its own, propaganda is an insufficient explanation; propaganda needs to tie into an ideational base to be effective.
[67] United States Department of State 1971a.
[68] United States Department of State 1971h.

Clearly, public refusal to securitize India was strong enough to cause Kissinger to harbor concerns about the possible backlash should the United States move to threaten India.

There are indications that, within the Nixon administration, Nixon and Kissinger's assessment of the Bangladesh crisis and their policy of siding with a military authoritarian government against democratic India was not universally accepted. Columnist Jack Anderson, in discussing how he received internal government documents on administration policy during the crisis, highlighted the dissonance some in the administration faced:

> During the India-Pakistan war, one of my sources told me we were bungling. Here was a conflict between a military dictatorship and the world's second [sic] largest democracy, and whose side did we – the largest democracy – come out on? The dictatorship.[69]

The comment of Anderson's source suggests that my central analytical claim, that democratic identity influences threat construction, which in turn limits the security options of leaders in democracies, has strong explanatory potential.

Nixon's efforts to securitize India did not go unchallenged. In Congress, critics of the administration pushed back. Senators Kennedy (D-MA) and Muskie (D-MN) disputed Nixon's assignment of blame to India and focused on Pakistan as the primary problem.[70] Kennedy, in rejecting the administration's policy and efforts to characterize India as the aggressor, dated the start of the crisis to Yahya's crackdown on the Awami League in March and linked West Pakistani military efforts in the east, particularly the treatment of minorities, to Nazi Germany. Kennedy argued that Pakistan, with the "military regime's brutal repression of democracy," and "jail[ing] of a political leader whose only crime was the winning of a free election," posed the real threat. Kennedy also desecuritized India, arguing that the refugees generated by Yahya's policy threatened the "economic stability and well-being of the world's largest democracy." Kennedy contrasted Nixon's efforts to open up China to his administration's apparent willingness to "alienate one-sixth of mankind in India – a democratic nation with whom we have had years of productive relations."[71] Kennedy also drew a parallel between Indian actions in East Pakistan and U.S. involvement in Vietnam. The linkage between threat and democracy is clear in Kennedy's statements. West Pakistan and President Yahya, through their aggression against democracy embodied in the repression in East Pakistan, posed the real threat to world peace and U.S. interests. Democratic India, victimized in the crisis and patient and reasonable in its response, posed no threat to the United States and indeed was working in America's interests.

---

[69] Rosenthal 1972. It is odd that Anderson refers to India as the second largest democracy when India's population in 1971 far outstripped that of the United States, making the United States the world's second largest democracy.

[70] Gwertzman 1971d.

[71] Senator Kennedy (D-MA) 1971.

Senator George McGovern (D-SD), then a presidential candidate for the Democratic Party, claimed that India's action in Bangladesh was justified and that West Pakistan had provoked the invasion.[72] Senator Fred Harris (D-OK) excoriated Nixon's policy toward the crisis and – drawing on Anthony Lewis's *New York Times* article – argued that, while India could be difficult to deal with at times, it was still "the largest nation in the world following our notions of political freedom." Harris also argued for congressional investigation of Nixon's policy toward the crisis, suggesting that political benefit could be had from opposing Nixon's policy.[73]

Senator Frank Church (D-ID) also pushed back against Nixon's policy and rhetoric. In discussing the crisis, Church emphasized that West Pakistan, not India, bore the brunt of the blame for the situation. Not only had West Pakistan imposed massive suffering – which Church detailed – but it had done so in response to elections. Church quoted one East Pakistani to exemplify his claim against Pakistan: "We voted for freedom; we were the majority in the whole country, east and west. We voted for freedom and we were killed." Church rejected the Nixon administration's labeling of India as an aggressor and argued that India's position was "consistent with our [U.S.] ideals" and that "there is a large measure of justice in India's cause." Church also cited India as the "only major democracy on the continent of Asia" and paralleled India's involvement in East Pakistan with American involvement in South Vietnam – making it extremely difficult to argue for the securitization of India because India reflected the United States both in form – democracy and values – and function – involvement in another state to facilitate self-determination.[74]

Representative Cornelius Gallagher (D-NJ) was even more explicit in invoking Indian democracy to delegitimize Nixon's approach.[75] Like other legislators, Gallagher argued that West Pakistan, through its brutal military action in the east, had created the situation and placed India in an untenable position vis-à-vis the refugees the action generated. Where Gallagher differed was his explicit appeal to Indian democracy as a critical factor in U.S.-India relations and a very nearly explicit reference to the importance of democratic identity in determining policy:

And we must never forget that India is the largest country in the world with a democratic tradition. Prime Minister Gandhi's electoral victory gave her nation new hope and new faith in India's hard-won traditions of democracy. Would it not then be wise for America to be very careful in its dealings with India? For the sake of our own oft-expressed traditions, should we not be disposed to consider India's position with sympathy and understanding?[76]

---

[72] *New York Times* 1971d.
[73] Senator Harris (D-OK) 1971.
[74] Senator Church (D-ID) 1971.
[75] Gallagher was chair of the House Foreign Affairs subcommittee.
[76] Representative Gallagher (D-NJ) 1971.

The media, particularly the *New York Times* as a central media vehicle covering the crisis, also pushed back against the Nixon/Kissinger rhetoric.[77] In an October editorial, the *New York Times* argued that India had acted with "remarkable restraint" given the tremendous economic and physical toll of the refugees fleeing Pakistani military action as well as the "shocking attack on Indian sensibilities" that accompanied the targeting of Hindus in the East Pakistan action. In advising Nixon, the author specifically identified India's "democratic achievements."[78] In a similar vein, a report on Gandhi's visit to the United States contrasted her as the "head of the world's largest democracy" against Nixon's "like" of "martial" Pakistani leaders. The reactions of Indian and American governments were contrasted as well. Gandhi described the situation in "East Bengal" not as "civil war," but as a "punishment of civilians ... it is a cynical way of getting rid of one's opponents." The U.S. approach emphasized geopolitics, focusing on maintaining a unified Pakistan out of concern that breakup would "throw President Yahya into the arms of Peking." The bloodletting in the future state of Bangladesh "has been viewed here [Washington] more in sorrow than in anger. There is virtually no moral indignation evident among policymakers." The wording of the article suggests that, in their concern for the situation in East Pakistan, Indian leaders evinced a more democratic values-oriented worldview than that of the Nixon administration. Indeed, the article reports that one of the chief complaints of the Nixon administration was that India talked too much of democracy.[79]

A letter to the editor published in the *New York Times* highlighted the democracy versus authoritarianism aspect of the conflict:

I am sure that in the present civil war in East Pakistan the sympathies of all freedom-loving peoples of the world lie with the Bengalis in the region ... The fact that in the first free elections held since the country's formation 23 years ago the Awami League party of East Pakistan won an absolute majority in the ruling body only adds insult to injury.[80]

The letter writer keys in to the issue of democracy and the transgression against the ideal as the critical source of sympathy for Western audiences as well as a fundamental sin of the West Pakistan government.

A *New York Times* editorial emphasized the democratic nature of India while pushing the Nixon administration to raise the level of economic aid to India.[81] Similarly, a later *New York Times* article emphasized the democratic credentials of the victims of West Pakistani aggression while arguing that the United States was well placed to "support democratic and peaceful

---

[77] Members of Congress regularly cited the *New York Times* on the crisis, suggesting it was a primary media vehicle for coverage. While it is true that the *New York Times* is seen as a liberal newspaper, political leaders from both parties cited it.
[78] J. Brown 1971.
[79] Welles 1971a.
[80] Gajwani 1971.
[81] *New York Times* 1971b.

development in Pakistan." The editorial continued, laying the groundwork for a potential securitization discourse with respect to Pakistan: "Continued blind backing for the military regime in Islamabad can only lead to disaster for this country's substantial interests in the Indian subcontinent."[82] The role of democracy both in identifying the victims and determining a peaceful future for Pakistan is strong within the argument. Additionally, the characterization of West Pakistan's government as a military regime in the identification of threat to U.S. interests supports an interpretation that, at least for the *New York Times* editorial board, democracy is perceived as nonthreatening while nondemocracy is viewed as at the core of a possible threat. This framing was present in an editorial reaction to the shipment of military equipment to Pakistan despite indications from the State and Defense Departments that the military aid program had been suspended and was under review. The United States, by supporting the Pakistani military, was "abetting an act of repression that is not only morally repugnant but which constitutes a serious threat to this country's own long-term interest in peace and democratic development on the Indian subcontinent."[83]

Anthony Lewis's December 6 editorial repudiated the Nixon approach, castigating the administration for blaming India for the crisis and comparing Yahya, with qualifications, to Adolph Hitler.[84] Democracy played an important role in Lewis's forceful critique. Yahya was using force to "wipe out the result of the [1970] election by force" because the "largest number of seats was won, democratically, by a Bengali party that favored effective self-government for East Pakistan." In dismissing the administration's efforts to blame India, Lewis highlighted the fundamental argument of this book, and why securitization of India was seen as wrong:

American policy toward the Indian subcontinent is as much of a disaster by standards of hard-nosed common sense as of compassion. India may be annoying and difficult, but she does happen to be the largest nation in the world following our notions of political freedom.[85]

An indication of the power of Lewis's argument lies in the frequency with which members of Congress, addressing the crisis and U.S. policy, cited it and requested inclusion in the congressional record.

Direct evidence of public acceptance or rejection of the Nixon/Kissinger securitization argument is sparse. Part of this scarcity no doubt arises from the timeframe of the early 1970s, but other factors play a role as well. Nixon and Kissinger, while demonstrating significant concern about the crisis behind closed

---

[82] *New York Times* 1971c.
[83] *New York Times* 1971a.
[84] Lewis compared the anonymous State Department official who blamed India to the scheming and duplicitous antagonist in *David Copperfield*: "The anonymous state department official who made the comment matched Uriah Heep in sheer oleaginous cynicism about the facts of the situation and about our own moral position" (1971).
[85] Lewis 1971.

doors, were reticent to discuss the matter in public. The relative secrecy cloaking the *Enterprise* policy exemplifies the Nixonian approach. Nixon and Kissinger's preference for avoiding public discussion on the matter suggests self-censorship. There were no compelling geostrategic reasons for secrecy; indeed, challenging a perceived Soviet proxy publicly would be in keeping with long-standing and future U.S. policy (North Korea, North Vietnam, Cuba, Afghanistan). On balance, from Nixon's point of view, there were good reasons to adopt a more public approach to the situation. Pakistan was a long-standing, if neglected, American ally. Pakistan was also the primary – although not only – conduit for negotiations with China. In August, India signed a treaty of friendship with the Soviet Union. Nixon and Kissinger's self-censorship and policy secrecy suggest that they felt, strongly, that they would be unable to make a compelling case for securitizing India to the public. The discursive evidence suggests that indeed this was the case. Consequently, public awareness of the situation was low because key policy makers refused to make it an issue of public debate. A second possible factor was the ongoing war in Vietnam. In the *New York Times*, for example, coverage of Vietnam outnumbered coverage of India's role in the Bangladesh crisis by a ratio of almost 3 to 1 over the eleven months between March 1, 1971 and February 1, 1972.[86] In the *Washington Post*, the ratio was even stronger at nearly 7 to 1.[87] Clearly, Vietnam occupied a dominant position in terms of media coverage and as a result was the central foreign policy concern for the public.

In combination, these factors had the effect of depressing public attention to the Bangladesh crisis. Consequently, polling on the matter was highly limited.[88] The only public opinion survey on the crisis occurred after the war had concluded. When the public was questioned as to which country engendered more sympathy neither India nor Pakistan fared very well.[89] An overwhelming number

---

[86] A search (keyword India AND NOT ad; there seem to be a number of advertisements for an Indian restaurant and cabaret that the ad keyword filters) of the *New York Times* for the period produced two thousand thirty-five articles, including news summaries, referencing India – although not necessarily in the context of the crisis, as India held elections during the period. A similar search for articles on Vietnam (the keyword search is only for Vietnam – many if not all of the advertisements dealt with Vietnam, for example, a campaign ad for Democratic presidential nominee George McGovern highlighting his antiwar position or a "Principles of Joint Treaty of Peace" full-page ad taken out by People's Peace Treaty) produced five thousand eight hundred fifty-nine articles, including news summaries, referencing Vietnam. While undoubtedly some of the articles in both searches are theoretically irrelevant – coverage of Indian sports, for example – the point that Vietnam carried far more media and policy weight in the public's eyes is still relevant.

[87] India's coverage was 652 while Vietnam's coverage was 4,542.

[88] It is difficult to measure the acceptance by the public of the security construction of India presented by policy makers. To a certain extent, the focus on policy maker securitization accepts the assumption that, as politicians, these actors are intimately aware of what policies and justifications they can or cannot sell to the public. Public opinion polling should offer some insight on the issue, but as will become clear shortly, polling data requires at least as much interpretation as political speech and is critically dependent on the content and the manner in which questions are asked (Moore 2004).

[89] Fourteen percent of the respondents felt sympathetic toward India while 23 percent felt sympathetic toward Pakistan.

of respondents (63 percent) indicated they had no preference between the two countries.⁹⁰ Given the foreign policy context, these results are not surprising. The fact that a dominant majority of the respondents had no preference – perhaps indicative of a basic lack of opinion – reflects the relatively low media priority of the crisis, the dominance of Vietnam, and the secrecy of the Nixon administration. In this context, the small preference for Pakistan in the poll, while not surprising given the Nixon administration's efforts to securitize India, is not likely indicative of general public reaction. The public simply did not engage deeply on the issue because it was not asked or forced to do so. A different question in the same poll as to opinions on Nixon's handling of the crisis also indicates a high level of disengagement within the public. On that question, nearly a quarter of the respondents (24 percent) were not sure as to their opinion on Nixon's handling of the war. Similarly, roughly a quarter of respondents held a poor, only fair, and pretty good (23 percent, 25 percent, 23 percent, respectively) opinion of Nixon's efforts.⁹¹ Since the question and the responses give no indication of whether the respondents thought Nixon had been too hard on India, the question only serves to support the claim that public engagement on the issue was minimal. More important, securitization did not take place.

Other polls from the same time offer at best indirect evidence on how the public perceived India. A majority (65 percent) of respondents identified Indira Gandhi as a person whom they respected a great deal (41 percent) or somewhat (24 percent). Only 4 percent indicated they had no respect for her at all.⁹² In keeping with the other polls, a large number of respondents (31 percent) either had never heard of her or were unsure. The large percentage of respect accorded Gandhi is particularly striking given that India had signed its treaty of friendship with the USSR two months prior to the poll. While respect does not translate into amity or affection, the poll does indicate that something, possibly India's shared democracy, helped to keep Gandhi in Americans' good graces even after a treaty with the Soviets. Another poll, positing a hypothetical situation of a communist attack against India, also presents indirect but supportive evidence.⁹³˙ A plurality of the respondents (48 percent) indicated they would send troops (8 percent) or material support (40 percent). A smaller number (38 percent) indicated they

---

⁹⁰ Louis Harris and Associates 1972b. Sixty-three percent of respondents felt sympathy for neither country (27 percent of the overall response), both countries (4 percent of the overall response), or were not sure (32 percent of the overall response).

⁹¹ Louis Harris and Associates 1972a.

⁹² Louis Harris and Associates 1971. It should be noted that the sample was strongly skewed toward women. Out of a sample of four thousand people, three thousand were women.

⁹³ Text of the question: "In the event a nation is attacked by Communist backed forces there are several things the U.S. can do about it. As I read the name of each country, tell me what action you would want to see us take if that nation is actually attacked – send American troops or send military supplies but not send American troops, or refuse to get involved at all. How about India, what action would you want to see us take if India is attacked?" (Gallup Organization 1971).

would refuse to get involved.[94] What is striking about this poll is not the no involvement rate; that would be expected to be sizable in light of the contentiousness and lack of popularity the war in Vietnam suffered from during its final years. The poll was, in effect, asking Americans if they would be willing to venture money and/or manpower for a similar war. Given that context, the high willingness to get involved is noteworthy. Again, there is no indication as to why a near majority of the respondents were willing to engage in another war while still fighting an unpopular one, making conclusions as to the rationales behind public support speculative, but shared democratic identity, and the common security construction that attends that identity, may have played a role.

Another indication that securitization was unsuccessful was the striking silence of the Nixon administration with respect to the move of the carrier task group *Enterprise* to the Bay of Bengal. The aggressive move was eventually justified through an appeal to the need to evacuate U.S. citizens from East Pakistan, but the administration did little to publically publicize or explain the maneuver.[95] Indeed, on December 15, Indian Ambassador to the United States Jha could not cite official U.S. comments on the *Enterprise* maneuver, instead referring to "a reliable source."[96] After the carrier group movement toward India had been firmly established, the U.S. government still refused to comment, leaving the explanation of the purpose of the movement to unidentified sources. These sources claimed that the United States' purpose was political and humanitarian, to pressure India *and* the Soviet Union to prevent further escalation of the conflict and to evacuate U.S. citizens.[97] Once again, U.S. policy makers linked India with the Soviet Union. More interesting, though, is the fact that the Nixon administration refused to publicly justify what was clearly a military move. This may be an indicator that, knowing efforts to securitize India were unsuccessful, Nixon sought to pressure India without having to mount an embarrassing climb down after it became apparent that the U.S. public and Congress would not support military involvement. Had securitization of India been successful, the administration would likely have been far more forthcoming regarding the deployment of U.S. military assets. The military purpose of the *Enterprise* deployment only came to public light after the war had ended and columnist Jack Anderson, through his syndicated column, revealed sensitive documents outlining administration policy and thinking. While Anderson's revelations do not contend that the Nixon administration intended to use force against India, they do highlight the aggressive nature of the *Enterprise* policy and belie the public explanations for the carrier group's movement. The evacuation explanation was a cover story, a justification rather

---

[94] Gallup Organization 1971.
[95] H. Smith 1971.
[96] Naughton 1971.
[97] Szulc 1971.

than rationale. Clearly, by opting for the covert use of force, the Nixon administration revealed it felt its efforts to securitize India had been unsuccessful.[98]

Conclusions

Given the lack of public engagement on the crisis, is it fair to say that the democratic identity of the public was a factor in the construction of the security issue? I argue that while the public did not actively engage on the issue, this case does support my central claim regarding the role of democratic identity in shaping security. Clearly, Nixon and Kissinger perceived India as a threat to U.S. interests in the region and globally. Indeed, one of the critiques of Nixon's policy is that it embedded what should have been a regional affair into the broader geostrategic security context. If Nixon and Kissinger perceived India as a threat, the question becomes: Why did they act as they did, keeping a low policy profile and minimizing public exposure? There is evidence that their effort to securitize India was incurring a significant domestic political cost, particularly in Congress. Yet this by itself does not carry much explanatory power. The ability of members of Congress to impose political costs on the president as a result of his policy choices stems from the policy preferences, implicit or explicit, of the public. Policies that run against the preferences of the public engender political costs, those that do not produce political gains. The fact that the public, as evidenced by the opinion polling, did not engage strongly on the issue indicates that policy preferences were implicit. Nixon's securitization efforts were half-hearted because he and Kissinger believed that ultimately they would not be successful. They said as much themselves, noting public affection for India and the willingness of the public to ignore the aggression of other democracies. Left unsaid, of course, was that the aggression by democratic India was against autocratic Pakistan. In this case, the expected public reaction, linked to preferences arising out of democratic identity, stayed the hand of the Nixon administration. While there are no indications that Nixon and Kissinger would have actually used force against India, there is clear evidence that public backlash against their preferred policies restrained Nixon and Kissinger and that the public's unwillingness to support those policies is tied to shared democracy.

The case beautifully illustrates the importance of democratic identity in shaping the security space of the United States, and in turn the behavior of political actors within it. Despite their clear perception that India posed a threat to the United States, or at least U.S. interests, their understanding of the security space – the same security space Congress and the media operated in as they put pressure on the administration – stayed their collective hand.

---

[98] Welles 1972.

3

Nuclear Games

The United States, India, and the Desecuritization of Nuclear Weapons

Historical Overview and Literature

On May 18, 1974, India conducted its first nuclear explosion test at its Pokhran test site. Code named "Smiling Buddha," and labeled a "peaceful nuclear explosion" (PNE) rather than a nuclear weapons test[1], the Indian policy and test took the United States by surprise.[2] The test was the product of a decision, made two years previously by Prime Minister Indira Gandhi, to manufacture and test a nuclear device based on existing designs. After the test, India's nuclear program remained quiescent until 1998, when India officially tested a nuclear weapon, prompting a nuclear response from Pakistan.[3] The Clinton administration imposed sanctions on both countries, although, at least in the case of India, many of these sanctions were removed relatively quickly. Following on from intentions declared in 2005,[4] in March 2006, President George Bush announced a controversial agreement to supply India with advanced civilian nuclear technology.[5] These three cases – the 1974 PNE, the 1998 nuclear weapons test, and the 2005 nuclear deal – comprise the empirical focus of this chapter.

Why does a nuclear program provide a test of theory? In 1974, it was yet another move by a state Nixon and Kissinger perceived, at least in 1971, as a threat to U.S. interests. The PNE demonstrated conclusive dominance of the subcontinent by India,[6] a fate Nixon and Kissinger sought to avoid in 1971.

---

[1] After the test, officials at the site – unable to use a secured hotline – conveyed the success of the test to Prime Minister Indira Gandhi over an unsecured phone line by reporting that "the Buddha has smiled" (Talbott 2004, 14). Interestingly, discussions of the event rarely use the code name (R. N. Burns 2007; Schrafstetter 2002).
[2] *New York Times* 1974f; Reston 1974.
[3] J. Burns 1998.
[4] Bush and Singh 2005.
[5] Bumiller and Sengupta 2006.
[6] *New York Times* 1974f; Weinraub 1974a.

Nuclear weapons are also, because of their massive destructive capabilities, easily securitized. Indeed, since the development of nuclear weapons, the onus has arguably been on political leaders to justify why such weapons are not a security issue rather than to justify their securitization. Public opinion polls regularly rate the spread of nuclear weapons as a top foreign policy concern. In this context, India's development of nuclear weapons provides a good opportunity to explore the desecuritization of nuclear weapons proliferation in the Indian context. This is particularly trenchant in the context of ongoing efforts by the United States to construct nuclear programs in Iran and North Korea as threats, a comparison I have commented on at length elsewhere.[7]

As in the case of the Bangladesh War, the predominant approaches to IR have a difficult time handling the U.S. response to India's nuclear program. Structural realism is split regarding the effect of proliferation.[8] At one end of the spectrum, Waltz argues that the spread of nuclear weapons increases international stability and should be encouraged, albeit at a slow pace.[9] On the other side of the spectrum, Mearsheimer largely sees the spread of nuclear weapons as detrimental to powerful states and doing little to reduce conflict.[10] Surprisingly, Waltz's approach to the issue is largely prescriptive, arguing that states should welcome the slow spread of nuclear weapons but saying little about whether they actually welcome the spread. The regular efforts of the United States to oppose proliferation (including significant pressure on the post-Soviet inheritors of the Soviet nuclear arsenal to relinquish their weapons), as well as the open-ended extension of the Non-Proliferation Treaty (NPT) in 1995, suggest that the U.S., is not prosaic about proliferation. Ostensibly, then, structural realism would predict a balancing effort against India by the United States for regional and global reasons. At the regional level, India's possession of nuclear weapons gave it unquestioned predominance in south Asia at the expense of Pakistan, the United States' professed ally in the region. At the global level, India would have imperiled – at least during the Cold War – U.S. containment strategy as well as reduced U.S. global military advantage. While containment as a motivating basis for U.S. policy disappeared after the end of the Cold War, the more general reasons under neorealism to oppose India's possession of nuclear weapons remain.

No doubt due to the prominence of nuclear weapons in global security concerns, significant academic attention has been paid to India's nuclear program. Much of the literature focuses on the global impact of India's nuclear weapons or more narrowly prescribing how the United States should deal with India's burgeoning arsenal.[11] Another set of literature focuses on explaining

---

[7] Hayes 2009.
[8] Roth 2007.
[9] Sagan and Waltz 1995.
[10] Mearsheimer 1990.
[11] A. Carter 2006; Ganguly and Mistry 2006; Levy and Ferguson 2006; Perkovich 1998, 2002; Schaffer 2002; Talbott 1999.

Indian nuclear policy choices.[12] These are traditional approaches to the issue of nuclear proliferation, and as such leave aside some very important factors. First, the literature largely does not address the remarkable permissiveness of U.S. policy toward India. Second, the literature largely assumes the threatening nature of India's nuclear weapons, failing to recognize that the threatening characteristics of the weapons are socially constructed. Finally, by neglecting the first two points, the literature leaves itself unable to provide an accurate sense as to how or if nuclear weapons have (or will) factor into U.S.-India relations – a critical point as India's place in the global hierarchy changes. While this chapter certainly does not remedy these issues, it does provide an important examination of the construction of U.S. security relations with India in the context of nuclear weapons, which in turn provides important insights on the variable meaning of nuclear weapons.

1974 PNE

India's 1974 PNE was potentially a significant security challenge to the United States. While India clearly attempted to frame the test in a nonthreatening manner, terming the test as a "peaceful nuclear explosion experiment," few states accepted that framing.[13] In fact, a State Department memo issued immediately after the event noted long-standing U.S. policy that made no distinction between a peaceful nuclear explosion and a nuclear weapons test.[14]

Remarkably, given this context, the Nixon administration made a concerted effort not to securitize India's PNE. When the explosion took place, Kissinger's reaction was muted. Internal State Department memorandums reference the department's "low-key" response guidance when dealing with the press.[15] State Department bureaucrats prepared a sharp criticism of the PNE, but Kissinger rejected it, stating that "public scolding would not undo the event, but only add to U.S.-Indian bilateral problems and reduce the influence Washington might have on India's future nuclear policy."[16] Kissinger instead made a more neutral statement. In a meeting with Pakistani foreign minister Aziz Ahmed shortly after the PNE, Nixon emphasized dialogue with India over forceful confrontation despite a litany of security concerns raised by Ahmed, many of them focused on the cooperation between India and the USSR.[17] In a separate meeting with Ahmed, Kissinger made it very clear that while the United States could make security guarantees vis-à-vis the Soviets, no such guarantees could be made

---

[12] Ganguly 1999; Kinsella and Chima 2001; Marwah 1977; Mehta 1998; Ollapally and Ramanna 1995; Sagan 1996; Walker 1998.
[13] Weinraub 1974a.
[14] Rush 1974.
[15] Rush 1974.
[16] Perkovich 2002, 183–4.
[17] United States Department of State 1974a.

with respect to India.[18] In a July memo to Prime Minister Zulfikar Ali Bhutto of Pakistan, Nixon refused to address at any level Pakistani security concerns regarding India.[19] In September of that year, Secretary of State Kissinger failed to single out India in an address to the UN on nuclear proliferation.[20]

In contrast to the events of 1971, the public construction of the issue reflected the Nixon administration's internal position. In the immediate aftermath of the explosion, a State Department spokesman did attempt to link India's nuclear blast to a threat to world stability while other officials suggested that the explosion could disrupt Indo-American relations.[21] However, as late as May 22 (four days after the test), the *New York Times* reported the Nixon administration was officially silent on the test.[22] In early June, Kissinger (somewhat remarkably) argued that India's nuclear explosion had not changed the balance of power on the Indian subcontinent, apparently because of India's limited resources.[23]

The lack of securitization of India's nuclear efforts is exemplified by the willingness of the Nixon administration to rejoin in mid-June a World Bank consortium aid program to India for the first time since aid was suspended in 1971.[24] The consortium did not ignore India's nuclear blast – the Indian representative was asked to make a statement on the PNE – but clearly the West, the United States in particular, did not view India's nuclear program as a significant threat.

In July, at an embassy dinner, Secretary of State Kissinger emphasized traditions shared between the United States and India as a factor in dealing with India's nuclear explosion:

We have shared many traditions together … we have shared traditions and now we share a new tradition. This has given rise to doubts in some quarters but I am confident we can solve it constructively.[25]

While Kissinger does not refer directly to shared democracy, there can be little doubt that democracy is one of the primary "shared traditions" to which Kissinger refers. The new tradition, nuclear weapons, fits into and is constrained by the broader web of shared traditions – democracy – and these shared traditions enable the constructive resolution of the problems raised by India's nuclear test.

In a major speech to the United Nations General Assembly, Secretary of State Kissinger, while highlighting the spread of nuclear weapons as a serious

---

[18] United States Department of State 1974b.
[19] United States Department of State 1974c.
[20] Gwertzman 1974.
[21] *Los Angeles Times* 1974; *The Washington Post* 1974a.
[22] Weinraub 1974b.
[23] Gelb 1974.
[24] Farnsworth 1974.
[25] McCardle 1974.

threat, claiming that "nuclear catastrophe looms more plausible whether through design, or miscalculation, accident, theft, or blackmail," refused to single out India by name.[26] Nuclear weapons proliferation was a major theme of the speech, but the possible threat posed by India was not.

During the first high-level meetings between the U.S. and Indian governments since the nuclear explosion, Kissinger claimed India had "a special role of leadership in South Asian and in world affairs," and that a powerful India would benefit world peace: "There is no reason to fear a powerful and strong India, and still less reason to prevent it from being so."[27] That these comments came in the wake of Kissinger's focus on nuclear weapons proliferation in his UN speech and further comments while in India highlighting nuclear weapons proliferation as a major threat to peace exemplifies the effort the Nixon and Ford administrations were making to securitize weapons proliferation while desecuritizing Indian nuclear weapons proliferation.[28] By September 1974, the United States agreed to resume shipment of uranium to India in return for guarantees that the Indian nuclear program would not use plutonium generated by the use of U.S. fuel for nuclear explosions.[29]

In October, less than a year after India's nuclear explosion, Secretary of State Kissinger promised new food aid to India and claimed the visit had established "a mature and good basis for the future relationship between the two countries." A joint communiqué issued during the visit emphasized the "broadening" nature of Indo-American relations.[30] Kissinger also for the first time accepted and praised India's nonalignment policy.[31] Securitizing India seemed far outside Kissinger's policy options despite proliferation concerns. Notable, however, is the general absence of democracy rhetoric. With the possible exception of Kissinger's July embassy dinner speech, the shared democratic tradition of the United States and India remained unmentioned. While official attention to the PNE was quite limited, the absence of democracy rhetoric does not match up well with the expectations of the approach I have set out, a point I return to in the conclusion to this section.

What security reaction there was to the India test overwhelmingly focused on proliferation generally, not on a potential threat posed by India's ability to manufacture nuclear devices.[32] In his syndicated column, Marquis Childs argued that the Indian PNE was "shattering" for the "long range survival of mankind," breaking the "fragile barrier" of the NPT.[33] Once again, when

[26] Gwertzman 1974.
[27] *New York Times* 1974c.
[28] During his trip to India, Kissinger claimed: "A world in which an ever increasing number of nations possess nuclear weapons vastly magnifies the risks of both regional and global conflict" (*New York Times* 1974c).
[29] *The Washington Post* 1974b.
[30] Weinraub 1974c.
[31] Marder 1974.
[32] Cowan 1974; Middleton 1974; Morgan 1974; O'Toole 1974.
[33] Childs 1974.

India poses a threat, it is not directly to the United States but to the control of proliferation. Here proliferation – aided by India's nuclear test – is the fundamental threat. One news analysis pointedly claimed India's nuclear development reframed India's international image as "less pitiful" without putting India into the category of "menacing."[34]

The editors of the *New York Times* did frame the blast in security terms. An editorial clearly constructed the test in security terms, indicating that "the military significance of this nuclear breakthrough will not be lost on India's neighbors – or others."[35] The test, in addition to inhibiting or reversing the "trend towards reconciliation in South Asia," marked "a dangerous move away from the world's essential efforts to render a nuclear holocaust impossible."[36] While the editors did single out India, they also sought to broaden the burden of blame. The editors argued that India's nuclear efforts were a reflection of the failed promises of the United States and the USSR to destroy their own nuclear arsenals as promised in the Non-Proliferation Treaty. In effect, the editors, by using the India test as a rhetorical vehicle, sought to securitize global nuclear policy. While the editors clearly construct the test in security terms, the threat to the United States and its citizens arises from nuclear weapons in general rather than Indian nuclear weapons specifically.

In another editorial, the *New York Times* argued that India's nuclear test posed a threat to the United States and the world, but not that India posed the threat directly. Instead, the editors argued that by testing and widening the circle of nuclear states, India's nuclear activities encouraged possibly threatening states to redouble their own nuclear efforts. The real threat posed by India's proliferation is not that India will use nuclear weapons, but that India's proliferation challenges the nonproliferation regime that keeps weapons out of the hands of those that truly do pose a threat:

> If nuclear weapons spread further – coming into the hands of demagogic dictators and even organizations of terrorists and criminals – dangerous instabilities will replace the relatively stable nuclear balance that now exists.[37]

Implicit within this argument is the idea that Indian democracy differentiates India from the states that pose a threat to global stability. The editors at the *Times* are not then seeking to securitize India – it is not India that poses a threat – but instead they identify proliferation as the key security issue.

---

[34] Simons 1974.

[35] A brief note on sources is in order. As was the case in 1971, the coverage of India's PNE was vastly disproportionate. The *New York Times* was dominant in its coverage, with 192 articles on or mentioning the explosion. *The Washington Post* and *Los Angeles Times* had roughly half the coverage of the *New York Times*. In the *Wall Street Journal*, the explosion barely warranted a mention two days after the fact, and in all was mentioned only fifteen times in the subsequent year of news coverage.

[36] *New York Times* 1974d.

[37] *New York Times* 1974b.

Nuclear Games

Interesting, the *New York Times* editorial staff returned to the theme of shared democracy when it praised efforts by Ford and Kissinger to reestablish normal relations – pointing out that "Asia's most populous democracy" was an important "symbol of political freedom, maintained in the face of economic poverty."[38]

Congressional reaction to the explosion was limited. Senator Edward Kennedy identified nuclear proliferation as a threat to world peace, but laid the blame on U.S. policy:

> The real failure to prevent the spread of nuclear weapons rests not with India, but with the United States, with the Soviet Union, with France, with China, and with Britain.[39]

Kennedy did not refer to Indian democracy, but he largely left India out of his threat assessment. Kennedy's larger purpose seemed to be pushing for a Comprehensive Test Ban Treaty rather than detailing concern over the Indian PNE specifically. Along similar lines, Representative Robert Price (R-TX) also focused on the threat of proliferation rather than the threat of Indian nuclear weapons, and emphasized strengthened U.S. support for the IAEA.[40]

More significant discussion of the PNE took place in the context of a debate over a bill funding international development assistance (IDA). During the debate, Senator Harry F. Byrd, Jr. (I-VA) complained that U.S. IDA enabled India to develop a nuclear capability that posed a direct threat to the United States:

> What it [IDA bill] does is permit countries like India to use her own resources to develop a weapon that could plunge this country into chaos and eliminate the world by the development and use of a nuclear weapon.[41]

In a long response, Senator Humphrey (D-MN) desecuritized the Indian nuclear program by contrasting it against the military and nuclear programs of the major powers. Humphrey also made an implicit desecuritizing argument by appealing to Indian democracy:

> May I say, before I sit down, that India is still a democracy. China is not. The nations of Southeast Asia are not. At least they still have elections in India. Of course, India has a population of 550 million people. It gets into bad habits as it watches the United States, the Soviet Union, Great Britain, and France.[42]

The argument is twofold. First, that India as a democracy poses less of a concern than nondemocratic China and nondemocratic states in southeast Asia. Second, India's behavior, insofar as it is problematic, can be traced directly back to the behavior of the existing nuclear powers.

---

[38] *New York Times* 1974a.
[39] Senator Kennedy (D-MA) 1974.
[40] Representative Price (R-TX) 1974.
[41] Senator Byrd (I-VA) 1974, 16085.
[42] Senator Humphrey (D-MN) 1974, 16087. The bad habits reference here is to India's nuclear test.

Public polling suggests that, as in 1971, the American public did not see India as a threat. As is typical of public opinion polling, no questions exist that speak directly to my argument, but there is some circumstantial evidence. In a 1975 poll, a majority of the respondents (64 percent) expressed a desire to strengthen ties (22 percent) or continue Indo-American relations as they were (42 percent). Only 19 percent felt the United States should lessen its commitments to India.[43] The poll, coming about six months after the PNE and in the midst of efforts by the Ford administration to improve ties with India, suggests the public did not construct India's nuclear advancement as a threat. The willingness of Americans to support and improve ties with India is remarkable in light of expressed concerns over the role of nuclear weapons in the world generally. In late 1973, nearly 70 percent of poll respondents felt nuclear weapons would be used should another world war break out.[44] In 1974, clear majorities, often approaching 70 percent, felt nuclear reactor sales and assistance should be restricted to prominent democracies and established allies including Australia, Israel, Japan, and West Germany.[45] In the same poll, 78 percent of respondents also expressed concern that "if too many countries get a nuclear capability, some irresponsible country is bound to set off a bomb that could blow up the earth in World War III."[46] A 1975 poll, emphasizing the allocation of limited governmental resources, found that 86 percent of the respondents felt the U.S. federal government should exert some (28 percent) or major (58 percent) effort to limit nuclear weapons.[47] Given these nuclear concerns, the willingness of Americans to support Indo-American relations, while not direct evidence on public perception and construction of India's possible nuclear threat, does powerfully suggest that India's nuclear program, filtered through the lens of shared democracy, was not securitized.

While India's 1974 PNE was commonly accepted to have moved India into the ranks of the nuclear powers, Indira Gandhi's government claimed at the time that the test was purely for peaceful, research purposes and that India would not weaponize its nuclear technology.[48] After the 1974 test, India's nuclear program receded into the policy shadows. There are indications that India's political leaders were surprised by the strength of the international political backlash, particularly from Canada – one of India's primary nuclear technology benefactors.[49] The international reaction pushed India's nuclear efforts out of the public sphere. While political leaders kept the nuclear option open, nuclear development was secret and no tests took place. Throughout the remainder of the 1970s and 1980s, lack of direction and bureaucratic

[43] Roper Organization 1975a.
[44] Gallup Organization 1973.
[45] Louis Harris and Associates 1974b.
[46] Louis Harris and Associates 1974a.
[47] Roper Organization 1975b.
[48] *Los Angeles Times* 1974.
[49] Trumbull 1974.

infighting characterized India's nuclear program while political ambiguity and ambivalence surrounded it.[50] Consequently, India's nuclear status, while important, was not a central concern of U.S. policy makers.[51] In the 1990s, India began efforts to restart its nuclear weapons program. The Clinton administration put significant pressure on the Indian government to prevent a nuclear test. The victory of the Hindu nationalist Bharatiya Janata Party (BJP), which had long advertised a pro-nuclear weapons policy, in 1998 doomed Clinton administration efforts to prevent a nuclear test.[52] On May 11, 1998, less than two months after the BJP took office, India tested its first official nuclear weapon. That the test took the U.S. government, including the Central Intelligence Agency and the Department of State, by surprise testifies both to India's low-key approach to its nuclear program since 1974 and to low prioritization by successive U.S. administrations of India's nuclear program. These circumstances explain the structure of the case study here. There is a large gap between the 1974 and 1998 tests because, quite simply, little was happening.

The 1998 Nuclear Tests

President Bill Clinton's reaction indicates the strength of democratic identity for constructing the security environment. The testing came after years of U.S. pressure on India designed to avoid just such an event. Clinton was under no illusions regarding the significance of the tests, saying that the tests "were unjustified" and that they "clearly create a dangerous new instability in their region," as he declared the imposition of sanctions. However, Clinton also sought to prevent U.S. sanctions policy from being interpreted as the initial stage of securitization. He claimed he had "long supported deepening the relations between the United States and India," and, more important from the perspective of the theoretical framework presented in this book, highlighted Indian democracy:

It simply is not necessary for a nation that will soon be the world's most populous nation – it already has the world's largest middle class – that has 50 years of vibrant democracy, a perfectly wonderful country, it is not necessary for them to manifest national greatness by doing this. It is a terrible mistake.[53]

---

[50] Perkovich 1998.
[51] Strobe Talbott perhaps best describes the lack of attention paid to India and its nuclear program: "When the senior staff meeting ended, I returned to my office and settled behind the desk to read the *New York Times*. I skimmed articles on the front page about the latest Arab-Israeli tensions and drug trafficking in the Caribbean but skipped a feature article about India. That country could hardly have been further from my mind. *In government, it is often said, the urgent drives out the merely important.* India – the world's second most populous country, its largest democracy, and the most powerful country in a region that is home to nearly a quarter of humanity – seemed permanently stuck in the latter category" (2004, 2; emphasis added).
[52] J. Burns 1998; Talbott 2004, 26–7.
[53] Clinton 1999c.

Clinton went on to praise European integration and an "undivided democratic Europe at peace." Two points stand out in Clinton's characterization of the situation. The first is his recognition of Indian democracy. The second is his claim that the India test represented a "mistake" by India, rather than a malicious premeditated act. The combination communicates to the audience that India, as a democracy, would not purposely act in a threatening manner. During the same news conference, Clinton also directly addressed the motivation behind his decision to assess sanctions. In response to a question about Indian nuclear intentions, Clinton made it clear sanctions were mandated by law (the Glenn Amendment) and were not imposed as the result of a U.S. assessment of threat:

Well, I don't know about my ability to influence them [India]. I just know what the United States law *requires*, and it's a very stiff sanctions law. It basically says, no more aid.[54] (emphasis added)

The law, according to Clinton, left the executive "no discretion." As for Indian intentions, Clinton continued to emphasize nonsecurity explanations for India's nuclear policy, claiming India tested nuclear weapons because it had been "underappreciated in the world as a great power." Even as Clinton punished India, he took great pains to keep U.S. policy away from the realm of security, and democracy played a central role in that effort.

Clinton made similar arguments three days later in a radio address to the U.S. public. In that address, Clinton explained that, while the United States was imposing sanctions, India had "the world's largest middle class and 50 years of vibrant democracy to its credit."[55] Clinton argued that Indian democracy, among other factors, was a fundamental reason for the United States and India to be "close friends and partners for the 21st century." In a television interview that same day, Clinton linked Indian democracy to a political (rather than security) approach as he discussed how to move beyond the Indian nuclear tests:

And we have to go back to the Indians and say "Lets find a way to protect your security and honor the greatness of your democracy without becoming a nuclear power. This is a bad thing, but let's minimize this."[56]

A week after the explosion, Clinton again emphasized India's democratic credentials:

But, I can tell you that my view is we need, instead of saying we are not going to talk, we are not going to go here, we are not going to go there, what we really need to think of is you know Pakistan has been a good ally of ours, India has been arguably the *most successful democracy in history* in the last 50 years because they have preserved the democracy in the face of absolutely overwhelming diversity and difficulty and pressures

---

[54] Clinton 1999c, 745.
[55] Clinton 1999b, 769.
[56] Clinton 1999a.

Nuclear Games

internal and external, and they can't get along over Kashmir and they have some other tensions, and then their neighbors sometimes turn up the tensions a little bit. We have got to find a way out of this.[57] (emphasis added)

The reaction is clearly one of dialogue and understanding rather than concern for security. Of principal importance in characterizing India is its democratic nature. Clinton furthers these sentiments a month later when he describes India:

India is a very great nation, soon to be not only the world's most populous democracy, but its most populous country. It is home to the world's largest middle class already and a remarkable culture that taught the modern world the power of nonviolence. For 50 years Pakistan has been a vibrant Islamic state, and is today a robust democracy. It is important for the world to recognize the remarkable contributions both these countries have made and will continue to make to the community of nations if they can proceed along the path of peace.[58]

Important to note here is Clinton's language and how he seeks to draw on Indian democracy to desecuritize India's nuclear weapons.[59] Despite the fact that India had detonated a nuclear weapon in a region well known for tension and instability, setting off a nuclear response by Pakistan, Clinton's focus is on highlighting and linking India's democratic nature with a normal politics approach emphasizing dialogue and understanding.[60]

Clinton was not alone in his focus on Indian democracy. Immediately after the test, Republican Speaker of the House Newt Gingrich, seeking to redirect the securitization focus toward China, challenged Clinton's reaction by highlighting Indian democracy: "Look how angry he [Clinton] is at a democracy and how tolerant he is of a dictatorship [China]."[61] A month after the nuclear tests, Senator Connie Mack (R-FL) criticized what he perceived as Sino-centric U.S. foreign policy, arguing, "the United States is helping the largest single-party authoritarian government in the world [China] suppress the development of the largest democracy in the world [India]." The India-U.S. relationship should be the focus of U.S. foreign policy according to Mack: "We have a common bond with the Indian people based on a commitment to democracy, freedom, and the rule of law." Mack went on to defend India's

---

[57] Office of the Prime Minister 1998.
[58] Clinton 1998.
[59] I say *desecuritize* in this context not because India's nuclear weapons had been securitized, but because nuclear weapons and proliferation in general have been securitized.
[60] Exemplifying this desecuritized approach is a letter from Clinton to congressional leaders that in part dealt with the India nuclear issue: "Since the mandatory imposition of U.S. sanctions, we have worked unilaterally, and with other P-5 and G-8 members, and through the United Nations to dissuade India and Pakistan from taking further steps toward creating operational nuclear forces, to urge them to join multilateral arms control efforts, to persuade them to prevent an arms race and build confidence by practicing restraint, and to resume efforts to resolve their differences through dialogue" (Clinton 2000, 2023).
[61] Bennet 1998.

nuclear tests, arguing that India had broken no international laws and that "India's 50-year history demonstrates peaceful intent exercised within a democratic society." According to Mack, instability in the region could be traced to *Chinese* proliferation and U.S. foreign policy that had been broadly supportive of China. Mack carefully contrasts peaceful, democratic India against authoritarian, oppressive (and thus expansive and aggressive) China. The real threat for Mack was not India but rather "internally oppressive and undemocratic" China, a state that had forced India to remain outside the NPT and Test Ban treaty for self-defense (Mack highlighted China's own nuclear weapons and argued China was occupying Indian territory with claims on more).[62]

Some policy makers did attempt to securitize India's 1998 nuclear tests. Republican chair of the Senate Foreign Relations Committee Jesse Helms claimed India's nuclear program constituted "an emerging nuclear threat to the territory of the United States."[63] In the House of Representatives, Dan Burton (R-IN), quoting newspaper reports of health effects in villages near the nuclear testing, argued that government indifference to suffering was an indicator of India's "real warring intentions." The area, Burton argued, could "become the epicenter of a World War-III type nuclear conflict," presumably involving the United States. The key to India's intentions for Burton is the apparently undemocratic behavior of the government, ignoring the harmful effects of policy on the public. Indeed, the impression Burton gives is that, through testing, the Indian government willingly imposed such harm in the pursuit of a military luxury.[64] Senator Tom Harkin (D-IA) responded forcefully to the India test, calling for the U.S. government to "be prepared to exercise the full range and depth of sanctions available under law." Harkin drew a parallel between the India nuclear test and the surprise 1941 Japanese attack on the U.S. naval station at Pearl Harbor, purposely paraphrasing Roosevelt in calling the day of India's first tests "a day that will live in infamy, for the Nation of India." Harkin also referenced the *weaponization* of India's nuclear capabilities twice in an eighteen-hundred-word speech.[65] These references to Pearl Harbor and weaponization are clearly an effort by Harkin to construct the Indian nuclear tests as a threat to U.S. security.

History serves as testimony to which argument was successful. The public and policy makers in general did not accept the efforts to securitize India. Indeed, an amendment to the National Defense Authorization Act for Fiscal Year 1999 offered by Senators Brownback (R-KS), Feinstein (D-CA), Warner (R-VA), and Levin (D-MI) roughly a month after the initial nuclear tests exemplifies the lack of securitization.[66] In the amendment, the senators censured both

---

[62] Senator Mack (R-FL) 1998.
[63] Bennet 1998.
[64] Representative Burton (R-IN) 1998.
[65] Senator Harkin (D-IA) 1998.
[66] The amendment was titled "A Sense of the Senate on Nuclear Tests in South Asia."

India and Pakistan for their nuclear weapons tests but focused on diplomatic approaches to resolving the regional tensions and looked forward to eventually removing the sanctions. The senators kept the nuclear tests and the U.S. response to them firmly within the structure of normal politics and away from security.[67] In a further demonstration that securitization of the India nuclear tests had failed, the U.S. Senate voted in July 1998, only three months after India's first test, to lift agricultural sanctions on India and Pakistan, the heaviest of the sanctions imposed after the nuclear tests. In November of that year, the United States eased the ban on access to credit and military training programs. Interesting, in October 1999, the United States lifted most of the sanctions imposed in 1998 on India, but kept them in place for recently turned autocratic Pakistan. A U.S. spokesman at the time indicated that the military coup overthrowing the government of Nawaz Sharif was the primary reason sanctions against Pakistan remained in place.[68]

Polling data from after the test indicates that the public accepted the desecuritized construction of India's nuclear program. When questioned about the possible threat posed by India's nuclear program to world peace, a minority (47 percent) indicated India's possession nuclear weapons would pose a "serious threat" to world peace. An equal number indicated Indian nuclear weapons would not pose a serious threat, with 6 percent expressing no opinion.[69] This compares favorably against the 61 percent of the respondents that indicated it was "a bad thing that the atomic bomb was developed."[70] The threat construction of India also compares favorably against that of nondemocratic states, where significant majorities of the respondents indicated possession of nuclear weapons posed a serious threat to world peace.[71] In a different survey, an even more significant drop in threat perception occurred when the survey respondents were questioned about the threat posed to the United States by India's nuclear weapons. For that question, only 26 percent responded that India's nuclear weapons posed a "serious threat to the United States," while 69 percent indicated they did not.[72] As was the case with the more general question about world peace, nondemocracies registered significantly higher levels of threat perception.

Desecuritizing Proliferation: 2005 U.S.-India Nuclear Deal

On July 18, 2005, President George W. Bush announced a deal with India whereby the United States would supply India with advanced nuclear technology

---

[67] Senator Brownback (R-KS) 1998, S6864.
[68] BBC News 1999.
[69] Gallup Organization 1998a.
[70] Gallup Organization 1998c.
[71] Including Iraq (89 percent), Iran (83 percent), Pakistan (66 percent), China (61 percent) (Gallup Organization 1998b). By contrast, for democracies ranging from Brazil to Israel, minorities of the respondents indicated nuclear weapons possession posed a threat to world peace.
[72] Cable News Network et al. 1998.

in contravention of long-standing U.S. policy and accepted nonproliferation practice.⁷³ Despite significant differences in political ideology and leadership style, there are striking similarities in the use of democratic terminology by the Clinton and Bush administrations when referring to India's nuclear program. In a press conference with Indian Prime Minister Manmohan Singh following the announcement, Bush highlighted India's democracy as a fundamental basis for cooperation:

> I'm proud to stand here today with Prime Minister Singh, the leader of one of the world's great democracies ... India and the United States share a commitment to freedom and a belief that democracy provides the best path to a more hopeful future for all people. We also believe that the spread of liberty is the best alternative to hatred and violence. Because of our shared values, the relationship between our two countries has never been stronger. We're working together to make our nations more secure, deliver a better life to our citizens and advance the cause of peace and freedom throughout the world.⁷⁴

The challenge for Bush, as for Clinton before him, was to desecuritize *Indian* nuclear weapons in a context where nuclear weapons and their proliferation had been securitized. To do so, Bush and his administration relied on shared democracy and the attending package of linked values and interests. Implicated in Bush's statement is the logic that underlies much of the scholarship in constructivism: (democratic) identity plays a crucial role in determining interests.⁷⁵ India wants the same things as the United States because it is democratic like the United States. Therefore, *Indian* nuclear weapons pose no threat. Moreover, there is a heavy emphasis on cooperation and partnership. The implicit message is that the United States *trusts* India. The concepts of cooperation and partnership both depend heavily on trust. The members of the target audience know from their own lives that these concepts require trust. Notable beyond the heavy emphasis on democracy is the linkage between democracy and peace. Implicitly, the message here is that India, as a fellow democracy, could not pose a threat to the United States because shared democracy means shared peace. Interesting, this may also be an example where academic findings (democratic peace) find their way into the policy process and in the process produce outcomes rather than just explain them.

In a February 2006 interview, Bush again referenced India as a "great democracy" before affirming that U.S.-India cooperation is "reaching new heights."⁷⁶ Also in February, National Security Advisor Stephen Hadley answered press questions regarding the Bush administration's proposed nuclear deal with India. In his opening statements, Hadley told reporters President Bush had set

---

⁷³ United States Office of the President 2005.
⁷⁴ Bush 2005.
⁷⁵ Acharya 2001; Adler 1997; Hopf 1998; Katzenstein 1996; Vaughn 2000; Wendt 1999. On the role of implication in language, see Chilton 2004, 35–9.
⁷⁶ Bush 2006.

Nuclear Games

strengthening U.S.-India ties as a priority of his administration's foreign policy. India, the president had argued, was:

a country with whom we not only had common interests, but common values – committed democracy – and that he [Bush] saw India playing a role on a global stage, and a potential ally and partner for the United States in dealing with global issues ... on a whole range of issues, global in significance, we are now a partner with India. It has moved beyond just narrow bilateral issues, moved beyond even regional issues to India and the United States seeing how they can cooperate together on a global range of issues.[77]

Clearly, President Bush and his administration felt that the democratic nature of India was an important characteristic for explaining the U.S. policy of cooperation. U.S. Secretary of State Condoleezza Rice noted that autocratic Pakistan did not warrant the same treatment as India because "Pakistan is not in the same place as India."[78]

The message of shared democratic identity is repeated throughout comments made by the Bush administration about India. In March 2006, Undersecretary R. Nicholas Burns referred to India as "peaceful democratic India."[79] In April 2006, Assistant Secretary of State Richard Boucher, addressing a meeting of Indian business leaders, emphasized cooperation and Indian democracy:

Perhaps most importantly, we believe that one of India's greatest contributions in the coming decades can be in its stand for democracy. Many countries around the world are deciding to act on their democratic aspirations, while some others are wary. We know that India will stand beside us and the world community in assisting those who choose freedom. We hope that India will work with others on education, judicial training, free media, technology, independent elections commissions, rule of law and other foundations of democratic societies.[80]

The emphasis on Indian democracy and all that means in terms of cooperation, trust, shared interests, and values is a consistent point of emphasis for the Bush administration. Clearly, administration officials are appealing to an audience for which democratic identity strongly influences threat construction.

The emphasis on India's democratic governance extends to the halls of Congress. Senators as disparate as Biden (D-DE) and Specter (R-PA) have made reference to India's democratic governance in their comments on the nuclear deal. Senator Joseph Biden's remarks on the nuclear deal ground U.S.-India relations in shared democracy:

It has become cliché to speak of the U.S.-India relationship as a bond between the world's oldest democracy and the world's largest democracy – but this cliché is also a

---

[77] United States Office of the President 2006.
[78] United States Office of the President 2006.
[79] R. N. Burns 2006.
[80] Boucher 2006.

fact. Shared political values are the foundation for our relationship, a firm belief in the dignity of man and the consent of the governed.[81]

Clearly for Biden the relationship between the two states is more than traditional interstate relations; he describes it as a "bond." Also clear is the source of the deep and trusting nature of the relationship: democracy. President Bush echoed these sentiments two weeks later when he signed the bill of which Biden was speaking in support. India and the United States, Bush claimed, were "natural partners ... united by deeply held values."[82]

In early 2007, Senator Arlen Specter, commenting on a recent trip to India, made a balance of power assessment of India's role as a counterbalance to China in U.S. foreign policy:

I think it is especially important to see the Nation of India develop with its 1.1 billion people as a counterbalance, so to speak, to China with 1.3 billion people. We have in India a democracy, contrasted with the authoritarian government which prevails in China and, in the long run, the incentives and the productivity of free people in a democracy should be quite a counterbalance.[83]

What is remarkable about this quote is Specter's assessment of threat. China poses a potential threat to the United States not because it has the largest military in the world or nuclear weapons. Instead, the possible threat of China is tied to its authoritarian government. Conversely, India serves as a counterbalance against the Chinese threat simply because it is a democracy. The implicit argument is that India's democratic governance naturally allies it with the democratic United States, and that a democratic India naturally poses no threat to the United States. Tellingly, it is after he links threat assessment (or lack thereof) to Indian democracy that Specter goes on to discuss his change of heart on the U.S.-India nuclear deal. While Specter claims to have been swayed by India's argument that the NPT is discriminatory, it is unlikely he would have found these arguments compelling were they coming from nondemocratic states like North Korea or Iran.

Public opinion polling on the nuclear deal is extremely limited. An NBC News/*Wall Street Journal* poll in March 2006 indicated that public support for the nuclear deal was split, with opposition to the deal outpacing support by 54 percent to 41 percent.[84] However, there is no indication within the poll as to why opposition surpassed support. Certainly, polling indicates Americans hold a generally favorable view of India. An August 2005 poll suggests Americans were open to Bush's desecuritized construction of India and its nuclear program. Questioned about the relationship between the United States and India, a clear majority of respondents (62 percent) indicated India was either a

---

[81] Senator Biden (D-DE) 2006, S11823.
[82] Baker 2006.
[83] Senator Specter (R-PA) 2007, S537.
[84] NBC News et al. 2006.

close ally (20 percent) or friendly (42 percent). Only 3 percent of respondents indicated India was unfriendly or an enemy.[85] These numbers were echoed in another Harris poll a year later (17 and 45 percent respectively).[86] These high favorability numbers come despite widespread recognition that India possesses nuclear weapons.[87] This matches up well with long-term trends of generally favorable perceptions of India. In 2000, 76 percent of Americans felt India was an ally (15 percent) or a friendly non-ally (61 percent).[88] A 2001 poll found India's favorability in the eyes of the public stood at only 58 percent,[89] but by 2005 75 percent of respondents saw India favorably.[90] A year later, India's favorability rating had fallen back to 66 percent, roughly consistent with its rating of 69 percent as of March 2008.[91] Despite the variation in poll ratings, clearly India maintains a broadly favorable position in the eyes of the public. It consistently ranks among the top ten nations in terms of favorability. Obviously, polling does not speak for itself and thus it is not clear what factors drive positive public perceptions of India. It is telling, however, that democracies dominate the top of the favorability rankings. If democracy does play an important role in structuring public threat assessment, India's high rankings are consistent with what we would expect of public opinion.

Conclusions

In general, the case of U.S. nuclear policy toward India supports the proposed framework. The very nature of nuclear weapons, notably their massive destructive power, almost automatically makes them a potential security issue. Polls of the public regularly register high public concern over the use and proliferation of nuclear weapons. Thus, nuclear policy makes for fertile security ground. What is remarkable about the Indo-American relationship is how desecuritized the U.S. approach has been toward the Indian nuclear program. Indeed, the broader case of U.S.-Indian nuclear relations can be argued to be a negative security policy case akin to the negative war cases that pose a problem for democratic peace theory generally. As expected, U.S. political leaders regularly refer to Indian democracy in their efforts to desecuritize the Indian nuclear program and U.S. cooperation with that program.

Of the three nuclear policy cases, the 1974 case least fits with my theoretical expectations. Kissinger, the primary executive branch foreign policy maker in this case (Nixon was likely preoccupied by the cresting Watergate crisis), rarely if ever made reference to the democratic nature of India to justify the

[85] Harris Interactive 2005.
[86] Harris Interactive 2006.
[87] Pew Research Center for the People & the Press and Council on Foreign Relations 2005.
[88] Saad 2000.
[89] Moore 2001.
[90] Moore 2005.
[91] J. Jones 2006; Saad 2008.

desecuritized approach the United States had taken. Indeed, the event – seen as important by a number of proliferation experts at the time[92] – garnered little official attention. In contrast, the 1998 and 2005 nuclear policy cases line up well with theoretical expectations. The 1974 case is problematic, but not insurmountably so. It occurred at a very unique time in U.S. political history as Nixon confronted possible impeachment over the Watergate scandal. Nixon would resign from the presidency on August 9, 1974 – less than three months after Smiling Buddha. It is reasonable to believe the scandal overshadowed all other political developments, including the Indian PNE, decreasing public attention and thus decreasing the need for the administration to take an active security position. The Watergate scandal also decreased the amount of resources available within the administration to deal with foreign policy matters. Nixon and Kissinger marshaled the few resources available into brokering a deal between Israel and Syria over the Golan Heights.[93] A breakthrough on the Golan Heights issue combined with warming relations with the Soviets, it was hoped, would ease some of the domestic pressure, or at least cement Nixon's foreign policy legacy.[94] Moreover, there is little evidence that the low-key approach to the Indian PNE needed to be justified in public; the public opinion polling evidence, while circumstantial, suggests the public did not see the Indian nuclear program as a possible threat. Thus, while the 1974 case does not fit neatly within the predictions of the framework, neither does it pose a significant problem. It is also worth considering that the 1974 explosion came shortly after the Nixon administration had so badly calculated its response to the Bangladesh War. The lessons learned from that experience, notably that Americans were not going to see democratic India as a threat, likely played a role in shaping Nixon and Kissinger's lack of response to India's nuclear development.

Democratic Identity and Security in Indo-American Relations

Taken together, the 1971, 1974, 1998, and 2005 cases strongly suggest democratic identity plays an important role in how security policy is constructed. In the 1971, 1998, and 2005 cases, the appeal of policy makers to Indian democracy strongly correlates with efforts to desecuritize the relationship. The reverse is also true. When U.S. policy makers sought to securitize India, they avoided mentioning Indian democracy and often sought to portray India as undemocratic. The 1974 case proves a partial exception, with Indian democratic identity playing a far less substantial role. However, as discussed previously, the unique domestic political context of Watergate occupied a central focal point

---

[92] Dye 1974; *New York Times* 1974e.
[93] Gelb 1974.
[94] McCurdy 1974. Interesting, this behavior is the opposite of that expected by scholarship on the diversionary conflict hypothesis (Clark 2003; Fordham 2005; James and Oneal 1991)

for politicians of all stripes and for the public. There is also anecdotal evidence that the Watergate scandal altered Nixon's foreign policy priorities, shifting his focus to the Middle East, where a peace breakthrough held the promise of easing his domestic political position as well as acting as a positive guarantor of Nixon's place in history. In all cases, there is significant evidence that the public did not accept efforts to securitize India. Thus, regardless of the caveats, the importance of public democratic identity for security policy construction has been remarkably powerful and consistent over time.

The cases also speak to the literature in significant ways. The 1971 case, finding that American securitization of India rested in the minds of Nixon and Kissinger but not in the broader public, lends support to Widmaier's argument that the vagaries of interdemocratic relations can be traced to identity dynamics in the leadership.[95] At the level of the public, however, there is little indication that the economic identity of a fellow democracy (liberal versus social democratic) plays a significant role in threat construction. The 1971 case directly counters the argument put forward by Oren that democratic leaders can, should they desire to, easily manipulate the identity of the self and the other to justify power-based policy calculations.[96] At a personal level, Nixon and Kissinger clearly constructed, along power political lines, India as a threat to the United States and its interests. Yet, despite the clear assessment of threat, Nixon and Kissinger were constrained by their belief that they would be unable to successfully securitize India in public. Underlying this constraint was Nixon and Kissinger's belief that the public would refuse to accept a fellow democracy as a threat. In Oren's theoretical reality, Nixon would have simply reconstructed the United States or India in such a way that India would no longer qualify as a democracy, thus removing the constraints on what was clearly an important and pressing policy preference for Nixon.

The 1974 PNE case poses a problem for claims, like that made by Gelpi, that democratic leaders externalize violence in response to domestic political troubles.[97] Despite the fact that Nixon faced the one of most significant domestic political challenges to a sitting president in U.S. history, he, along with Kissinger, took a very low-key approach to Smiling Buddha. The two virtually ignored the event in public and implemented a decidedly accommodating policy toward India. Given the existing latent securitization of nuclear weapons and the weak relations between the United States and India, the 1974 PNE provided an exemplary opportunity to make a securitization move. That they did not presents a problem for Gelpi and similarly minded scholars. It also suggests the power of the shared democracy inhibition on securitization so clearly highlighted in the 1971 case.

[95] Widmaier 2005.
[96] Oren 1995.
[97] Gelpi 1997.

When it comes to anticipating the relationship between the United States and India as a rising power, these chapters suggest the future is a positive one. The shared democratic identity of both countries acts to inhibit securitization, making it possible – indeed likely – for the United States and India to keep their relationship in the realm of normal politics. While there may be times where either side or both are unhappy with a given outcome, these outcomes will be understood within the context of normal political practice. Negotiation and compromise will be the rule, and policy makers will have much greater flexibility pursuing both knowing the possibility of securitization remains remote.

PART II

THE NONDEMOCRATIC "OTHER": THE SINO-AMERICAN RELATIONSHIP

The relationship between China and the United States presents an important opportunity to examine security within democracy when the external state is politically relevant and nondemocratic. Since World War II, China has been one of the most politically relevant nondemocratic states in terms of U.S. policy and the international system in general. Accordingly, it makes an attractive research target – as the mountain of research on China by U.S.-based scholars attests. The chapters in Part II examine two important focal points in Sino-American security relations: (1) the 1995–6 Taiwan Straits crisis, when the Clinton administration eventually sent two aircraft carrier battle groups to the region in response to Chinese aggression toward Taiwan; and (2) the 2001 downing of a United States EP-3 surveillance plane and its subsequent captivity in the hands of the Chinese.

The U.S.-China relationship presents several opportunities to probe the theoretical framework I outline in Chapter 1. First, and most important, including case studies of focal points in U.S.-China security relations allows for observation of the processes of democratic security when the external state is not a democracy. There can be little dispute regarding the nondemocratic nature of the Chinese regime. It meets none of the criteria established by Dahl. Elections, with the possible exception of some at the local level,[1] are nonexistent, violating both the Downs and Schumpeter criterion.[2] Contravening Bollen's definition emphasizing minimization of elite political power, elite circles of the Communist Party clearly contain most, if not all, of the political power in China.[3] Finally, Babst's four criteria (finances controlled by a popularly elected legislature, the executive controlled by a popularly elected government, secret

---

[1] Chen and Zhong 2008; Li 2002, 2003; O' Brien and Li 2000; Shi 1999.
[2] Downs 1957; Schumpeter 1942.
[3] Bollen 1980.

ballot with freedom of press, and independence) are obviously absent.[4] While some scholars argue China is in the process of democratizing,[5] China is not now, and has not been in the past, a democracy. Indeed China may be in the process of institutionalizing a single-party authoritarian state as well as actively pushing back against what has become a normative expectation of democratization.[6] Regardless of the measure, China provides a clearly nondemocratic contrast to India's democracy.

Second, China is a highly politically relevant state. It is the world's single largest state in terms of population. The U.S.-China relationship is regularly considered one of the most important for global stability. China has the world's largest military in terms of manpower and, as one of the permanent members of the UN Security Council, has an internationally recognized nuclear arsenal. Economically, China is a force drawing global attention. The Chinese economy ranks as the second largest in the world, and the growth rate over the last decade has ranged from more than 8 percent in 2000 to more than 14 percent in 2007.[7] Sino-American trade ties are very strong, and China sits at an important geostrategic location, with several important trade routes between southeast Asia and the United States running along the Chinese coast.

Third, in important ways, the U.S.-China relationship represents the antithesis of the Indo-American relationship. While the U.S.-India relationship contains relatively weak geostrategic, institutional, and economic linkages, these linkages abound in the Sino-American relationship. The United States enjoys strong trade ties with China while Indo-American trade ties are underwhelming. Despite similarly sized populations, the Chinese economy, at 5.92 trillion USD (2010 figures), far outweighs India's at 1.72 trillion USD.[8] Annual bilateral trade in 2010 between the United States and China tops 474 billion USD, placing China in second place (behind Canada) in total trade flow with the United States and far ahead of India ($49.9 billion total annual trade).[9] China also contrasts India in terms of military strength. Having detonated its first nuclear weapon in 1964, China has gone on to develop a missile-based nuclear capability while India (consciously) rejected militarization of its nuclear capacity until 1998. Chinese conventional military capabilities are also generally assessed as significantly greater than those of India.[10]

---

[4] Babst 1972.
[5] Brzezinski 1998; Gilboy and Heginbotham 2001; Gilley 2004; Harding 1998; J. Thornton 2008.
[6] D. Lynch 2007; Nathan 2003.
[7] World Bank 2012.
[8] World Bank 2012.
[9] OECD 2010. U.S. imports from China are significantly more valuable than exports. In 2010 imports were $382.9 billion while exports were $91.8 billion.
[10] International Institute for Strategic Studies 2012.

The security implications of Sino-American relations occupy significant attention in the IR literature, as I discuss later in this chapter.[11] In part, this attention can be attributed to the size of the countries, but in part it stems from a deep divide over assessing whether China poses a threat to the United States. Given that whole books have been and will continue to be written on the subject, there is obviously insufficient space here to address the arguments comprehensively. Broadly speaking, the debate roughly follows the boundaries of (and is dominated by) neorealism and neoliberal institutionalism. The "China Threat" argument holds that China as a rising military power will – either incidentally or purposely – reorder the international balance of power.[12] This reordering will bring China and the United States into conflict. The primary question here is how the United States maintains an advantageous balance of power without resorting to war. Careful management of trigger points (e.g., Taiwan, South China Sea territorial claims) is a high priority. In general, however, the China threat approach is pessimistic about the possibilities of avoiding conflict. Even if this argument is accepted, the policy outcome remains ambiguous. Will/should the United States balance rising Chinese power externally through alliances or internally, or both? Without a sense as to how China is constructed in the domestic context, scholars cannot adequately explain policy outcomes.

To be fair, the logic of balance of power might operate to suppress the use of force. While China's power projection capabilities are limited,[13] its large ground forces and air force have the potential to make any military engagement a prolonged, costly one for the United States. While commentators generally hold that China will not achieve parity with U.S. military forces in the short to medium term, some point out that parity is not necessary to make U.S. policy makers think twice about a military engagement.[14] A number of scholars also argue that the shared possession of nuclear weapons should prevent the United States and China from escalating issues to the point of conflict.[15] These two neorealist stories expose the fundamental ambiguity of neorealism regarding security outcomes in the international system. The logic cuts both ways, and without an understanding of the processes that produce security – which is an ideational condition – as opposed to the use of force – which is a materially based phenomenon – the ambiguity is difficult if not impossible to resolve.

The primary counter to the neorealist China threat argument derives from neoliberal institutionalist claims regarding the pacifying effects of economic interdependence.[16] As of March 2012, the Chinese government owned $1.17

---

[11] Thomas C. Berger provides a nice review of the expectations for regional security in east Asia generated by realism, liberalism, and constructivism (2000).
[12] Roy 1996.
[13] H. Brown et al. 2003.
[14] Christensen 2001.
[15] Asal and Beardsley 2007; Gaddis 1986; Geller 1990; Waltz 1990.
[16] Copeland 1996; Gartzke and Li 2003; Keohane 1984, 1988; Oneal and Russet 1997; Oneal et al. 2003; Papayoanou 1999.

trillion worth of United States government debt obligations, amounting to over a quarter of U.S. foreign debt and almost 8 percent of U.S. annual GDP.[17] Should the Chinese leadership choose to stop buying U.S. debt, the U.S. federal government would quickly face significant financial difficulties. The large Chinese dollar reserves pose a related risk to the U.S. economy. Should Beijing decide to sell its dollar holdings, the value of American currency would crash along with the stability of the U.S. economic system. The large economic consequences to both sides of the conflict should, according to neoliberal theory, dampen the potential for the use of force.[18] As is the case with neorealism, the neoliberal approach can cut both ways. As with neorealist-based approaches, a principal weakness of neoliberal institutional theories lies in their general reluctance to address the security process in favor of focusing on one possible outcome (the use of force). Thus the expectation that economic interdependence pacifies interstate relations does not directly comment on the argument of this book. Securitization does not necessarily lead to the active use of violence, only the removal of the issue from normal politics. Securitization is a critical step in the path to the use of force, but it is not tantamount to the use of force. Accordingly, it is not clear that an economic inhibitor on the use of force would similarly act as an inhibitor on securitization. Additionally, because economic interdependence focuses on the conditions that constrain the use of force, arguments based on this foundation struggle to address the converse – that is, why states use force.

Both neorealist and neoliberal institutionalist approaches operate at the systemic level in an effort to understand how structural forces alter macroscopic patterns of state behavior. Therefore, application to the Sino-American relationship exposes the difficulty these approaches have regarding processes and mechanisms that produce outcomes. The materialist basis of much of the debate means that, with a few exceptions,[19] Sino-American relations have largely escaped the attention of ideational approaches. Without a far better accounting of ideational factors, the debate over the present significance and future trajectory of U.S.-China relations will produce decreasing returns. Thus, the relationship presents an invaluable opportunity to explore how ideational factors like identity shape security processes as well as the mechanisms by which security is constructed.

The Sino-American Literature

Unlike Indo-American relations, relations between China and the United States have been the subject of an immense amount of scholarship. While a discussion of the general Sino-American literature is important for contextualizing the

---

[17] United States Department of the Treasury 2012.
[18] U.S. economic relations with Taiwan complicate the economic interdependence arguments, particularly in the case of conflict over Taiwan. Taiwan also serves as a significant trade partner to the United States, accounting for $63 billion in annual trade in 2010 (OECD 2010).
[19] Johnston 1995; D. Lynch 2007.

cases, the volume is such that only a brief overview of the literature is appropriate for this introduction.[20] Given the focus of this book, the focus here rests primarily on security relations between the United States and China and the factors that affect those relations.

Not surprising given the ideological divides of the twentieth century as well as direct and proxy conflict (Korea and Vietnam) between the United States and China, security is one of the central themes in the literature on the relationship between the two countries. Before 1972, strategic security confrontation defined the Sino-American relationship. The 1950–3 Korean War institutionalized confrontation between the United States and China.[21] After the war, U.S. policy in the Pacific consisted primary of containing China. Two years before Nixon took office, 90 percent of the public held an unfavorable opinion of China, and 70 percent considered China the greatest threat to U.S. security.[22] Modern Sino-American relations were born in a security context. Indeed, for much of the 1970s, Sino-American relations revolved around two issue areas: resolving differences over Taiwan and defining a mutually acceptable program of security cooperation.[23] (In)security plays a central role in Harding's history of Sino-American relations. Chapter titles and section headers warn of hostility, complications, stalemate, disenchantment, and disillusionment. On the positive side of the security ledger, Sino-American rapprochement was driven by the need for the United States to pursue strategic security vis-à-vis the Soviet Union.[24] Sino-American mutual interests revolved around security with an emphasis on reducing the danger of confrontation and conflict and restraining the Soviet Union. For the United States, China was also seen as a means to end the war in Vietnam.

With the normalization of relations in the late 1970s, economic issues took on increasing importance in the relationship, an importance reflected in the literature. Economic issues, however, exist within the broader security context, vying with security to be the primary shaping force of U.S.-China relations. In Johnston and Ross's 1999 edited volume on accommodating the rise of China, consisting of eleven chapters written by multiple authors, strategic and economic relations comprised the primary (indeed almost

---

[20] It is important to emphasize the goal here is not to provide a comprehensive overview of the literature on U.S.-China relations, much less the far more expansive comparative literature on China. With respect to Sino-American relations, replicating the efforts others have dedicated to spelling out the various theoretical approaches to Sino-American relations would be of little utility (Friedberg 2005; Johnston 2003).

[21] Christensen 1996.

[22] Harding 1992, 3.

[23] Harding 1992. Taiwan plays a predominant role in the security relationship between the United States and China within the literature. Since the first case – the 1995–6 Taiwan Straits crisis – is centrally about the U.S.-China relationship as mediated by Taiwan, I leave discussion of the relationship between Taiwan and Sino-American security relations to the literature overview in that chapter.

[24] Mann 1999.

exclusive) focus.[25] Although he does not explicitly point these two themes out, Christensen's analysis of zero and positive sum arguments regarding the rise of China also reflects the security/economic dichotomy.[26] Indeed, economic interdependence is the defining element of the U.S. engagement policy.[27] In discussing the extensive Sino-American relationship in the early 1990s, Harding focuses almost exclusively on economic factors: trade, tourism, and military sales.[28] Christensen's outline of the positive-sum view of U.S.-China engagement emphasizes the importance of economic engagement and interdependence for the optimistic view of the future of Sino-American relations.[29] The role of economic interdependence does not lend itself to a singular evaluation. Lampton points out that the growth of economic interdependence made fertile ground for nationalist appeals in both China and the United States, raising the risk of conflict.[30] Christensen's zero-sum approach also emphasizes the importance of economic interdependence, but rather than see it as a positive force, the approach argues economic interdependence has the potential to undermine the linkages between the United States and allies in east Asia (Japan, South Korea) and friendly states in the broader region (Philippines, Singapore, Thailand) because they increasingly owe their economic stability and success to linkages with China. Thus economic interdependence is a double-edged sword depending on the goal of policy. If the goal is to alleviate the security dilemma (positive sum), regional economic interdependence provides a compelling answer. However, if the goal is to limit China's influence and power (zero sum), interdependence alone is the wrong approach.

While economics slowly grew to challenge security as the primary motivator of U.S.-China relations, the end of the Cold War and the 1995–6 Taiwan Strait Crisis renewed the importance of security concerns. Kim observes that in the aftermath of the Taiwan Strait Crisis, the discourse over the rise of China shifted from "'the rise of China' chorus in the marketplace" to the "rise of China threat."[31] The future of Sino-American relations in the literature is contentious. Many argue that conflict between the United States and China is inevitable owing to a lack of a stable balance of power and institutions capable of resolving conflicts.[32] Christensen's zero-sum discussion emphasizes the inevitability of conflict between China and the United States given their mutually exclusive goals of primacy in east Asia – a point supported by Shambaugh's earlier assessment of east Asian security.[33] Here economic development poses a problem because it enables a future Chinese military challenge to the United States. Others agree with the general assessment, but cite different reasons, notably

[25] Johnston and Ross 1999.
[26] Christensen 2006.
[27] Johnston 2003; M. Lynch 2002.
[28] Harding 1992.
[29] Christensen 2006.
[30] Lampton 2001.
[31] S. Kim 1998, 3.
[32] Bernstein and Munro 1997a, 1997b; Friedberg 1993.
[33] Shambaugh 1994.

the divergence of national identity across the Taiwan Strait.[34] Taiwanese independence also plays a critical role in Carpenter's more materialist-oriented prediction of conflict between the United States and China.[35] Opponents to these positions argue that China is a status quo power unlikely to challenge the United States regionally, much less globally.[36]

Economics and security do not comprise the only themes in the literature on Sino-American relations. Human rights, for example, play an important part.[37] However, economics and security – much as in U.S.-China relations itself – are the dominant discourses. Overall – possibly reflecting the emphasis placed on security – the literature seems to indicate a consensus that the Sino-American relationship is a fragile one and vulnerable to significant and dramatic disruption.[38] Initial U.S. engagement with China was founded in the strategic calculus of the Cold War. China, an enemy of the Soviet Union, became a "friend" of the United States.[39] Denied that grounding with the breakup of the Soviet Union and with illusions of democratization ruptured by the 1989 events in Tiananmen Square, U.S. policy became fragmented and inconsistent.[40] Freeman describes relations in 1996 as focused on the "adverse consequences of estrangement and strategic hostility" rather than the benefits of friendship.[41] Chinese Premier Li Peng described U.S.-China relations as "highly volatile."[42] Lampton argues the relationship between the United States and China will remain a mix of contention and cooperation ("at best") in perpetuity.[43] Levine characterizes the relationship as "wracked by contention" over a wide range of issues, most of which focus on economics (trade) or security (arms transfers, Taiwan). Misunderstandings and suspicions undermine any effort to improve relations between the United States and China, keeping the relationship unstable. Indeed, the title of Levine's chapter – "Sino-American Relations: Practicing Damage Control" – sums up the fraught nature of relations between the countries.[44] The apparent tenuousness of the relationship is striking, particularly in the context of the accepted importance of Sino-American ties.

Efforts to account for the role of the American public in the literature on U.S.-China relations are far more advanced than in the literature on U.S.-India

---

[34] T. C. Berger 2000.
[35] Carpenter 2005.
[36] Johnston 2003; Nathan and Ross 1997; Ross 1997. Johnston's argument is generally in this group, but much of his article centers on a critique of the concepts of status quo and revisionist power in International Relations literature. Interestingly, this position seems at odds with his earlier findings suggesting that Chinese strategic culture encourages militaristic responses to international crises (Johnston 1995).
[37] Chan 2002.
[38] Harding 1992.
[39] Levine 1998.
[40] Levine 1998, 96–7; Mann 1999, 96.
[41] Freeman 1996, 3.
[42] Freeman 1996.
[43] Lampton 2001.
[44] Levine 1998.

relations. Levine argues long-term U.S. policy must be grounded in American democratic political culture.[45] Harding also emphasizes the importance of domestic considerations in his history of Sino-American relations, particularly elite opinion and the way the events in Tiananmen influenced foreign policy.[46] Harding also notes that shifting domestic contexts had an impact on relations, but these points are less about security per se and more about the role of the "second image" in policy. Indeed, at one point Harding clearly dismisses the importance of the public, noting that negative public opinion of China does not preclude a normal working relationship between the United States and China. Lampton disagrees, arguing domestic audiences play a critical role in Sino-American relations. The interaction between global economic forces and domestic politics gives political leaders incentives to adopt unilateral, nationalistic policies. More broadly, Lampton claims political leaders in the United States and China face two critical constituencies, the domestic and the global. For example – discussing the controversy surrounding the invitation of Chinese dissident Fang Lizhi to a reception held by President George H. W. Bush during his visit to China – Lampton notes the conflict between the personal-level importance Bush attached to China and the moral sensibilities of the American public.[47] The Chinese wanted Fang disinvited while the U.S. domestic media and public saw the situation as a moral test for the new administration, bringing domestic forces into conflict with Bush's own desire to prioritize U.S.-China relations. An analogous situation confronted the Bush administration in the aftermath of the 1989 events in Tiananmen Square. While the administration wanted to restore relations, powerful members of Congress – Senator Jesse Helms, for example – sought to distance the United States from China. Consequently, "Tiananmen" drove "a wedge between the executive and legislative branches on issues regarding China policy."[48] Mann also claims some importance for domestic politics, albeit at the upper levels of the policy elite rather than an interaction between policy makers and the public.[49] Occasionally, the public does play a role, as in the aftermath of Tiananmen Square in 1989, pushing the administration toward a policy it would not otherwise choose.[50] Generally, however, Mann's narrative portrays the United States side of Sino-American relations as dominated by individual-level decision-making and bureaucratic processes. Congress and the public have only become involved sporadically and were not generally considered in the foreign policy making of Sino-American relations.[51]

[45] Levine 1998, 108.
[46] Harding 1992.
[47] Lampton 2001, 18–20.
[48] Lampton 2001, 21.
[49] Mann 1999. He notes, for example, that Nixon was fastidious in preparing the ground for his 1972 trip to Beijing, cultivating support among Republicans beforehand.
[50] Suggesting support for the focal points case selection approach.
[51] Where the public was considered, the image presented by the U.S. government was at odds with the picture confronting policy makers. In the 1980s, for example, while China remained

In his book on Sino-American relations during the Korean War, Christiansen comments on the importance of domestic political mobilization, arguing for the necessity of developing a "concept of national political power, defined as the ability of state leaders to mobilize their nations' human and material resources behind security policy initiatives."[52] On the surface, this emphasis on domestic political mobilization bears similarities to the approach presented in this monograph. However, there are distinct differences between Christiansen's approach and that presented here. First, Christensen's aim is to develop a framework applicable across polities, while mine seeks to establish conditions that influence the emergence of a state of security, with a specific focus on the role of democratic identity. Second, Christensen's factors for domestic mobilization emphasize materialist factors (ability to raise taxes, immediacy of threat), although he does incorporate ideational elements (consistency with past responses, the novelty and history of policy details within grand strategy). These differences aside, Christensen's approach and that proposed here complement each other, and I share Christensen's criticisms of realist "black boxing" of domestic factors. Further, there is an element of what might be called "proto-securitization," particularly in Christensen's comments on Truman's use of communist-democracy ideology to build support foreign policy. Harding and Lampton also note the role of ideology in Sino-American relations, but like Christensen they do not make the connections between the public, ideology, identity, and security. These approaches are more generally foreign policy analysis frameworks that include a wide range of variables in their efforts to understand the why and how of U.S. policy toward China. Lampton is specific in invoking all three levels of analysis in developing his understanding of the processes that shape U.S. policy with respect to China. In doing so, Lampton and the other authors leave aside explicit theorizing on how policy makers and the public interact to affect U.S. security policy in a systematic way.

Clearly, my approach fits within the general security focus of scholarship on Sino-American relations. That said, my approach makes significant contributions to understanding U.S.-China relations. First, this book contributes the relatively scarce constructivist literature on U.S.-China relations.[53] The argument over whether China poses a threat or not, and over U.S. policy toward China in general, largely assumes a rationalist and materialist basis. Marc Lynch's critique of the discussion regarding the perceived failure of engagement draws this point out very well.[54] Lost in the debate over whether China is or is not a threat is the critical distinction that threat is not an objective, material

---

a possible partner against the Soviets, Reagan administration officials hid their concerns about China. The public was treated to "positive images of a friendly, changing China" (Mann 1999, 149).

[52] Christensen 1996, 11.
[53] What work there is on the ideational elements of U.S.-China relations has tended to focus on China (Johnston 1995; D. Lynch 2007).
[54] M. Lynch 2002.

reality.[55] Instead, political leaders and analysts construct it. The ability to act on this construction, particularly in the security context, relies on the willingness of the public to accept the construction – a point largely absent from scholarship on Sino-American relations. This is the second contribution of the book: the explicit focus on the relationship between policy makers and the public in the context of the security policy process. While there is significant attention paid in the literature to domestic politics (especially as compared to the literature on India), these discussions largely leave aside the role of the public itself. In discussing the battles over policy at the upper levels of government – particularly between the legislative and executive – scholars have generally left aside what empowers these debates: the public.

Roadmap and Theoretical Expectations

The chapters on the 1995–6 Taiwan Strait Crisis and the 2001 EP-3 incident follow the pattern set by the India cases. In each, I begin with an issue overview and a review of relevant literature. I then move on to the case itself, analyzing the security constructions of political leaders in the United States with particular attention to how shared democratic identity structures the security arguments. In both chapters, I end with an empirical and analytical summary. The EP-3 chapter wraps up tying the U.S.-China cases back to my general theoretical framework.

As is the case with the India cases, the central aim of the following chapters is to examine how U.S. policy makers attempt to construct their security policy vis-à-vis the American public. To reiterate, my claim is that the democratic identity that binds the imagined community together acts as a constraint of the foreign policy options available to leaders. At the psychological level, leaders may construct threats and formulate security policy using very different rationales than what they present in public. In the case of China, and in the chapters to follow, the argument leads to the following expectations. When attempting to securitize an external nondemocracy, U.S. policy makers are anticipated to emphasize the external state's nondemocratic characteristics and identity. When attempting to desecuritize a nondemocratic state, policy makers will emphasize the democratic characteristics and identity of that state. With respect to the 1995–6 case, those who sought to construct China as a threat should highlight the lack of Chinese democracy as well as autocratic-democratic nature of the cross-strait conflict. Those who opposed the policy will emphasize China's democratic characteristics in an effort to undermine the existential threat argument. Similar dynamics should play out in the 2001 case as well. As securitization theory suggests the success of these efforts can be measured by public support for the policy. If securitization is successful, the public accepts the existential threat argument as well as the identification of the threat and the policy prescription.

---

[55] The contentiousness of the discussion reinforces this point.

4

Near Miss

China and the United States in the 1995–1996 Taiwan Strait Crisis

Historical Overview and Literature

The United States[1] has a long history of emotional, political, and strategic attachment to Taiwan dating back to Truman's insertion of the Seventh Fleet into the Taiwan Strait, effectively ending the major military phase of the Chinese civil war and sanctioning the creation of an independent Taiwan.[2] At that time, the U.S.-backed Kuomintang (KMT) led by Chang Kai-shek had been driven off the mainland by Mao Zedong's communist forces and governed only a few offshore islands, the most significant of which was Taiwan. Truman's action established a new status quo, separating Taiwan – the Republic of China (ROC) – from the People's Republic of China (PRC) on the mainland.[3] It also established a tradition of U.S. military and diplomatic support for the government of Taiwan. In 1954, President Dwight Eisenhower signed the Mutual Defense Treaty, committing the United States to the defense of Taiwan. From this point until Nixon's efforts to normalize relations with the PRC, the United States maintained a significant military presence on the island. The historic visit in 1971 by Henry Kissinger to lay the groundwork for a visit by President Richard Nixon and Nixon's own visit in 1972 marked both the beginning of

---

[1] It is important to be clear as to the purpose of this overview. The goal here is not to provide a comprehensive review of U.S.-China relations or the role of Taiwan in those relations. I seek to provide a historical context for the case. To that end, I only provide a brief summary of the history of Sino-American relations focused on the importance of Taiwan. Far more complete histories are available, notably by James Mann and Robert Ross.

[2] Ross 1995. Truman was actually reacting to the spread of communist influence in east Asia and the political problems that presented rather than out of a specific concern for Chang and the KMT.

[3] For the sake of expediency, the terms *China* and *PRC* will be used interchangeably. Similarly, *Taiwan* and *ROC* will both refer to the functionally independent government on the island of Taiwan.

the process of normalization of relations between the United States and China and the beginning of the end of normal relations with Taiwan.

From the outset, the issue of Taiwan was omnipresent. The Chinese politburo made it clear that the removal of U.S. forces from Taiwan was a "crux issue."[4] The joint communiqué issued at the end of Nixon's visit (also known as the Shanghai Communiqué) clearly outlined the importance of Taiwan as an issue. The Chinese claimed Taiwan was the "crucial question obstructing the normalization of relations between China and the United States," and demanded the removal of all U.S. military forces and installations from the island. The Americans agreed to draw down U.S. forces on the island with the ultimate goal of complete removal and acknowledged that "all Chinese on either side of the Taiwan Strait maintain there is but one China and that Taiwan is a part of China," but reaffirmed U.S. interest in the peaceful settlement of the Taiwan issue.[5]

Taiwan continued to be a central issue when the United States and China finally normalized relations in 1979.[6] The Chinese government refused to accept official U.S. relations while America maintained official relations with Taiwan. In order for the United States to upgrade its relations with China, it would have to sacrifice its thirty-year-old ties with Taiwan. In what has been called the "Second Communiqué," the United States under the Carter administration reaffirmed the Shanghai Communiqué and once again recognized that Taiwan was part of China.[7] In a domestic press release accompanying the release of the Second Communiqué on December 15, 1978, the Carter administration went into detail regarding the changes required by the agreement. Official relations with Taiwan, including the Mutual Defense Treaty, would be abrogated on January 1, 1979. All remaining military personnel would be withdrawn within four months. As the Nixon administration did in the Shanghai Communiqué, the Carter administration emphasized the importance of a peaceful resolution to the dispute between Taiwan and China, continuing a position that might allow – but not require – the United States to take action in support of Taiwan should China exercise military options to force reunification.[8]

---

[4] Ross 1995, 37.
[5] United States Department of State 1972.
[6] The long gap between the Shanghai Communiqué and the final normalization of relations was not planned. Nixon and Kissinger originally intended to normalize relations in Nixon's second term, a point made clear by both Mann and Ross. However, as was evident in the case study on India's 1974 PNE, Watergate consumed much of Nixon's energies, making normalization almost impossible. President Ford also promised to normalize Sino-American relations, but again had to wait until a possible second term as he was in a tough primary battle with more conservative elements – namely Ronald Reagan – in the Republican Party. Interesting, while domestic politics clearly play a role in policy making, the role of the public in policy making is once again present only by implication.
[7] J. Carter 1978a.
[8] J. Carter 1978b.

The Second Communiqué and the official establishment of relations with China was not the final word on U.S.-Taiwan relations. The same year that China and the United States officially recognized each other, the United States Congress passed Public Law 96–8, the Taiwan Relations Act.[9] The act mandates a U.S.-Taiwan relationship far deeper than the Second Communiqué suggests. The act makes clear that with the exception of official relations – a function to be filled in large part by the unofficial American Institute in Taiwan – the United States would be required to treat Taiwan as a sovereign foreign country. U.S. laws would apply to Taiwan as they did to any other foreign state and U.S. treaties signed with Taiwan before January 1, 1979 would remain in effect unless legally terminated. While the act does not commit the United States to intervening in a military confrontation between China and Taiwan, it strongly reinforces the demand for a peaceful resolution to the situation, going so far as to predicate Sino-American relations on the peaceful evolution of Sino-Taiwanese relations: "The United States decision to establish diplomatic relations with the People's Republic of China rests upon the expectation that the future of Taiwan will be determined by peaceful means." Any effort by China to force reunification with Taiwan (e.g., military force, economic sanctions, etc.) would be considered by the United States as "a threat to the peace and security of the Western Pacific area and of grave concern." To this end, the act mandates that the United States supply Taiwan with military equipment "of a defensive character" and requires the president to maintain the capacity to resist any means of coercion that threatens the security or social and economic systems of Taiwan. The act also requires the president to inform Congress of any threat to Taiwan and stipulates that Congress as well as the president should determine the appropriate course of action. This passage is extraordinary because it explicitly removes from the executive branch its traditional purview over foreign relations. The passage is also remarkable because U.S. policy to that point toward China had been made by a select few policy makers at the top of the foreign relations hierarchy, largely without the input of the public or Congress.[10] Congress clearly sought to reign in the ability of the president to negotiate away the independence of Taiwan.

In 1982, President Ronald Reagan together with Premier Zhao Ziyang issued the third joint U.S.-China communiqué.[11] Along with the previous two communiqués and the Taiwan Relations Act, the "Third Communiqué" provides the foundation for Sino-American relations. In accordance with the previous two communiqués, the Third Communiqué reiterated that Taiwan is part of China and that the dispute between Taiwan and China is an internal matter for the Chinese. Unlike the previous two communiqués, the Third Communiqué took on the issue of U.S. arms sales to Taiwan. Acknowledged in the communiqué

---

[9] United States Congress 1979.
[10] Mann 1999, 370.
[11] Reagan 1982.

as a source of tension between the United States and China, the issue of U.S. sales of military hardware to Taiwan is the primary subject in the communiqué. Responding to Chinese pressure (the communiqué affirms the "Chinese side stated that it would raise the issue [arms sales to Taiwan] again following normalization"), the Reagan administration claimed the United States had no long-term policy for selling arms to Taiwan. Accordingly, the communiqué sets out a long-term trajectory for U.S. policy, committing the United States to capping qualitative and quantitative arms sales to the levels of "recent years" and to gradually phasing out arms sales to Taiwan entirely.

As was the case with the Second Communiqué, the Third Communiqué was not the final word on U.S. sales of weapons to Taiwan. On the domestic front, the Taiwan Relations Act committed the United States to the continued sale of defensive weapons systems to Taiwan. Internationally, at roughly the same time as the Third Communiqué was being negotiated, the United States agreed to six "assurances" proposed by Taiwan to govern U.S.-Taiwan relations.[12] In agreeing to the assurances, the Reagan administration promised:

1. The United States would not set a date for termination of arms sales to Taiwan.
2. The United States would not alter the terms of the Taiwan Relations Act.
3. The United States would not consult with China in advance before making decisions about U.S. arms sales to Taiwan.
4. The United States would not mediate between Taiwan and China.
5. The United States would not alter its position on the sovereignty of Taiwan, which was that the question should be decided peacefully by the Chinese, and would not pressure Taiwan to enter into negotiations with China.
6. The United States would not formally recognize Chinese sovereignty over Taiwan.

Clearly, the issue of Taiwan and U.S. support of the island and its government had not been conclusively resolved. The ambiguity of U.S. commitments to China regarding Taiwan would remain a central focal point for Sino-American tensions. After the end of the Cold War and the disintegration of the overarching strategic environment that formed the primary foundation of Sino-American relations, the difficulties between China and the United States over U.S.-Taiwan relations would dramatically increase. Only ten years after the apparent weapons sales limitations of the Third Communiqué were negotiated, the very China-friendly President George H. W. Bush laid the groundwork for the 1995–6 crisis with his decision to sell F-16 fighters to Taiwan.[13]

---

[12] United States Department of State 1982.
[13] T. Friedman 1992; Ross 2000.

The 1995–1996 Crisis

I do not intend to provide a comprehensive historical overview of the 1995–6 Taiwan Strait Crisis (also called the Third Taiwan Strait Crisis). Others have performed this task, and in much greater length and detail than is possible here.[15] However, as with the preceding overview of Sino-American relations as moderated by Taiwan, a brief summary of events is helpful. The Taiwan Strait Crisis is actually two separate crises conjoined by two common threads: Taiwanese democracy and China's fear of Taiwanese independence.[16] The crisis traces its immediate roots to an invitation extended by Cornell University to Taiwanese President Lee Teng-hui to give the 1995 commencement address. Lee's visit would be the first by a Taiwanese leader since formal diplomatic recognition had switched from Taipei to Beijing in 1979. Lee accepted the invitation, but the United States government under President Clinton initially indicated to China that a visa would not be granted to Lee. Domestic politics changed the political calculations for the Clinton administration as both the U.S. House (396–0) and Senate (97–1) overwhelmingly passed resolutions in May of that year calling on the Clinton administration to grant Lee a visa.[17] The Clinton administration relented and issued Lee a visa, and Lee visited Cornell in June to deliver his commencement address. Chinese response to the Clinton administration's policy reversal was harsh, warning of future reprisals and placing the responsibility for "severe damage to Sino-U.S. relations" on Washington: "If the United States refuses [to revoke the visa], then the United States will bear the full consequences and pay its price."[18]

The full Chinese response took shape in July, when the Chinese military fired missiles off the coast of Taiwan.[19] A month later, the Chinese military conducted more intensive exercises combining air and naval missile tests with naval live fire artillery exercises. China's apparent goals were to intimidate Taiwan, introduce instability, and ultimately end President Lee's career in the lead up to the first democratic presidential elections on the island due to be

---

[14] Mann 1999, 270.
[15] Garver 1997.
[16] The International Crisis Behavior project lists the crisis as beginning on May 22, 1995 when the Clinton administration announced a visa for Lee Teng-hui and ending on March 25, 1996 when Chinese military maneuvers ended after the Taiwanese presidential election [http://www.cidcm.umd.edu/icb/dataviewer/].
[17] United States Congress 1995. The bill in the House was House Concurrent Resolution 53 and in the Senate was Senate Concurrent Resolution 9.
[18] *New York Times* 1995a; Tyler 1995a.
[19] Faison 1995.

held in 1996.[20] Foreshadowing efforts the following year, China also sought to influence Taiwan's December 2 legislative elections.[21] In November, the Chinese military once again held military exercises. The Chinese government clearly stated that these joint land, naval, and air exercises – including amphibious landings – were specifically aimed at preventing Taiwanese moves toward independence.[22] By the end of the November exercises, China was probing U.S. military officials as to possible U.S. reactions to a military crisis over Taiwan.[23] The U.S. policy response in 1995 was restrained. President Bill Clinton and Secretary of State Warren Christopher sent private letters to Chinese President Jiang Zemin and Foreign Minister Qian Qichen respectively, and the U.S. aircraft carrier *Nimitz* along with several support ships cruised through the Taiwan Strait in December.[24]

After November 1995, the crisis seemed to abate. China announced no new military exercises and U.S.-China relations began to thaw.[25] While Beijing complained about the *Nimitz* transit through the Taiwan Strait, relations were strong enough to permit a long-scheduled visit by the amphibious dock landing ship USS *Fort McHenry* to Shanghai.[26] However, China's concerns over possible Taiwanese independence and its opposition to Lee Teng-hui did not subside. In January 1996, China issued a clear warning to the United States that if Lee won the March 1996 presidential elections, China had prepared military strike plans, including missile strikes, that could be put into action on short notice. The Chinese warnings also included an implicit threat against the United States. The press at the time reported a Chinese official claiming Beijing was not concerned with a possible military response by the United States to a Chinese attack on Taiwan because U.S. leaders "care more about Los Angeles than they do about Taiwan," an implicit threat that China might use nuclear weapons against the United States.[27]

The apparent lull in the crisis ended on March 5 when Beijing announced a new round of nuclear-capable M-series missile tests in the run-up to the Taiwanese presidential election on March 23.[28] Unlike the 1995 tests, which took place in the open sea 80–100 miles from Taiwan, the new tests would target waters much closer to Taiwan. With their closer proximity to Taiwan, the tests had the potential to blockade the principal Taiwanese commercial

---

[20] *New York Times* 1995b; Tyler 1995b, 1995e.
[21] Tempest 1995.
[22] Ross 2000, 102.
[23] Tyler 1995c.
[24] Garver 1997; Mann 1999. The transit was a first for a U.S. aircraft carrier since 1979. It was low key, however, and was only reported in the United States a month after it occurred and explained by U.S. officials as a bad weather diversion (Associated Press 1996b).
[25] Tyler 1995c.
[26] Faison 1996b; Tyler 1996c.
[27] Tyler 1996a.
[28] Reuters 1996.

shipping ports of Keelung in the north and Kaohsiung in the south.[29] Five days later (March 10) Chinese leaders announced a new round of live fire naval and warplane exercises that would close a significant portion of the Taiwan Strait and last through the presidential election.[30] In contrast to its response to China's 1995 war games, the Clinton administration reacted by sending two aircraft carrier battle groups (CBG), the *Independence* and *Nimitz*, to the waters near Taiwan.[31] The deployment marked the largest U.S. naval force in the region since the end of the Vietnam War.[32] By March 13, as the live exercises were under way, Beijing signaled to the United States that Taiwan would not be invaded or attacked.[33] The day before Taiwan's scheduled elections, Beijing's rhetoric once again became bellicose; Chinese officials warned the United States that the People's Liberation Army (PLA) could "bury an enemy intruder in a sea of fire" and claimed that an invasion of Taiwan could be mounted with just six hours of preparation.[34] In the end, the Chinese were unsuccessful in their openly avowed effort to politically weaken President Lee. Lee was elected with 54 percent of the vote, better than the 50 percent he sought as a political mandate. Combining Lee's – who favored raising Taiwan's international profile but not outright independence – vote tally with that of his pro-independence opponent Peng Ming-min indicates that 75 percent of the voters in the presidential election voted for a leader at odds with Beijing's clearly stated and demonstrated desires.[35]

The importance of China's military buildup and the U.S. response is not easy to overstate. Andrew Nathan writes that the tests were "one of the most frightening ... military crises in the post-cold war era ... [u]ndoubtedly the exercises were a turning point in the relations between the United States and China."[36] Ross argues that the events of 1995–6 were the closest China and the United States have come to crisis in thirty years, and that they were a "critical turning point in post–Cold War U.S.-China relations."[37] An unnamed Western diplomat at the time of the crisis presaged both assessments: "I think 30 years from now people are going to look back at this summer [1995] as a turning point, but I'm afraid it's going to be a turn for the worse."[38]

Not surprising, given the magnitude of the crisis and the popularity of Sino-American relations in the International Relations literature, the events of 1995–6 have received significant attention. What is surprising is the

[29] Tyler 1996b.
[30] Tyler 1996d; Tyler 1996h.
[31] Tyler 1996f.
[32] Pinsker 2003.
[33] Tyler 1996e.
[34] Faison 1996a.
[35] Tyler 1996g.
[36] Nathan 1999, vii.
[37] Ross 2000.
[38] Tyler 1995d.

relative lack of engagement in the literature on ideational factors as well as the dynamics internal to the United States. Much of the literature focuses on the strategic implications or approaches associated with the outcomes or causes of the conflict, or on the causes of the conflict, particularly those sourced to China or Taiwan.

The scholarship on the crisis is heavy with strategic analysis. The predominance of strategic analysis is such that one scholar complains: "American security analysts treat states as amoral essences and are little interested in decisive domestic political forces."[39] Analytical focus rests on the calculation and counter-calculation of China, Taiwan, and the United States isolated to strategic imperatives assumed to be generated by the international system.[40] The Chinese sought to change the supposed Taiwanese trajectory toward independence, and the United States, in response, sought to reassure Taiwan as well as its allies in the region that Washington held dear its security guarantees. Some even argue for the need to eliminate domestic politics – that is, Congress – from U.S. foreign and security policy calculations.[41]

A notable weakness in the literature, as Edward Friedman points out, is the lack of serious engagement with the idea that states are something other than unitary (and strategically rational) actors. Where there is attention to the role of domestic factors in shaping the crisis, the literature pays *considerably* greater attention to the internal political and identity dynamics in China and Taiwan than those in the United States. For example, Friedman emphasizes the role of Chinese nationalism in fueling the crisis.[42] In his well-cited book on the subject, Garver proves the exception by providing a relatively balanced analysis.[43] Across the board, two assumptions reign. First, that for the actors involved, the security threat is self-evident. While this assumption is merited in the case of Taiwan (which had missiles lobbed at it), it leaves open a wide range of questions for both China and the United States, specifically how and why the issue of Taiwan came to be seen as a threat. These questions are critical because of the contentious nature of U.S.-China relations and the central place Taiwan occupies in that relationship. Understanding how and why issues become matters of security in the Sino-American relationship has important ramifications for the relationship in the future as well the role Taiwan will play in that future. The second assumption is that the actors are strategically rational. Yet scholars in security studies are increasingly showing that other logics are operative. As one of the pivotal points in the Sino-American relationship, failure to analyze the Taiwan Straits crisis through other, more sociological lenses means scholars and policy makers have an incomplete understanding of how

---

[39] E. Friedman 1997, 8.
[40] Hickey 1998; Nathan 1996; Pinsker 2003; Ross 2000; Scobell 2000.
[41] Hickey 1998.
[42] E. Friedman 1997.
[43] Garver 1997.

the events in 1995–6 came to pass, where those events fit in the relationship between China and the United States, and how the dynamics that drove the events might contribute to future situations. Obviously my analysis of the case does not comprehensively address these points, but it does make an important contribution by tying social structures to policy outcomes in the United States and analyzing the process by which Chinese behavior came to be understood as threatening.

The Case

Rhetorical Foundations of Engagement

The debate over China and its actions in the Taiwan Strait took on the contours of the division of power in Washington. The executive branch, embodied in the Clinton administration, steadfastly sought to keep U.S.-China relations out of the realm of security. Conversely, Congress – both houses – pushed hard to make China a security issue. As the overwhelming majorities voting for the nonbinding resolution pushing Clinton to grant President Lee a visa suggest, the issue was not a partisan one, although Republicans were far more outspoken in their effort to securitize China than Democrats.

In 1995–6, the Clinton administration was in a difficult position when it came to dealing with China. On both the domestic and international scenes, the administration's energy and political capital were depleted or otherwise committed. Domestically, Clinton's first administration had seen significant policy failures – notably health care reform – and scandal seemed ever present. On the foreign policy front, the administration was dealing with a full-fledged crisis in the Balkans with the breakup of the former Yugoslavia and the ensuing bloodshed. Peace process negotiations in that conflict came to a head at the same time crisis broke out in the Taiwan Strait. China had also been an ongoing problem for the Clinton administration. While a candidate for the presidency in 1992, Bill Clinton strongly criticized President George H. W. Bush for his China policy, accusing him of "coddling" the regime in Beijing.[44] In his first year as president, Clinton sought to tie renewal of China's Most Favored Nation (MFN) trading status to improvements in human rights. The policy was largely a failure; China refused to make even token concessions, forcing Clinton to either deny MFN status at great economic cost or to grant MFN status at great political cost. In the end, Clinton paid the political cost, making a very public policy reversal.

The failure of Clinton's human rights-MFN linkage, and his administration's policy response, formed the rhetorical and policy foundation of Clinton's response to the crisis that would emerge a year later. With the failure of the MFN linkage policy obvious, the Clinton administration turned to a policy of engagement as the means to pursue U.S. interests in democratization and

[44] *New York Times* 1992.

human rights in China. On announcing his renewal of China's MFN status in May 1994, Clinton argued that revoking MFN status would do less for democracy and human rights in China than his new policy of engagement:

> To those who argue that in view of China's human rights abuses we should revoke MFN status, let me ask you the same question that I have asked myself over and over these last few weeks as I have studied this issue and consulted people of both parties who have had experience with China over many decades. Will we do more to advance the cause of human rights if China is isolated or if our nations are engaged in a growing web of political and economic cooperation and contacts? I am persuaded that the best path for *advancing freedom* in China is for the United State to intensify and broaden its *engagement* with that nation.[45] (emphasis added)

To further cement the relationship between democratization and engagement, Clinton cited two of the most successful examples where U.S. political and economic influence had given rise – at least in part – to Asian democracy:

> But I believe that over the long run we're more likely to make advances if there's more contact with the Chinese, not less; if there's more economic growth, not less – we saw that in *Taiwan and Korea* – and if we are free to explicitly and aggressively pursue our human rights agenda, as we would with any other country.[46] (emphasis added)

In a press conference the same day, National Security Advisor Anthony Lake, Assistant Secretary of State for Human Rights John Shattuck, Assistant Secretary of State for Asian and Pacific Affairs Winston Lord, and Assistant to the President for Economic Policy (shortly to be secretary of the treasury) Robert Rubin reiterated Clinton's argument regarding the connection between engagement, democracy, and human rights in China. National Security Advisor Anthony Lake argued that the new approach would enable the administration to pursue human rights as actively as before:

> [T]he President wanted to adopt a new approach aimed at the same strategic objectives and to make a clear decision to delink and has done so ... the President's decision is designed to lay the basis for a long-term, sustainable relationship with China through which we can pursue both our human rights interests and our security and economic interests as well. [W]e will be now pursuing a very active human rights policy with China in the context of that broader relationship.[47]

Robert Rubin reinforced the connection between engagement as a policy and the explicit expectation that the policy would result in improvements in the state of democracy and human rights within China:

> Senior administration people agreed from the beginning the revocation of MFN did not make sense, that *democracy* and *human rights* could be better served by *engagement*, integration into the global community of China ... the President put enormous

---

[45] Clinton 1994b.
[46] Clinton 1994b.
[47] Lake 1994.

emphasis on what is the best way to accomplish human rights objectives. And it was this *engagement* and integration of China to the rest of the world that – was his judgment, was the best way to *accomplish our human rights objectives*.[48] (emphasis added)

Engagement, however, would not produce the quick results linkage had sought. It was by its very nature a long-term approach, a point made by Clinton and reiterated by Assistant Secretary of State for Human Rights John Shattuck:

And, finally, you have to look at the long-term and not just what is happening from week to week or day to day. And over the long-term, the development of nongovernmental organizations, a civil society, legal reform, parliamentary exchange we believe can have a major impact on Chinese society and human rights.[49]

These points would occupy a central role in the administration's defense of its China policy. In December 1994, Deputy National Security Advisor Samuel (Sandy) Berger repeated the connection between engagement and democratization:

That is, that we believe deeply that trade, that engagement does ultimately open societies and help to open societies, but we also believe that it's not sufficient, that we also need to vigorously work with countries to strengthen democratic institutions within those countries on a bilateral and in this case a multilateral basis.[50]

In the crisis, engagement would prove an important bulwark for the Clinton administration as it sought to ward off congressional efforts to securitize the events in the Taiwan Strait.

1995–1996: Engagement versus Securitization
As the historical overview indicated, the immediate origins of the crisis can be traced to the issuance of a visa to Lee Teng-hui to visit Cornell. The Chinese reaction did not begin in earnest until July, but both sides of the securitization dynamic that would follow began to present their approaches early. In May 1995, Congress members highlighted the importance of Taiwanese democracy in their push to grant Lee a visa. Senator Frank Murkowski (R-AK) explicitly drew on the democratization of Taiwan, suggesting democracy and shared democratic identity as the basis of political leverage: "When we look at the significance of President Lee in the development of Taiwan – they'll have free elections this year – keeping him out was a situation that had to end, and I'm glad to see President Clinton move on it."[51] Never before had the issue of a visa for a Taiwanese president been an issue, but never before had Taiwan been a democracy (or, more accurate, on the verge of full-fledged democracy). It was

---
[48] Rubin 1994.
[49] Shattuck 1994.
[50] S. Berger 1994.
[51] Greenhouse 1995.

Taiwan's democracy that made the visa an issue, suggesting that members of Congress felt the juxtaposition of Taiwan and democracy would resonate with the public in a way Taiwan and authoritarianism had not previously.

At the same time, the Clinton administration sought to downplay the visa and focused on the importance of Sino-American relations: "Let me just reiterate something I said yesterday. Our relations with China are fundamentally important to the United States, given China's size, its power, its history, and its location in the world. We will continue to pursue good relations between the United States and China."[52] Despite the avowed importance of U.S.-China relations, the administration was vulnerable. The importance placed on Taiwanese democracy by members of Congress suggests shared democratic identity would resonate with the public. The Clinton administration's defensiveness over the visa issues, particularly the emphasis on democratization, suggests that administration officials also felt shared democracy was the basis of their political vulnerability. The administration did not want to be seen as favoring authoritarian China over democratizing Taiwan:

> He's [Lee Teng-hui] someone for whom we have great respect, as you know. We've said that before. He's done a very fine job in leading Taiwan to a future which we hope will be based on political and economic reform. We have great respect for him. He will be treated very well when he comes to the United States.[53]

Assistant Secretary of State for Asian and Pacific Affairs Winston Lord went further, claiming:

> With respect to Taiwan, generally, this Administration, I would argue, has been friendlier to Taiwan than any previous Administration, strictly within the unofficial context. The review that we undertook and the changes we made last September, in terms of upgrading, particularly our commercial and economic ties and other steps we took, was the most comprehensive review since 1979. Therefore, we have been very friendly toward Taiwan in an unofficial sense, even as we maintain relations with Beijing and don't change the basic policy that has been pursued by several Administrations of both political parties and different ideological viewpoints.[54]

The administration's efforts to present its Taiwan policy as the friendliest toward Taiwan of any administration suggests the Clinton White House was concerned that congressional emphasis on shared U.S.-Taiwanese democracy would resonate with the public, and as a consequence damage the political standing of the administration. While the arguments here are not securitizing moves, the initial language presents important insights into the role shared democracy, or lack thereof, would play in the battle over securitization that would take place over the ensuing year.

---

[52] N. Burns 1995a.
[53] N. Burns 1995b.
[54] Lord 1995.

Near Miss: China and the United States

Starting in June, the Clinton administration worked to keep Sino-American relations out of the realm of security as China announced, and in July executed, plans for missile tests and military exercises in the Taiwan Strait area. The concept of engagement played a central role in these efforts to keep U.S.-China relations within normal politics. On June 29, Assistant Secretary Lord, arguing against the claim that the United States sought to contain China – a reference to the security policy of the United States during the Cold War[55] – explicitly referenced engagement:

> That [containment] is emphatically not United States policy. We seek to engage China, not contain it. Containment would imply that we treat China as an enemy [which would be] a self-fulfilling prophecy.[56]

A little over a week later, State Department spokesman Nicholas Burns again called on engagement to defuse an effort – this time from the press – to securitize China:

> Q: What would you say to those who say that Vietnam would be an important ally as a hedge against Chinese expansionism?
>
> MR. BURNS: Oh, I wouldn't put it in those terms. I wouldn't put it in those terms at all because we have a policy towards China which is grounded in engagement. The President and the Secretary have talked about that many times. That was a decision made at the beginning of this Administration – way back in 1993 – that that should be the proper posture for the future of U.S.-China relations. So I would never describe U.S.-Vietnamese relations in that fashion.[57]

As Chinese military maneuvers progressed in July, the Clinton administration walked a very tight line, seeking to dissuade the Chinese from acting militarily against Taiwan while countering securitizing moves against China. To this end, the Clinton administration moved quickly, coupling abstracted references to peace and stability in the region with engagement to both express disapproval and counter potential securitizing moves. On July 24, Nicholas Burns presented the peace and stability position, conscientiously avoiding any framing that suggested Chinese actions were threatening:

> Q: Nick, do you have anything to report upon your exchanges with the Chinese on the missile exercises now that the exercises have been going on for four days now?

---

[55] It is important to note here that containment was a policy arising out of a successful securitization. The policy of containment arose out of the claim that the Soviet Union presented an existential threat to the United States both physically (i.e., might attack the United States) and ideologically/politically (i.e., Soviets were aggressive in expanding the geographic scope of communism, potentially to the United States and its allies). Containment policy also bore the hallmarks of the suspension of normal politics associated with security: that is, centralization of power and removal of policy/issue from normal political decision-making processes.

[56] Sciolino 1995.

[57] N. Burns 1995c.

MR. BURNS: We've been in contact with the Chinese Government on the issue of the missile exercise. We do not believe this test contributes to peace and stability in the area. It's been the long-standing policy of the United States to seek to promote peace, security, and stability in the area of the Taiwan Strait. This is in the interest of the United States, the People's Republic of China, and Taiwan.[58]

When a reporter questioned whether the United States or its allies in the region might be taking steps to counter China's activities, Burns shut down the issue: "I think I've detailed how we feel about the test, what we've done about it, and I'd just leave it there."

Four days later on July 28, Secretary of State Warren Christopher made what was billed as a major speech on U.S. foreign policy in the Asia-Pacific. In it, Christopher again highlighted the engagement policy, reiterated the long-term nature of the policy, and – as Clinton did a year previous – tied it to democratization:

The second element of our Pacific strategic [sic] is our policy of *engagement* with the other leading powers of the region, and, as I said, including especially our former cold-war adversaries. In that connection, of course, few nations are able to play as large a role in shaping Asia's future as is China. With its vast population, its geographic reach, its rich history of cultural influence across Asia, its growing military power and its new economic dynamism, China is just unique. As we shape our policy and as we conduct our diplomacy with China, *we must not allow short-term calculation to divert us from pursuing our long-term interests.*[59] (emphasis added)

What is interesting to note here is that Christopher avoids any mention of Chinese governance in his description of the state and its uniqueness. This is not particular to the secretary of state; while the Clinton administration could not argue that China was a democracy – public awareness and the relatively recent events in Tiananmen Square made such a claim largely impossible – not once did Clinton or his surrogates mention China's style of governance. The Clinton administration's avoidance of the authoritarian nature of China's government suggests awareness that the lack of shared democracy may work to the advantage of those who sought to securitize China. Moreover, discussing the current nature of China's governance would undermine engagement's message to the audience of China's long-term potential for democratization.

Christopher went on to reinforce the oppositional nature of engagement vis-à-vis securitized policy approaches and tied the approach to democratization:

The policy of *engagement* reflects the fundamental understanding that our ability to pursue significant common interests and to manage significant disinterests, would not be served by any attempt to *isolate or contain* China. We do not intend to try to do so ... This policy has produced enormous benefits for the United States as well as for China and Taiwan. It has helped to keep the peace, and it has helped to fuel prosperity on both

---

[58] N. Burns 1995d.
[59] Christopher 1995.

Near Miss: China and the United States

sides of the Strait, and it is *certainly helping to propel Taiwan's flourishing democracy.*[60] (emphasis added)

According to Christopher, peace in the region – the opposite of the existential threat required for securitization – could only be attributed to engagement, and as a consequence security policies like containment or isolation would only impair efforts to return the region to its peaceful state. Moreover, transitioning Sino-American relations into a security framework would damage the ability of the United States to replicate with China the process that resulted in the democratization of Taiwan.

Throughout August, the Clinton administration held to its dual line of engagement while carefully pushing China to suspend military operations. On August 1, Defense Department spokesman Kenneth Bacon, following on from his State Department colleagues, emphasized dealing with China within normal politics:

Q: Can you make any comment on the *New York Times* article ... regarding Beijing seeing the United States as plotting to thwart the PRC? Can you respond to that specifically with regard to the military conspiring to undermine China militarily?

BACON: We are not conspiring to undermine China militarily. Quite the opposite. We believe strongly in the one China policy. We see China as an emerging world power and a country with which we want to have *constructive relations*, and we're working hard to have *constructive relations* with China. Of course constructive relations require constructive activity by both partners, and we are working to realize that on both sides of the relationship.[61] (emphasis added)

Note that once again the administration refrained from mentioning the nature of China's emerging power. While Bacon does not reference engagement, he twice claims the United States sought to have "constructive" relations with the PRC, a positive term communicating a normal, working, positive relationship. The argument here is not a realpolitik one: that yes China is authoritarian but the United States cannot afford to securitize China because of economic interests. Instead, it is an effort to bypass the nature of China's governance by focusing not on China but on the relationship. Two weeks later, Bacon – while denying the U.S. military had contingency plans – was forced to react to further Chinese military activity:

Q: China began its latest round of military exercises in the China Sea today. Since you have had more time to find out about the exercises, do you have any new comment on this, and more specific comment on this latest round of exercises?

BACON: We want to see peace and stability in Asia, and particularly in the Straits of Taiwan. We believe this is in our interest, in China's interest, and in the interest of the people of Taiwan. So we're hopeful that China will not be overly provocative in these exercises. We also believe that it would be helpful to China – and for the cause

---

[60] N. Burns 1995d.
[61] Bacon 1995a.

of stability in Asia – if China were to resume its security dialogue with us which has been interrupted recently, and we hope that will happen.[62]

Bacon, like his colleagues in other branches of the executive branch, sought to downplay China's military activity. "Peace and stability" were in the interests of all the parties according to Bacon, a positive statement that avoids suggesting Chinese activities may present a threat to peace, stability, or the United States. Rather than directly confront the issue and criticize China, Bacon used positive terminology – "hopeful" – while suggesting Chinese activity might be provocative without being threatening. He concludes with a call for China to return to the normal, indeed democratic-sounding, "dialogue" that characterized relations until recently.

Through the end of August, the Clinton administration had made its position clear. It sought to avoid securitizing China and used the concept of engagement (with its implicit linkage to *future* democracy) as a tool for defusing potential securitizing moves. When the administration did comment on China's behavior, critiques were couched indirectly and using positive terminology. The Clinton White House sought to keep Sino-American relations clearly in the realm of normal politics. Starting in September, however, the administration confronted increasing efforts to securitize China by members of Congress. In making a securitizing move and criticizing administration policy toward China, Representative Peter King (R-NY), employed an approach directly opposite to that deployed by the Clinton administration. King regularly focused on China's governance type, contrasted Taiwanese democracy against Chinese authoritarianism, and emphasized the irrationality of the Chinese regime as well as its threat. In sending First Lady Hillary Clinton to a United Nations conference on women's issues hosted by China, the Clinton administration was "providing the veneer of moral respectability" to an "outlaw regime such as the People's Republic of China," which "routinely trample[s] the human rights of all its citizens," including the "execut[ion of] 16 political dissidents in preparation for this [women's] conference."[63] From the outset, King predicated his assessment of China on the political character of the government in Beijing. However, the women's conference was not the real problem for King. By sending the First Lady, Clinton had cast doubt "on the willingness of the United States to resist mainland China's increasingly aggressive actions against Taiwan." This was no small matter for King; after outlining the long relationship between the United States and Taiwan and the important role trade with Taiwan played in the U.S. economy, the representative turned to the crux of the matter:

Taiwan's greatest achievement, however, has been its attainment of an open, democratic society ... Taiwan now has a robust political system, with a particularly combative

---

[62] Bacon 1995b.
[63] Representative Peter T. King (R-NY) 1995.

Near Miss: China and the United States

National Assembly. In March 1996 the President, heretofore elected by the legislature, will be elected by popular vote. This will mark the *first time in the history* of China that a President has been democratically elected.[64] (emphasis added)

Not only was Taiwan a democracy, like the United States it was a groundbreaking democracy, the first in all of Chinese history. King went on to characterize the PRC's reaction to this historically momentous occasion:

Unfortunately ... Taiwan's economic might and its *embrace of democracy* have *enraged* the PRC which has reacted *aggressively* ... The PRC's response to President Lee's visit has bordered on the *hysterical*.[65] (emphasis added)

The Chinese reaction to the Taiwanese embrace – a very positive term suggesting a positive and willing conversion – of a democratic style of governance had been greeted by the "outlaw" communist authorities on the mainland with rage and aggression. King's use of the terms *enraged*, *hysterical*, and *aggressive* ties into a construction of nondemocracies as irrational and unpredictable and willing to use force to resolve political disputes. Having laid the groundwork for constructing China as a threat based on its nondemocracy, King completed the securitizing move by arguing the Chinese posed an existential threat not only to Taiwan – a state of value as a fellow democracy – but directly to U.S. interests:

Clearly the PRC is attempting to use the threat of invasion to intimidate the people of Taiwan into rejecting President Lee and adopting a docile foreign policy. If the PRC is successful in carrying out this extortion and *subverting the democratic process in Taiwan*, the United States will only be encouraging *further PRC aggression* in the region against Japan and the Philippines and we will be severely marginalized as a Pacific power. In short we will have allowed the PRC to establish Asian hegemony.[66] (emphasis added)

Failure of the United States to treat China as the threat it was would result in the loss of Taiwanese democracy as well as aggression against long-standing – and democratic – U.S. allies and the loss of U.S. influence in a large, critical region of the world. While King did not argue that China would strike directly at the United States, the threat to the United States was no less pressing. King's assessment of threat – to the United States, to its allies, and to democracy in general – was tied directly to the authoritarian nature of China's regime. While there is a strategic aspect to King's argument – the loss of U.S. influence and the rise of PRC hegemony – his securitizing move was at its core predicated on the nature of the regimes involved. It was not fundamentally a strategic argument, and would not succeed unless it tapped into a public democratic identity.

---

[64] Bacon 1995a.
[65] Bacon 1995a.
[66] Bacon 1995a.

King's approach to China would set the pattern for ensuing efforts to securitize China. In October 1995, Representative Elton Gallegly (R-CA) made similar arguments while urging President Clinton to take a strong stand:

[I]t must be made clear by the President that our support for the freedom and democracy of Taiwan cannot be compromised and that continued attempts by Beijing to intimidate Taiwan or to undermine the political stability in Taipei, through the use of missile and artillery firings off the coast of Taiwan are unacceptable ... *They [Taiwan] are a strong democracy committed to the freedoms enjoyed and promoted by the United States and other democracies throughout the world.*[67] (emphasis added)

Clearly, shared democracy with Taiwan plays a central role in Gallegly's assessment of the situation. Like King, Gallegly contrasts free and democratic Taiwan against the military response of Beijing. His call for uncompromising support of Taiwan and a "clear" stand by Clinton suggests support for a move to security politics, and certainly a critique of the Clinton administration's relatively gentle approach designed to maintain the issue within normal politics.

In October, the Clinton administration pushed back against the congressional securitizing argument. At the end of the month, President Clinton met with Chinese President Jiang Zemin in New York. While the meeting was conducted largely out of the public eye, the administration sought to defuse congressional securitizing moves by once again highlighting its policy of engagement and indicating that the New York meeting would begin a process of dialogue – essentially, that there was no need to move Sino-American relations into the security realm.[68] More significant was a speech given by Secretary of Defense William H. Perry, the administration's first major speech on China policy. In keeping with the administration's overall counter-securitizing strategy, Perry raised the policy of engagement at the outset of the speech:

These factors [world's most populous country, fourth largest economy in the world, major military power, nuclear power, permanent seat in the United Nations Security Council] lead to the inescapable conclusion that China is becoming a major world power. As China does so, it is inescapable that China's interest will sometimes harmonize and sometimes conflict with those of the United States. The government of the United States recognizes this fundamental fact. Our response to it is a policy of comprehensive *engagement* with China.[69] (emphasis added)

Note that once again there is no mention of China's governance, only a reference to occasional (implicitly normal) conflicts of interest between the two countries that engagement is designed to address; no securitization is required. Perry proceeds to reiterate what the administration means when it talks about engagement. In contrast to the characterizations of an irrational China made by members of Congress, engagement was designed to account for "important

---

[67] Representative Elton Gallegly (R-CA) 1995.
[68] McCurry 1995.
[69] W. H. Perry 1995.

common interests and that these interests make dialogue more rational than confrontational."⁷⁰ Thus, the implicit claim is that those in Congress who seek confrontation are the irrational actors in the situation, not the governments of the PRC and the United States. Perry emphasized the critical core of engagement as a counter-securitization discourse: the long-term promise of democratization in China:

This dialogue will help us reinforce *positive developments* in China and encourage China to become a stabilizing influence in the region and in the world ... *In the long run, change is coming to China.* For example, while Beijing still abuses human rights activists, market reforms are leading to the rapid development of laws that place increasing constraints on government and ultimately will empower citizens to defend basic civil rights.⁷¹

Indeed, there was already evidence the promise of democratization was being realized:

While the ruling Communist Party often practices politics in the old Cold War ways, there is growing experimentation at the village level with democratic elections.⁷²

Engagement was the only way to proceed according to Perry:

The direction of these changes suggests it is more likely than not that long-term change in China will favor our interest. *Seeking to contain and confront China can only slow down the pace of this change.*⁷³ (emphasis added)

Perry's, and by extension the administration's, argument was simple. Confronting or containing (i.e., securitizing) China would actually impede democratization in China. The policy of engagement would eventually produce a democracy in China and eliminate whatever (vaguely mentioned) problems the United States and China faced currently. Keep Sino-American relations within the realm of normal politics, the argument claims, and shared democracy will become a reality. The counter-securitizing move depends not on China currently operating as a democracy, but that it will be in the future.

While the press noted Chinese military maneuvers in November, members of Congress were largely silent on the issue. The Clinton administration remained upbeat and consistent in claiming the "longstanding policy of the United States [is] to seek to promote peace and security and stability in the area of the Taiwan Straits. This is in the interest of the United States, the People's Republic of China, and of Taiwan. We hope that both Taiwan and the People's Republic of China will refrain from any actions which would increase tensions in the area."⁷⁴

---

⁷⁰ Bacon 1995a.
⁷¹ Bacon 1995a.
⁷² Bacon 1995a.
⁷³ Bacon 1995a.
⁷⁴ N. Burns 1995e.

Beginning with the new congressional session in January 1996, the securitizing effort began again in earnest. Like his predecessors in the effort to securitize China, Representative Gerald Solomon (R-NY) grounded his securitizing move in the nature of China's governance:

The editorial [to be included in the Congressional Record] alludes to the obvious differences between *Communist* China and *democratic* Taiwan in terms of human rights, democratic development, and economic performance. The only area left out is foreign policy orientation. Taiwan is unabashedly pro-Western and pro-United States. Communist China is unabashedly the opposite. It is a *rogue regime*, an enemy of freedom and yes, an *enemy of the United States.*[75] (emphasis added)

Solomon uses democratic Taiwan to accentuate the nondemocratic nature of the PRC regime. Fundamentally, the securitizing move – and there can be no doubt this is a securitizing move as Solomon labels China as "an enemy" – like those that came before is predicated on the nondemocratic nature of the government in Beijing. Later that month, Representative Sherrod Brown (D-OH) – in discussing China's threat to democratic Taiwan – implicitly connected China's autocratic regime to the reported threat that China would use nuclear weapons against the United States.[76] Speaker of the House Newt Gingrich made a related securitizing move in early February when he claimed the United States faced a future nuclear threat from "China or Iran or Korea or some place like that." He went on to envisage an angry China launching a nuclear strike against Los Angeles.[77] Here Gingrich securitizes China by tapping into the latent securitization already in place with respect to nuclear weapons. He also implicitly grounds his assessment of the threat to regime type by grouping China with Iran and North Korea. The common link between the three and the unnamed "someplace like that" is authoritarian governance.

February 1996 marked an intensification of securitizing efforts and a very limited expansion of the counter-securitizing effort to Congress. On the first day of the month, a securitizing move by Representative Stephen Horn (R-CA) heralded an innovation, connecting China to significant security threats in the past. Horn started by underlining the autocratic nature of China by contrasting it against democratic Taiwan:

This free election is the culmination of years of reform in the political process in Taiwan. It is an obvious contradiction to those who say that Asian cultures cannot and do not support widespread democratic reforms. That is the view by many of the autocrats of Asia. Sadly, it is also the view within some Western circles. March 23 will be an historic date in the advance of freedom during this troubled century. There is no freedom for the 1.1 billion people of mainland China. There is growing economic freedom. But the

---

[75] Representative Gerald Solomon (R-NY) 1996a.
[76] Representative Sherrod Brown (D-OH) 1996.
[77] Sciolino 1996.

aging Communist oligarchy that rules the People's Republic of China is out of step with the aspirations of its own dynamic citizenry.[78]

It is to the communist government of the PRC that Horn traces the threat to both Taiwan and the United States, noting that the "government in Beijing ... [has been] threatening the lives of not only the people of Taiwan, but even the United States. In an appalling turn, the veiled threat of nuclear destruction has been leveled against Taiwan and the United States."[79] Horn then connects the current events to a period in which U.S. and Chinese forces faced each other in direct conflict:

> Shortly before the invasion of South Korea in June 1950, it was suggested by the American Secretary of State that the Korean peninsula was outside of direct United States interests. This played a large part in encouraging the leaders of North Korea that the United States would not interfere with their plans to reunify Korea by force. The recently dedicated memorial on the Mall to the thousands of Americans who died to prevent aggression is proof that they were wrong.[80]

The analogy of the Korean War functions to tie the claimed Chinese threat to concrete historical events. The possibility of armed conflict between the United States and China is no mere hypothetical; it has happened before and may happen again. China remains communist and the United States is at risk, by failing to treat China as a security threat, of allowing history to repeat itself. Using the historical analogy grants legitimacy and immediacy to Horn's claim of a Chinese threat and strengthens his regime-based securitizing move. Were the communists no longer in power, however, the analogy would fail.

A week later, in arguing for a forceful U.S. response, Senator Paul Simon (D-IL) left no doubt as to the connection between governance type and the threat posed to the United States:

> Mr. President, the best way to avoid force or to avoid giving a *dictator* and a *dictatorship* the appetite *that will not be satisfied with conquering one area* is to make clear that that will be resisted by the community of nations. I am not talking about the use of American troops, but I think American air power clearly ought to be brought to bear if such an eventuality should take place.[81] (emphasis added)

Simon clearly calls for a securitized response to China when he argues that authoritarian regimes inherently pose a threat through their expansionist tendencies, a threat that can only be countered through extraordinary means. If the authoritarian regime sees the community of nations debating the appropriate response, it will act aggressively. Simon's call for a strong security response backed by the willingness to use force explicitly removes the issue from normal political processes and places it into the realm of security.

---

[78] Representative Stephen Horn (R-CA) 1996.
[79] W. H. Perry 1995.
[80] W. H. Perry 1995.
[81] Senator Paul Simon (D-IL) 1996.

With the rising military tensions in the Strait and the increasing pressure from congressional securitizing moves, the Clinton administration became more direct in its refutation of a Chinese threat. On the same day Senator Simon made his securitizing move, Secretary of Defense Perry specifically argued that China did not pose a threat to the United States:

> At this point at least, with the present level of concern but no imminent danger, I don't believe we will make a statement more definite than that ... I am concerned about the military maneuvering the Chinese are doing to – in not so subtle ways – threaten Taiwan, to try to influence their election ... I'm concerned about the military buildup that's going on in China today. I do not see this as a threat yet, but I am concerned.[82]

Later in February, Senator Sam Nunn (D-GA) mounted a rare congressional defense of the administration's desecuritized approach to China. Like members of the Clinton administration, Nunn focused on engagement and its promise of long-term change:

> American engagement is essential. We are not likely to significantly affect events over the short run, but – by engaging in dialog about our mutual interests and our grievances, by speaking in clear terms in this dialog; by participating in China's development; by greater military transparency between our countries; by helping to educate China's next generation of intellectuals, which we are doing by assisting it in alleviating some of its economic and institutional problems – its evolution is more likely to be in directions favorable to peace and stability in the Pacific as well as to American interests ... Even were China to embark on a process that we would call democratization, the development would be a lengthy one.[83]

The hallmarks of the Clinton administration's counter-securitizing approach are evident here. Nunn emphasizes the long-term nature of the policy and the promise that China will eventually evolve domestically in ways favorable to peace and stability in the region, that is, in a democratic direction. While Nunn does not go as far as Perry does in his October speech, the senator also cites evidence of the potential for China's future progress:

> It [China] has modified its social and cultural control over its people, so that its authoritarian government, while still harsh, has moved far from the reign of terror of the Cultural Revolution days. While far from acceptable by our present standards, by every conceivable measure, China's treatment of its own people in 1996 is far better than at the time of President Nixon's opening in 1972 and President Carter's normalization in 1979.[84]

The message here is the same as in Perry's speech: engagement works. While China is not yet a democracy, it is moving in that direction. The United States should keep Sino-American relations within normal politics to guarantee the peaceful future offered by shared democracy.

---

[82] Associated Press 1996a.
[83] Senator Sam Nunn (D-GA) 1996.
[84] Bacon 1995a.

As the military exercises intensified in March 1996, political pressure pushed the Clinton administration to become more aggressive in its approach even as it denied that China posed a threat. During the 1995 military exercises, the administration avoided mentioning the fact that China was conducting military exercises in the Taiwan Strait, usually admonishing China to act in a responsible way or in a manner that would contribute to the peace and stability in the area. Statements spoke to U.S. interests in peace, but did not express concern at Chinese actions. The shift in tone by March 5 was evident in comments made by Nicholas Burns:

> I think, as we've said before, these missile exercises are designed to intimidate the people of Taiwan before the Taiwanese elections. We're concerned by this announcement and by this prospective action. Our Embassy in Beijing today has expressed these concerns to the Government of the People's Republic of China, and that expression of concern will be reiterated to the Chinese Embassy here this afternoon by a senior official of the State Department. Those concerns are well known. Those concerns have not changed. There have been missile tests in the past which we found to be unproductive and destabilizing.[85]

Despite the harsher rhetoric from the Clinton administration, it still sought to avoid securitization:

> Our judgment is that there is no imminent threat of a Chinese invasion or attack or military action against Taiwan. We do not believe there is an imminent threat. We've said that consistently over the last two months, and we stand by that judgment ... When we say there's no imminent threat of a Chinese attack or military action on Taiwan, that really gets to a political question, a question of political motivation. We don't believe it's there – the motivation to attack. We believe the motivation is to intimidate.

An emphasis on engagement also remained at the forefront. Various spokespersons for the Clinton administration, including the foremost civilian authority on defense matters, Defense Secretary William Perry, would echo Burns's claim that Chinese actions did not pose a threat.[86] At one point, State Department spokesman Glyn Davies argued that a Chinese warning to the United States to stay clear of the Taiwan Strait was not a threat:

> Q : Do you have a response on the Chinese Premier's warning that the U.S. naval forces should not sail through the Taiwan Straits?
> MR. DAVIES: Our reading of this so-called threat is that there was no threat; that if you read Chinese Premier Li Peng's words carefully – and we have people who are paid to do that – they in fact have not threatened U.S. forces operating near Taiwan. That's what we come up with as we look carefully at those statements.[87]

On March 6, the day after Burns's press conference, Assistant Secretary for Human Rights John Shattuck cited engagement and the gradual, long-term

---

[85] N. Burns 1996a.
[86] W. J. Perry 1996.
[87] Davies 1996.

nature of its effects in waving off an argument that U.S. policy had not changed China's human rights record.[88] The following day – March 7 – while Nicholas Burns warned of consequences should China's missile testing go wrong,[89] he also claimed the United States saw no threat in Chinese behavior. In response to a direct question regarding the possibility of changing Chinese military behavior through isolation, Burns again turned to engagement:

> We are opposed to any policy, and we would not follow a policy of isolating China. We are engaged in a policy of discussion and activity and, in general, engagement with China. China is too big a country to be isolated. China plays too important a role in the world to be isolated, so therefore we must work with China.[90]

Even as the United States took military steps to address the situation, the Clinton administration constructed the moves in a desecuritized frame. As the *Independence* and *Nimitz* CBGs moved into position, Nicholas Burns claimed the largest U.S. naval presence in the region since the Vietnam War was there to "monitor" the situation.[91] The ambiguous response prompted a reporter to push for a more detailed reaction:

> Q: Since your analysis is that there is no Chinese plan to attack Taiwan – that there's no military danger to Taiwan – could you kind of explain in greater detail why two aircraft carriers are being sent to the area?
>
> MR. BURNS: To note the great concern that the United States has over the testing of missiles in close proximity to Taiwan and the introduction of live-fire exercises. The general climate that's been created by that, which we think is not conducive to peace or a constructive discussion of issues. It notes our interest. We are a Pacific power. We are a Pacific country. We have all sorts of interests in that part of the world, in the western Pacific. It notes those interests. It's a signal meant to convey the strong interest that we have in a peaceful outcome to these differences.[92]

While the United States had sent a massive amount of military hardware to the area near Taiwan, suggesting the Clinton administration was responding to political pressure on the issue, Burns used language emphasizing the opposite. The CBGs were there to facilitate a climate that would allow for peace and "constructive discussion of issues."

An exchange on March 7 highlights the difficulty facing the administration and its efforts to keep China from being securitized. At the same time as the Taiwan Strait Crisis, the Helms-Burton Act was making its way through Congress. The act strengthened U.S. sanctions against Cuba. Supportive of the measure, a reporter challenged Burns as to the difference between the countries.

---

[88] Shattuck 1996.
[89] Tyler 1996b.
[90] N. Burns 1996b.
[91] N. Burns 1996c.
[92] W. H. Perry 1995.

The difference is that China is a very large country with over a billion people in Asia which is a global power and whose actions have a critical impact on United States national security interests. We believe that in the case of China, it being a vastly different country culturally and historically and politically and economically than Cuba, the only correct policy is to try to work through differences while you *engage* them on those differences ... Cuba is the *only authoritarian country in the entire hemisphere* ... Cuba has isolated itself. It's out of touch. It's got policies that made sense perhaps for leftist revolutionaries in the 1960s – that are completely antiquated. It deserves to be isolated, and it is effectively isolated ... Cuban policies are *repressive at home*, antiquated in terms of Cuban foreign policy. They are a *major violator of international law*. They're close to our shores. They're out of step with the hemisphere. They deserve to be isolated. They can be isolated, and they will be isolated until the regime changes; until one day when democracy comes to Cuba. That will be a great day.[93] (emphasis added)

Interestingly, Burns used the same type of language toward Cuba that members of Congress used in their securitizing moves with respect to China. Burns focused on Cuba's authoritarian nature as the central reason why the country needed to be isolated, that is, security measures arising from securitization. The threat would only be gone when Cuba became a democracy. Cuba was stagnant and unchanging. With China, by contrast, the United States was engaging on the difference between the two countries. China was changing, dynamic, moving forward in the way engagement promised while Cuba was beyond the redemption of engagement. Certainly, there are strategic elements to the argument here, but the appeal to democratic identity is predominant. Burns's effort to draw distinctions between China and Cuba, however, highlights the vulnerability of the administration to securitizing efforts grounded in the democratic identity of the public.

Not surprising, the uptick in China's military behavior in March prompted an increase in congressional securitizing moves. On March 6, Senator Frank Murkowski (R-AK) cited the threat posed to the United States from Chinese nuclear weapons and explicitly raised the issue of China's actions in Tiananmen Square in 1989 before arguing that the United States "cannot idly watch a peaceful, democratic ally – which Taiwan is – be threatened."[94] The next day Senator Paul Simon repeated his call for a strong U.S. position and raised doubts as to the administration's claims that China would not attack Taiwan:

While it is probable that China will not invade Taiwan in the near future, or launch a missile attack, people struggling for leadership power sometimes do irrational things. And public officials are risk-takers. No one becomes a United States Senator without taking risks, and no one moves into leadership in China without taking risks. The lesson of history is that dictators who seize territory and receive praise for it from their own controlled media are not likely to have their appetite satisfied with one bite of land. If China should turn militaristic and seize Taiwan, that would be only the first acquisition.

---

[93] N. Burns 1996b.
[94] Senator Frank Murkowski (R-AK) 1996.

Mongolia to the north is a likely next target, and as we should have learned from Hitler, dictators can always find some historic justification for further actions. I personally would favor a strong response with air power by the United States and other nations, if an attempt were made to invade Taiwan or an appropriate military response if they launch a missile attack, but the means of responding militarily do not need to be spelled out.[95]

As with his previous call for strong action, Simon underlined the threat posed by dictators. What is new here is his reference to Hitler, which draws on a historical analogy where an aggressively expansive dictator far from U.S. shores posed a grave threat to the United States. The message is clear: China's distance does not eliminate the threat to the United States. As before, Simon's securitizing move is directly predicated on the nature of China's government.

A major codified securitizing move in Congress came on March 19, when House Concurrent Resolution 148, titled "A concurrent resolution expressing the sense of Congress regarding missile tests and military exercises by the People's Republic of China," passed the House of Representative by a vote of 369–14.[96] The bill itself strongly indicated that China posed a threat to the United States and its interests. According to the bill, China was guilty of:

> intense efforts to intimidate Taiwan ... that threatens to undermine stability throughout the region ... threat[s] to use military force against Taiwan ... [conducting] military maneuvers and tests [that] have included the firing of 6 *nuclear-capable* missiles [which caused] the interruption of international shipping and aviation lanes threaten[ing] both Taiwan and the political, military, and commercial interests of the United States and its allies.[97] (emphasis added)

The litany of offensive actions at least partially ties into existing securitization when it specifies Chinese missiles as "nuclear capable." The resolution clearly calls for an unambiguous securitizing move:

> [T]he United States is committed to the military stability of the Taiwan Straits and United States military forces should defend Taiwan in the event of invasion, missile

---

[95] Senator Paul Simon (D-IL) 1996. The use of historical analogies – notably Simon's reference to Hitler and Murkowski's reference to Tiananmen Square – are suggestive of work in the foreign policy analysis literature on the role of analogical reasoning in the decision-making process (Houghton 2001; Khong 1992). There is a significant difference, however, between the use of analogies here and the scholarship on analogical reasoning. That literature focuses on the cognitive processes whereby policy makers use (and abuse) historical analogies in their effort to develop, assess, and select policy options. It says almost nothing about the role of analogies in the interaction between policy makers and the public. Indeed, Khong partitions off the use of analogies in the justification of policy as part of the "skeptics'" argument against analogical reasoning as an individual-level heuristic (1992, 8). However, Khong's discussion raises interesting questions regarding the use of analogies in the public sphere: Why are they used in the securitization process and what impact do they have? The securitization approach used in this monograph and the presence of analogies in securitizing moves suggests a possible avenue of future inquiry regarding the role of analogy in the securitizing move writ large.

[96] The Senate version of the bill passed two days later by an even stronger margin: 97–0.

[97] Representative Christopher Cox (R-CA) 1996a.

attack, or blockade by the People's Republic of China, [including] maintain[ing] its capacity to resist any resort to force or other forms of coercion that would jeopardize the security, or the social or economic system, of the people of Taiwan, consistent with its undertakings in the Taiwan Relations Act.[98]

While the bill does not specifically highlight the authoritarian nature of the PRC, it does underline the democratic nature of the ROC and in doing so implicitly highlights the nondemocratic nature of the government in Beijing:

[T]he United States and Taiwan have enjoyed a longstanding and uninterrupted friendship, which has only increased in light of the remarkable economic development and political liberalization in Taiwan in recent years [as] has reached a historic turning point in the development of Chinese democracy, as on March 23, 1996, it will conduct the first competitive, free, fair, direct, and popular election of a head of state in over 4,000 years of recorded Chinese history.[99]

Where the bill does not specifically cite the authoritarian nature of the regime in Beijing, supporters of the bill went to great pains to highlight it. Representative Benjamin Gilman (R-NY) accused the administration of appeasement, an allusion connecting the Chinese government to the Nazi threat of World War II. Gilman argued that the administration's "accusations about isolation, containment, and political transition periods avoid hard questions of how to deal pragmatically and effectively with a *totalitarian* government with enormous resources to cause *havoc*"[100] (emphasis added). Not only did Gilman identify the Chinese leadership as totalitarian and sourcing instability to that totalitarian nature, he challenged the engagement concept and the claim of future democracy on which it depends. Gilman also drew a parallel between the crisis and the Korean War, repeating the securitized historical linkage Stephen Horn made in February. Gilman summed up his assessment of threat, and the central role governance plays in that assessment, neatly: "Democracies and dictatorships are fundamentally different and will always clash."[101]

Representative Gerald Solomon (R-NY) used historical analogy and China's regime type in his securitizing move:

But, first of all, let me say this: Why should the United States *come to the rescue* of a small island country halfway around the world? Let me tell you why: Because we are proud Americans and we pay our debts. For those that might not be able to remember, because the people of Taiwan, they came to our rescue. We, the United States of America, standing shoulder to shoulder *against the Japanese imperialists* that threatened our freedoms. Do you remember that in World War II? Shoulder to shoulder they stood with us when we were about to lose that war. Then standing shoulder to shoulder again, for 40 years, they were an *integral link in the chain of defense* against the spread of deadly, atheistic communism, that threatened the freedoms of every single American

---

[98] Bacon 1995a.
[99] Bacon 1995a.
[100] N. Burns 1996a.
[101] Representative Benjamin Gilman (R-NY) 1996.

in this world. They stood as one of the strongest links in that chain of defense against the spread of that deadly communism.

So, yes, we have a moral obligation to defend them against that same deadly, atheistic communism that now threatens their very freedoms, that democracy, that is similar to our own.[102] (emphasis added)

Solomon uses the historical analogy to draw a parallel between the Japanese in World War II and the Chinese in 1996. Just as the Japanese fifty years prior, the Chinese posed a direct threat to the United States and its democracy. Just as in World War II and the Cold War – the two supreme and universally recognized security threats to the United States in the twentieth century – the United States needed to stand once again "shoulder to shoulder" with the Taiwanese against a common threat. The centrality of governance type in the threat construction is overwhelming. The "imperialist" Japanese corresponds to the "deadly, atheistic" communists of China. In both cases, the external regime was not democratic, and because of that, it threatened the core of the United States: democracy.

Gilman and Solomon typified the pattern of securitization. Representative Dana Rohrabacher (R-CA) argued that in the face of the "largest and most heinous opponent and oppressor of people on this planet, the Communist dictatorship in China," the United States needed to "reassert to those dictators on the mainland of China that we side with the democratic people of the world, especially in the Republic of China, and we will not tolerate their expansionism or their threats or any other activities that threaten their neighbors."[103] Enid Waldholtz (R-UT) claimed that "what is at stake here is not just the viability of democracy in Taiwan, but the peace and security of the entire Asiatic region and the world."[104] Toby Roth held that the "United States will assist the democracies of the world in defending against tyranny and oppression" and complained: "My only argument with the resolution I am going to vote for is I do not think it is explicit enough."[105] Peter Deutsch (D-FL) asserted that, in the face of "Beijing's carefully crafted strategy designed to suffocate democracy in Taiwan ... The American people will not tolerate such a grave threat to our own national security."[106] George Nethercutt (R-WA) concluded: "It is right for America to defend Taiwan's progress and prevent an autocratic and militaristic Chinese regime from threatening Taiwan and our Pacific allies."[107]

Christopher Cox (R-CA), the original sponsor of the legislation, sums up the argument thus:

It is very, very important that the United States of America make clear to the People's Republic of China that a war of aggression waged against the democracy on Taiwan

---

[102] Representative Gerald Solomon (R-NY) 1996b.
[103] Representative Dana Rohrabacher (R-CA) 1996.
[104] Representative Enid Waldholtz (R-UT) 1996.
[105] Representative Toby Roth (R-WI) 1996.
[106] Representative Peter Deutsch (D-FL) 1996.
[107] Representative George Nethercutt (R-WA) 1996.

Near Miss: China and the United States

will not be accepted, not by the United States, not by the free world, and that is the world that Taiwan is joining, because right now, in the days ahead, Taiwan is preparing for the first ever free, fair, open, and democratic elections of a head of government in nearly 5,000 years of Chinese history. Communism, which continues to reign in the People's Republic of China, is the antithesis of democracy ... Right now, the People's Republic of China is *threatening freedom in the world* because they are threatening this military invasion ... Naked military aggression targeted against a *democracy* is something that everyone here should understand *threatens each of us*.[108] (emphasis added)

Central to Cox's construction of the threat, as is the case in the collective congressional securitizing move, is the autocratic nature of the authorities in Beijing. This authoritarian nature is the fundamental basis for the threat construction. It is not a construction based on strategic security or economic security, it is a construction predicated on an identity rooted in democracy. That identity gives discursive power to the shared democracy with Taiwan and the threat posed by Chinese communism. Without shared democratic identity, military aggression against democracy in Taiwan would not pose a threat to Americans.

Public Response

The March 23 election in Taiwan and the subsequent termination of China's military maneuvers effectively ended the crisis. As the preceding data indicates, there was a concentrated effort by members of Congress to securitize China, and an equally concerted effort by the administration to counter those efforts. In both cases, although more obliquely in administration discourse, the arguments of both sides were grounded in the governance of China and Taiwan as it related to the United States.

At the outset of the crisis, China was not a central concern for the public. In a June 1995 poll – prior to the start of China's first military exercises – only 6 percent of respondents indicated China was the most serious foreign policy issue facing the United States.[109] In August 1995, despite two months of Chinese military exercises, the public was ambivalent toward China. Roughly equal numbers saw China as a friend (25 percent) and an enemy (24 percent), with a plurality (45 percent) indicating China was neither a friend nor enemy of the United States.[110] For reference, another poll conducted in August showed a large majority of Americans (64 percent) felt Taiwan was a close ally (14 percent) or a friend (50 percent) of the United States. Only 5 percent indicated Taiwan was an enemy and less than a quarter felt Taiwan was neither friend nor enemy.[111] The polling on China was not a product of general public ignorance of China or the nature of the regime in Beijing. Another August poll showed the vast majority of respondents (82 percent) placed the status of personal freedoms in China at 5 or

---

[108] Representative Christopher Cox (R-CA) 1996b.
[109] NBC News and *Wall Street Journal* 1995a.
[110] Louis Harris and Associates 1995a.
[111] Louis Harris and Associates 1995b.

lower on a 10-point scale, with almost a quarter of respondents placing China at 1 – the lowest level of personal freedom.[112] At the same time, two-thirds of Americans felt the United States should not get involved in the internal affairs of China, even at the cost of ignoring human rights.[113] Also in August, Americans felt Sino-American relations were stable: only 22 percent indicated relations were getting worse. The majority thought relations were "staying about the same" (53 percent) or improving (16 percent).[114]

The ambivalence toward China and the relative lack of engagement by the public early in the crisis is not surprising. In the early months, the security narrative was dominated by the Clinton administration, which sought to keep Sino-American relations within normal politics. The public was disengaged because the Clinton administration, like a police officer at the scene of an accident, was waving the public by while announcing there was nothing to see. However, there are indications that engagement as a strategic tool borrowing future Chinese democracy to desecuritize China in the present would be problematic. Taiwan – a semi-state that had held legislative elections since 1980 and was preparing for its first presidential election – enjoyed a far more favorable perception than China. The large pool of respondents who indicated China was neither friend nor enemy, particularly compared against Taiwan, also suggests China did not enjoy the benefit of public doubt that democratic external actors did.

As congressional securitizing moves gathered force, public opinion began to shift. By September, China had moved from the least recognized U.S. foreign policy issue (out of six options) to third, ahead of relations with Russia, North Korea's nuclear program, and economic instability in Mexico.[115] Only trade relations with Japan and the ongoing war in Bosnia outranked China. By the end of the first week in November, respondents felt China was essentially tied with North Korea in terms of perceived military threat to long-standing U.S. ally Japan.[116] While there is no pre-crisis poll to compare this result to, the comparison is astounding. In the eyes of Americans, China was perceived as aggressive as North Korea, a state that made no secret of its antagonism toward the United States and against which the United States had deployed military force for nearly fifty years. The response – particularly compared to the disengagement evident in early polls – suggests a significant shift in threat construction was occurring among the public.

This shift, however, was unstable and public opinion was far from coherent. In January, during the lull in the crisis, the polls indicated the public had

---

[112] Gallup Organization 1995.
[113] Times Mirror 1995a.
[114] Times Mirror 1995b.
[115] In May, 6 percent of respondents indicated China was the most important issue. In the September poll, the number was up to 11 percent. (NBC News and *Wall Street Journal* 1995b).
[116] Gallup Organization et al. 1995. Forty-two percent indicated China; 43 percent indicated North Korea.

Near Miss: China and the United States

a marginally favorable view of China. A slight majority (49 percent) indicated it viewed China favorably while 45 percent felt negatively toward China.[117] Responses to a February poll regarding U.S. military involvement in the event of a Chinese invasion of Taiwan demonstrated strong American unwillingness to use military force in the region. Only 29 percent of respondents felt the United States should fight in the event of a Chinese assault on Taiwan.[118] A similar number (26 percent) felt the United States should send an aircraft carrier to decrease China's influence on Taiwan's election.[119] The use of force, at least in January and February, was not an option for the public.[120] Admittedly, the use of force is not a proxy for securitization, but these results suggest securitization had not occurred. At the same time, however, there is significant evidence that Americans were broadly sympathetic to Taiwan. In the February Harris poll, 62 percent of respondents indicated they thought of Taiwan as a separate and independent country, and 56 percent supported a Taiwanese bid for United Nations membership even if doing so angered China.[121] Over two-thirds (69 percent) felt Taiwan should reunify with the mainland only if the Taiwanese wanted to. Only 2 percent supported Beijing's contention that Taiwan should be reunited under any circumstances, and a remarkable 18 percent said reunification should never occur.[122] In January and February, the public seemed of two minds on the situation in the Taiwan Straits. While unwilling to commit U.S. military forces to Taiwan's defense and marginally favorable toward China, Americans were also strongly supportive of Taiwan's nation-state aspirations, to the point of being willing to anger China. The inconsistency suggests public opinion was unsettled. In the context of the discursive security battle in Washington and the lack of external cues from the region, the inconsistency is understandable.

In March, public opinion resumed its trend toward support of the congressional position. A poll in the second week of March showed a ten-point swing in U.S. perception of China toward the negative. Now Americans by an eleven-percentage point margin (54 percent to 43 percent) viewed China negatively.[123] By contrast, Taiwan's favorability remained very high at 64

---

[117] Gallup Organization et al. 1996a. The poll was a version of the feeling thermometer. A negative or positive sign on the response indicated the general feeling toward China while a numerical value (1–5) indicated the strength of the feeling, with 5 being the strongest feeling. It is worth noting that while the favorable view of China was slightly larger than the negative view, the strongly negative responses of -4 and -5 (total: 15 percent) were stronger than the strongly positive responses (total: 9 percent).

[118] Louis Harris and Associates 1996c.

[119] Louis Harris and Associates 1996a.

[120] It should be noted again that securitization does not necessarily mean the use of force. The polling at the time was, however, exclusively concerned with the possible use of force. Other options were not explored.

[121] Louis Harris and Associates 1996d.

[122] Louis Harris and Associates 1996b.

[123] Gallup Organization et al. 1996b. The extreme responses became increasingly unbalanced toward the negative end as well. The very positive response (+4 and +5 combined) remained consistent at 8 percent. However, the very negative response (-4 and -5) increased to 18 percent.

percent.[124] A separate poll showed over half (52 percent) agreed that the United States had "vital interests" at stake in the confrontation between China and Taiwan.[125] The public also reversed its position on sending CBGs to the region, approving Clinton's aircraft carrier deployment by a margin of 54 percent to 35 percent.[126] The public also became markedly more willing to deploy U.S. forces to counter China, suggesting congressional securitizing moves were gaining traction. While respondents in February overwhelmingly (65 percent) refused to fight China if it attacked Taiwan, by March the numbers were nearly even; 43 percent of respondents favored the use of force to defend Taiwan to 46 percent against, another major swing in opinion.[127] The hardening of U.S. opinion against China indicates that securitizing moves – grounded in the democratic identity of the public – had been remarkably successful as external events lined up with the discourse. While public opinion in favor of the use of force to protect Taiwan had not reached a majority by the end of the crisis, the success of the congressional securitizing move – as indicated by the large swings in public opinion – suggests that, had the crisis continued, support for the use of force would have reached a majority.

Conclusions

The case of the Taiwan Strait Crisis provides compelling support for my central analytical claim. The theoretical framework holds that the democratic identity of the public plays an important role in constructing threats. In the case of China, the theory expects leaders who seek to securitize China would emphasize the nondemocratic nature of China's regime, while those who seek to counter that securitizing move would highlight China's democratic characteristics. In Congress, the primary political center behind the securitizing move with respect to China, China's authoritarianism was front and center in the security argument. The claimed threat from China was traced directly to the authoritarian regime in Beijing. Indeed, many members of Congress argued that China posed a threat not just to U.S. interests, but also to U.S. democracy itself. The emphasis on China's government, and the contrast against U.S. and Taiwanese democracy, is undeniable. Members of Congress acted exactly as the theory anticipated they would, and the massive changes in public opinion in March 1996 suggest the grounding of the securitizing move in democratic identity found resonance with the public. The successful securitization of China in the public also suggests an explanation for the deployment of two carrier task groups by the Clinton administration, a move at odds with U.S. policy to that point. It seems plausible that the Clinton administration deployed the

---

[124] Gallup Organization et al. 1996c.
[125] ABC News and *Washington Post* 1996b.
[126] ABC News and *Washington Post* 1996a.
[127] Gallup Organization et al. 1996d.

carrier groups to head off more drastic action from a Congress empowered by a successful securitizing move.

The role of the engagement concept in the Clinton administration's effort to keep Sino-American relations within normal politics also indicates support for the theoretical approach of this book. It is true that the Clinton administration did not appeal to Chinese democracy to defuse securitizing moves, but in the context of the 1989 Tiananmen incident and public awareness of the regime in Beijing, such a claim would not have been credible and thus politically useless and potentially counterproductive. What the engagement concept does, however, is borrow from the possible future democratization of China in the effort to defuse securitizing moves aimed at China. In effect, the Clinton administration argued that securitization – possibly resulting in isolation, containment, or military response – would sacrifice China's future democracy. Sino-American relations should remain in normal politics because China would be a *future* democracy. In turning to engagement, the speaker was implicitly calling upon the assumptions underlying the concept – that China would eventually democratize – to support positions that opposed securitization. It served as a powerful discursive tool as long as policy makers periodically reminded the audience of those assumptions, which the Clinton administration did with two major foreign policy speeches (Christopher in July 1995 and Perry in October 2005) during the crisis.

The case also suggests why the claim of China's imminent democratization has been so pervasive in the popular and scholarly discussion over China's future. No doubt, some China scholars and scholars of democratic development do believe China will shortly adopt a more democratic form of government, but there are political reasons for supporting the democratization claim. As Mann points out, China policy has to a remarkable extent been the preserve of the executive branch;[128] the public and Congress have had relatively little input. Executive branch actors, particularly the presidency, have a vested interest in preventing the securitization of China. Yet the authoritarian nature of China's governance means they have precious little leverage to ward off securitizing moves, particularly by members of Congress. To make matters worse for the president, China is a particular type of authoritarian regime: a communist one. While it may be communist in name only, the name triggers automatic reference to the highly securitized foreign policy of the United States directed toward communist regimes during the Cold War. The claim of China's imminent or near future democratization enables those who seek to desecuritize China or to prevent the securitization of China in a particular context to borrow China's future democracy to desecuritize it in the present.

Finally, the strong presence of Republican members of Congress on the securitizing side of the equation suggests an important role for ideology and belief systems in the assessment of threat at the individual level. China, as one of

[128] Mann 1999.

the last communist states, represents the ideological opposite of traditional conservative belief systems in the United States. This ideological opposition may generate an expectation of threat, and those on the political right in the United States (generally members of the Republican party) will be more inclined (than if the external state were a right-wing nondemocracy) to interpret China' international behavior as threatening or give extra weight to potentially threatening behavior that supports the belief that left-wing nondemocracies are a threat. In effect, Republicans interpret Chinese behavior in a manner that reinforces their belief that far left ideologies (and the regimes that proclaim them) pose a threat to the United States. Psychologists refer to this as motivational bias, and this phenomenon may explain why Republicans are more willing to make a securitizing move with respect to China than (typically more politically left) Democrats.[129] It is worth noting, however, that while Republicans dominate the securitizing effort, there is some participation on the part of Democrats, in particular Democrats perceived as representing the left in the party. Sherrod Brown (D-OH) is one such example. Another example is Speaker Nancy Pelosi, who – while not outspoken during this particular incident – has a long history of hardline policy preferences toward China.[130] These observations suggest an interesting avenue of future research exploring the motivations behind the decision to make a securitizing move on the part of the individual, with a possible emphasis on macro-level structures that would lead to predictions regarding who will securitize and when they might do so.

---

[129] Frijda and Mesquita 2000. Khong notes a similar phenomenon in the psychology literature on Schema Theory (1992, 37).
[130] Salliday 1998.

5

Collision Course: The 2001 Hainan Island EP-3 Incident

Historical Overview and Literature

In the context of recent Sino-American relations, two focal points stand out: the 1995–6 Taiwan Strait Crisis and the 2001 collision between a U.S. Navy EP-3 surveillance aircraft and a Chinese J-8II fighter/interceptor.[1] The collision on April 1, 2001 between the top of the J-8II and the bottom of the EP-3 caused serious damage to both planes. As a result of the collision, the jet-powered J-8II crashed into the sea. The plane was not recovered and the pilot was pronounced dead. The turboprop-powered EP-3 also sustained significant damage, but was able to land, without permission, on the Chinese island of Hainan.[2] The crew was held for eleven days under generally good conditions until the United States issued the "two sorries" expressing condolences for the loss of the Chinese pilot and apologizing for landing without permission. The Chinese government released the EP-3 crew on April 11, 2001 and eventually shipped the dismantled EP-3 back to the United States.[3]

Remarkably, given the significance of the EP-3 incident as one of only three major crises to break out in Sino-American relations since the normalization of relations, academic work on the incident is sparse. Despite its small size, the

---

[1] There are two other possible focal points, but for different reasons they are less useful than the cases I have selected. The first is the 1999 U.S. bombing of the Chinese embassy in Belgrade. While the incident was highly publicized, the United States was the accidental "aggressor," making the case unsuitable from the standpoint of examining securitizing moves in the United States – although research examining Chinese securitization should find it very useful. A second focal point might be a series of confrontations between U.S. surveillance ships and the Chinese navy in the South China Sea region (Shanker and Mazzetti 2009). These confrontations were much lower in profile than the 1995/1996 and 2001 events and thus were largely resolved out of the public eye.

[2] Rosenthal and Sanger 2001.

[3] CNN 2001a; Prueher 2001; Sanger and Perlez 2001; C. Smith 2001.

literature displays two clear trends. First, there is a significant focus on legal and policy lessons. Within the policy-oriented literature, two foci emerge. One is a clear emphasis on what happened and the policy-related response within the U.S. government.[4] The second focus rests on the dynamics of conflict resolution (i.e., negotiation) between the United States and China or related analysis of the legal implications of the conflict.[5] In this literature the primary concern is a procedural treatment of policy and how policy responses can be modified so that future engagements of a similar type might be handled better. To that end, political processes, identity dynamics, and threat constructions – the central points of concern for this book and for questions about the present and future of U.S.-China relations – are largely unexamined.

Second, there is a remarkable amount of attention to issues of identity and language as factors in how events transpired during the EP-3 incident.[6] Communicative action plays an important role in much of this scholarship, but without clear implications for Sino-American security relations. Like the policy-oriented literature, studies on communicative action focus on communication dynamics specific to the EP-3 incident (e.g., the crisis was driven by failure to use metaphors to communicate clearly). These are not efforts to understand how either side constructed the incident or what those constructions might say about U.S.-China security relations. There are, however, tantalizing hints of such analysis. Scholars analyze Chinese efforts to manipulate international and U.S. domestic public perceptions of the incident.[7] Others note that perceptions of causation differ between the U.S. and Chinese cultural contexts.[8] In the end, however, both the communicative and policy-oriented literatures largely treat the incident as a one-off, offering some concrete or problem-solving lessons for practice but otherwise divorced from the larger U.S.-China relationship. In this narrow focus, the scholarship largely accepts the assumption that the incident was inevitably crisis-like in nature. In this chapter, I challenge that assumption by looking at the discursive process by which the incident was constructed in public by political actors. In doing so, I contribute to the understanding of why the events transpired as they did as well as what the incident means for Sino-American relations.

The Case

Bush versus Congress

Much like his predecessor, George W. Bush criticized the previous administration over its China policy as he ran for the presidency of the United States. In

---

[4] Blair and Bonfili 2006.
[5] Donnelly 2004; Tuosheng 2006; Valencia and Guoxing 2002; Xinbo 2007; Yee 2004.
[6] Callamari and Reveron 2003; Cheng 2002; Gries and Peng 2002; Slingerland et al. 2007.
[7] Callamari and Reveron 2003.
[8] Gries and Peng 2002.

the campaign, Bush effectively abandoned the Clinton administration's policy of engagement with China, arguing China was a "competitor" rather than a "partner."[9] This construction of China was evident as the administration struggled to keep the incident from escalating into a crisis and in particular sought to keep the incident from becoming constructed as a national security situation. An unnamed official was reported in the *New York Times* immediately after the collision as effectively saying a securitizing move would make the situation worse: "The question now is do we have access to the crew, when do we get the crew back, and how do we get the aircraft back. This is going to be a test of everyone's ability to stay cool and work things out."[10] From the outset, the media pushed a China-as-threat construction in press briefings. In an April 2 press briefing, White House spokesman Scott McClellan sought to avoid the question:

Q: I said, you're demanding immediate access to the crew.
MR. MCCLELLAN: To the crew, and to the aircraft.
Q: Or *what*? What's the other shoe?
MR. MCCLELLAN: I'm sorry?
Q: *What's the other shoe?*
MR. MCCLELLAN: Well, that's what we're continuing to discuss with Chinese officials.
Q: *When do you stop discussing and start acting?*
MR. MCCLELLAN: Well, again, when we have more information for you, I'll get that to you. But we continue to press – because that's our first priority, is the crew, that we have direct access to them
....
Q: China is threat to the United States?
Q: *Is China a threat to the United States?*
Q: It's about the same question, that if they are flying off the shore of San Francisco, do they do that?
MR. MCCLELLAN: I'd refer you to the Defense Department on that question. I'm not aware of any – [change of subject][11] (emphasis added)

At a press briefing the next day at the Department of Defense, a similar dynamic played out. Probing as to why the Department of Defense was taking a low-key approach to the incident, spokesman Rear Admiral Craig Quigley pushed back against the argument that the United States should implement a security response:

Clearly, we believe that there is a *diplomatic solution* to this incident and not a military one.

It is our aircrew. They are military people. There is a military aircraft on the ground. But if you think of a military solution to this, that's not the way ahead, Barbara. The way

---

[9] Bush 2000.
[10] Rosenthal and Sanger 2001.
[11] McClellan 2001.

ahead is a diplomatic one, and that's why the lead at this point – and I would expect it to stay – with the State Department.[12] (emphasis added)

At the same time, the administration did hint that while it was currently understanding of delays regarding the release of the EP-3 crew, if the situation continued a securitizing move might be possible:

> This is an *unusual situation* in which an American military aircraft had to make an emergency landing on Chinese soil. Our approach has been to keep this accident from becoming an international incident. We have allowed the Chinese Government time to do the right thing. But now it is time for our service men and women to return home, and it is time for the Chinese Government to return our plane.
>
> This accident has the *potential of undermining our hopes for a fruitful and productive relationship* between our two countries. To keep that from happening, our service men and women need to come home.[13] (emphasis added)

Here Bush justifies desecuritizing China's behavior by pointing to the unusual nature of the situation. The implication is that there is no standard operating procedure, and that the Chinese government needs time to determine how to proceed. According to an unnamed senior administration official, the administration's goal was to "issue a strong statement to the Chinese about what we are looking for, without overreacting."[14] However, the claim that the situation could "undermine" the current relationship between the two countries suggests the United States could move Sino-American relations out of the realm of normal politics. The implication is that the relationship could become securitized.

Not surprising given the security dynamic that developed during the 1995–6 crisis, members of Congress began efforts at securitizing the incident, and Sino-American relations more broadly. On April 3, two days after the collision, an unnamed Republican congressional aid made a securitizing move:

> If China wants to behave like a *rogue nation*, ignoring all the conventions of international law, this will indicate to us that they seek *confrontation over cooperation*. If they want to get members of the U.S. Senate upset over relations with China, this is the way to do it.[15] (emphasis mine)

The congressional aid does not explicitly refer to the nature of China's governance here, instead predicating the move on China as failing to observe the rule of (international) law. This "rogue nation" label suggests unpredictability and reminds the audience that China's government is not democratic (democracies are not labeled rogue regimes), although such a connection is not clear. The

---

[12] Quigley 2001a.
[13] Bush 2001b.
[14] Sanger 2001a.
[15] CNN 2001b.

"confrontation over cooperation" comment also suggests Sino-American ties may become a security matter.

Representative Christopher Smith (R-NJ) labeled the situation a "crisis situation," traced the source of the problem directly to Chinese governance, and linked the failure to observe rule of law with China's dictatorship:

> Madam Speaker, just let me say that the new tension created by the holding of 24 American servicemen by the People's Republic of China – a crisis situation that all of us want to see resolved immediately – only underscores anew how *the policies of the Beijing dictatorship are harsh and unreasonable* and how those policies have *continued to worsen and to deteriorate* with each and every passing year.
>
> Sadly, *universally recognized norms and international laws* have no meaningful application to the dictatorship. *The dictatorship in Beijing mocks the rule of law*.[16] (emphasis added)

While Smith refrains from making an explicit securitizing move in his statement, Smith does suggest China may be a security threat, particularly in the future. He claims Chinese policy is "harsh and unreasonable," suggesting that were U.S. interests to run up against those of China, no compromise would be possible. These policies, rather than improving with time, have worsened according to Smith, suggesting a trajectory that would make Sino-American conflict inevitable.[17] Not only does Smith tie his (implicit) threat assessment to Chinese governance – "dictatorship in Beijing" – he backs it up by underlining Chinese disregard for the rule of law, a core attribute of democracy. The implication here is not only that China is wholly undemocratic, but also that its parochial worldview will eventually put it in conflict with the universal, law-based perspective of the United States.

Also on April 3, Representative Clifford Sterns (R-FL) continued the pattern of implicit security moves. At the outset of his comments, Sterns took aim at the claim that economic engagement with China would result in eventual Chinese democracy:

> Mr. Speaker, in the last Congress and many before, many of us have heard predictions that have been made regarding China. Advocates last year stated that granting permanent normal trade relations to China would help bring reform to this Communist government, and establish a real friendship between our nations.[18]

Instead, Sterns argued, Sino-American relations had gotten worse. China's human rights record was as bad or worse, naturalized Chinese Americans were being arrested, and – of "larger concern" – China now held the EP-3 and its crew and was making "threatening" moves toward navy surveillance ships.

---

[16] Representative Christopher Smith (R-NJ) 2001.
[17] This also serves as a broadside against the notion of engagement. Chinese governance and policy has not improved despite international economic and political integration. Consequently, desecuritizing arguments based on borrowed future democracy are vacuous.
[18] Representative Clifford Sterns (R-FL) 2001.

He also highlighted Chinese actions in areas that had already been securitized: nuclear weapons and Iraq.

Other examples showing cracks within our forged relationship with China also bear noting, such as China's involvement with Pakistan's *nuclear bomb program* and their recent *questionable involvement in Iraq*, to name just a few.[19] (emphasis added)

Sterns ends his comments with an ominous call for a reevaluation of U.S. policy toward China while citing Chinese aggression: "Mr. Speaker, it is clear that our relationship with China needs to be carefully reevaluated. Since PNTR [Permanent Normal Trade Relations], we have seen aggressive behavior on their part."[20] By outlining a litany of problems in Sino-American relations traced back to the communist government of China, including recognized security issues like nuclear weapons and Iraq, Stern's call for a reevaluation of U.S. policy suggests China cannot be handled within normal politics. China – owing to its nondemocratic government – poses a threat to the United States both through direct actions like those taken against U.S. surveillance assets and indirectly through efforts to weaken nuclear nonproliferation and aid regimes like that in Iraq.

April 4 would mark the last day of significant security contestation over the incident. Congress went into Easter recess the following day, leaving the Bush administration largely in control of the policy narrative. As on the previous day, the administration walked a fine line between keeping the policy response within normal politics while suggesting possible securitization. White House spokesman Ari Fleischer, in responding to a question regarding damage to Sino-American relations, pointed both to the "fruitful aspects" of U.S.-China relations while warning of potential problems if the situation was not resolved:

Q: Ari, have U.S.-Chinese relations been damaged at this point?
MR. FLEISCHER: Keith, the President made it clear yesterday that he hopes that this accident will not turn into an international incident, and in his meeting with the Deputy Premier of China, they discussed the *fruitful aspects of our relationship with China* and our hopes to grow those aspects. The President said yesterday that in the event that our servicemen and women are not returned, that it *could damage U.S.-China relations*. And that is another reason why it's important for our servicemen and women to be allowed to come home.
Q: So it could damage U.S.-China relations; it has not so far?
MR. FLEISCHER: Again, what's important is the return of our servicemen and women. That's where the President's focus is.[21] (emphasis mine)

The administration's desecuritizing tactic remained centered on an appeal to the utilitarian benefits of the relationship. The terminology *fruitful* suggests the incident should remain within normal politics because the United States might lose out on practical benefits derived from the relationship. Not surprisingly,

---

[19] Representative Clifford Sterns (R-FL) 2001.
[20] Representative Clifford Sterns (R-FL) 2001.
[21] Fleischer 2001.

it mirrors Bush's own emphasis on the "fruitful and productive" relationship between the two countries. References to Clinton's policy of engagement are not in evidence, a direct result of Bush's campaign effort to criticize the Clinton administration's policy toward China and to redefine the relationship as one between strategic competitors. The Bush administration had in effect disowned the borrowed future democracy desecuritizing approach of the Clinton administration.

The Bush administration also received interesting support from Congress. Representative John Hayworth (R-AZ), while tracing the incident to "the Communist Chinese regime," and threatening "numerous [policy options] with serious repercussions for the Chinese regime in Beijing," also sought to put a break on his own securitizing move.[22] He did so by expressing his support for the Bush administration's diplomatic approach and praising Secretary of State Colin Powell's expression of "regret over the loss of life." Representative Heather Wilson (R-NM) in effect sought to undermine the authority of colleagues to make securitizing moves by deferring to the president, stating she was "supportive of the President's desire to keep this accident from becoming an international incident."[23] Similarly, Representative Jo Ann Davis (R-VA) argued that "politics should stop at the water's edge. We need to support our President."[24] Here the cost of disavowing engagement becomes clear. Members of Congress opposed to securitization cannot appeal to present or future democracy and thus turn to other discursive tools to counter securitizing moves, specifically by invoking executive branch purview over U.S. international relations policy.

While the Bush administration's position remained consistent from April 3, the securitizing move on April 4 became more explicit. Representative Brad Sherman (D-CA) claimed the EP-3 crew – and America – were being held "hostage" by the Chinese, suggesting both were under threat.[25] Representative Duncan Hunter (R-CA) introduced legislation revoking China's trading status, claiming the EP-3 situation was "indicative of the regard in which the *communist regime* in China holds our government.[26] The fact is, while we trade with China, they prepare for *war*" (emphasis added).[27] The linkage seems clear: China's regime type directly leads to a threat against the United States. Representative Dana Rohrabacher (R-CA) claimed that "[u]ntil our 24 military personnel are returned, they should be considered as hostages, being held by a hostile power."[28] While not explicit about the threat, Rohrabacher uses the

---

[22] Representative John Hayworth (R-AZ) 2001.
[23] Representative Heather Wilson (R-NM) 2001.
[24] Representative Jo Ann Davis (R-VA) 2001.
[25] Representative Brad Sherman (D-CA) 2001.
[26] The legislation had thirty-five cosponsors representing a broad spectrum of political positions, from strong conservatives like Hunter or Tom Tancredo (R-CO) to strong liberals like Bernie Sanders (I-VT) and Sherrod Brown (D-OH) (United States Library of Congress 2001).
[27] Yang 2001.
[28] Representative Dana Rohrabacher (R-CA) 2001.

term *hostages*, implying their personal welfare was at risk. More broadly, the concept of a hostile power suggests an immediate threat to the welfare of the United States. Representative James Traficant (D-OH) was similarly explicit in his appeal to China's regime type:

China now demands an apology, an apology for spying on a *country who has missiles pointed at us* ... China is now testing American resolve, piece by piece, incident by incident. Mr. Speaker, we need to tell it like it is. China is trying to determine what Congress and Uncle Sam will do when China attacks Taiwan. That is the way it is, folks. I say the dragon is going too far.

I yield back the fact that *an attack on Taiwan is an attack on democracy*, and, by God, that *should be considered an attack on the United States of America*.[29] (emphasis added)

For Traficant, Chinese action with respect to the EP-3 was indicative of a larger threat to Taiwan and the United States. Note that Traficant cites both the missiles targeted on the United States (an immediate existential threat to lives of citizens in the United States) as well as an attack on Taiwan (a more indirect threat to the U.S. political system) in constructing his securitizing move. While he does not reference China's governance directly, the claim that an attack on Taiwan would be an "attack on democracy" traces the threat construction indirectly – albeit strongly – back to the nature of China's government.

Representative Joseph Pitts (R-PA) was less explicit about the threat but more explicit about the nature of the Chinese regime when he claimed China owed the United States an apology:

Mr. Speaker, China's President should apologize to the United States for its *aggression* in the accident with one of our airplanes over international waters. This is not the first time Chinese Air Force fighter pilots have *recklessly* and *aggressively* flown by our slower-moving planes over international waters well outside of China's boundaries to *harass* our Air Force planes. They have done this repeatedly and have been warned of the danger. Unfortunately, this time, the Chinese fighter caused an accident.

This *reckless aggression*, the forced landing of our disabled plane, and now the holding of our crew and plane as *hostages*, and now *China's belligerence is outrageous*. It violates international agreements that China has signed; it *damages U.S.-China relations*.

President Bush should stand firm and strong and demand an apology from the *dictators in Beijing*, the immediate return of the American crew and plane. China is at fault on this one.[30] (emphasis added)

The threat posed by China in Pitts's statement is one of implication. Pitts relies on language implying violence when discussing the situation, using terms like *aggressive* and *belligerence* to characterize China and its behavior. He also refers to the EP-3 crew as *hostages*, a term suggesting the welfare of the captives

---

[29] Representative James Traficant (D-OH) 2001.
[30] Representative Joseph Pitts (R-PA) 2001.

is at risk. Pitts points to the "dictators in Beijing" as the fundamental source of the threat when he claims it is they who owe the United States an apology.

After April 4 and the departure of Congress for the Easter recess, the Bush administration was left largely in control of the narrative, and the message remained the same. On April 5, White House spokesman Ari Fleischer continued to emphasize the utilitarian reasons to keep the situation desecuritized:

> And during the meeting that the President had with Deputy Premier Qian Qichen, what they focused on in the Oval Office was entirely positive. They talked about the fruitful, growing relations between the United States and China, the many opportunities our two nations have, particularly in the area of trade, which are mutually beneficial. That was the tenor of the meeting. And the President continues to believe that there are many fruitful opportunities between the United States and China, particularly in the areas of trade.[31]

President Bush was similarly positive, if more vague during an April 5 press conference:

> The message to the Chinese is, we should not let this incident destabilize relations. Our relationship with China is very important. But they need to realize that it's time for our people to be home. We're working all diplomatic channels to affect our priority. There's discussions going on. And we'll continue to do so. My mission is to bring the people home.
>
> And as to whether or not we'll have good relations, my intention is to make sure we do have good relations. But the Chinese have got to act. And I hope they do so quickly.[32]

Interesting, Bush also began to draw on the engagement rhetoric that characterized his predecessor's efforts to keep Sino-American relations desecuritized. In responding to a question suggesting a trade-off between strategic (i.e., security) interests and economic interests, Bush essentially argued the trade-off was a false one, and that promoting U.S. economic interests would eventually produce a Chinese democracy:

> Q: In my region, we have strong economic interests in Asia as an export market. Would you please comment on the balance that you think should be struck between our strategic interests and our economic interests in Asia, including China?
>
> The President: I believe that China ought to be a trading partner of ours. I think it's in our economic interests to open up the Chinese markets to U.S. products, to U.S. agricultural products. *I not only believe it's in our economic interest, I believe it's in our interest to promote U.S. values.*
>
> And I believe *the marketplace promotes values. When people get a taste of freedom in the marketplace, they tend to demand other freedoms in their societies.* And so, I'm an advocate of China's entering into the WTO and I'm hopeful that the current situation ends quickly and our people come home.
>
> China is a strategic partner, a strategic competitor. But that doesn't mean we can't find areas in which we can partner. And the economy's a place where we can partner. And

---

[31] Fleischer 2001.
[32] Bush 2001a.

we've got some differences with China, long-term differences, spreading of weapons of mass destruction is an issue that we need to work with the Chinese on, as well as other nations in that part of the world.

Human rights is an issue, but *I believe trade will encourage more freedom, particularly when it comes to individual liberties. The marketplace is – the marketplace unleashes the opportunity for people to make choices, and so I continue to push for trade with China.*[33] (emphasis added)

It is difficult to overstate the significance of Bush's claims here. While he included his construction of China as a strategic competitor, he once again fell back on Clinton-era engagement language in his effort to desecuritize China and its relations with the United States. The question that prompted Bush's response suggested the United States could not pursue its economic interests – the primary rationale for counter-securitization to that point – and security interests simultaneously. Rather than defending the economic basis of his efforts to prevent securitization, Bush turned to the promise of China's democratic future to bolster his position. The concept of engagement came up again two days later during a televised interview with House International Relations Committee Chair Henry Hyde (R-IL). In response to a claim from co-host Mark Shields that China was a "Stalinist regime," Hyde agued for a policy of engagement instead of securitization:

Well, I don't think we should have any illusions about the character of the Chinese government, but it's out there. It's the largest country in the world in terms of population, and it's a reality, and we have to deal with it. Now, we can deal with it, at least attempt to deal with it, by *engagement*, by flooding the country with American marketers and servicemen. That's what most-favored-nation status is supposed to be about. It's called engagement. I haven't seen an awful lot of results from that, and how long we should continue that is another question. But I'm not for heating up another Cold War that could well turn into a hot war.[34] (emphasis added)

After Bush's March 5 interview, the administration curtailed commentary on the situation.[35] Bush himself limited his comments on the issue until the crew was released six days later, indicating only that the United States was working "behind the scenes" and pursuing a diplomatic solution.[36] Administration spokespeople were similarly restrained. White House spokesman Ari Fleischer's response to a loaded question regarding Chinese motivations emphasized the complexity of the situation and the importance of a diplomatic response:

Q: Some reports are saying that China is testing the waters and the strength of the United States and of this administration, how long President Bush can go on this, and this is going like 20 years ago, U.S. diplomats in Iran.

---

[33] Bush 2001a.
[34] Hyde 2001.
[35] Perlez and Sanger 2001.
[36] Bush 2001c, 2001d, 2001e.

MR. FLEISCHER: I think what took place was an accident. And now in the wake of that accident, both nations are involved in a delicate *diplomacy*, so that our men and women can come home. I think that's what's going on in the ground in China. I think it's a *complicated situation* on the ground in China. And that's where the matter stands.[37] (emphasis added)

Department of Defense spokesman Rear Admiral Craig Quigley responded similarly to a leading question from a reporter:

Q: And there continues to be a sense here that we need to just modulate what everybody's saying and let the diplomatic process play out? Because again, I'm struck by the fact that – I mean, these are 24 of your own – that you're not outraged about this. But everything that we know officially is very – we're very grateful and we're very happy that everybody's – What! These are 24 prisoners!
ADM. QUIGLEY: Diplomacy – well, I don't agree with your term.
Q: Twenty-four detainees!
ADM. QUIGLEY: Diplomacy, as the president said yesterday, can be a slow process, but that is the way ahead. There is not a military solution to this, it is a diplomatic solution. That process is under way. It will continue until we get to a successful resolution.[38]

The Bush administration clearly sought to keep the U.S. response, and Sino-American relations more broadly, desecuritized. When pushed, the administration emphasized the importance of diplomacy – a very normal political process – in resolving the situation.

Once the crew was released on April 11, the incident faded from public view. While the EP-3 remained in Chinese custody for over a month after the crew was released, news reports on the subject dropped off dramatically. In Congress, with a few exceptions, business went on to other issues. All but one of these exceptions were statements by members of Congress praising the merits of the EP-3 crew. On April 24, immediately after Congress's return from recess, Representative Dana Rohrbacher (R-CA) made the most explicit securitizing move of the incident, and in doing so derived his threat construction directly from China's regime type:

Mr. Speaker, one month ago, the *Communist regime* that *controls* the mainland of China *attacked* an American surveillance aircraft while it was in international waters. After being *knocked out of the sky*, 24 American military personnel, the crew of the surveillance craft, were held *hostage* for nearly 2 weeks. The *Communist Chinese* blamed us and would not return the crew until the United States was humiliated before the world ... How much more proof do we need that the so-called engagement theory is a total failure? Our massive investment in China, pushed and promoted by American billionaires and multinational corporations, has created not a more peaceful, democratic China, but an *aggressive nuclear-armed bully* that now threatens the world with its hostile acts and proliferation. Do the *Communist Chinese* have to *murder American*

---

[37] Fleischer 2001.
[38] Quigley 2001b.

personnel or attack the United States or our allies with their missiles before those who blithesomely pontificate about the civilizing benefits of building the Chinese economy will admit that China for a decade has been going in the opposite direction than predicted by the so-called "free traders."

We have made a monstrous mistake, and if we do not face reality and *change our fundamental policies*, instead of peace, there will be *conflict*. Instead of democratic reform, we will see a further retrenchment of a regime that is run by *gangsters and thugs*, the world's worst human rights abusers.

Let us go back to basics. The mainland of China is *controlled* by a rigid, *Stalinistic Communist party*.

[...]

Yes, the *Communist Chinese* are arming themselves to sink American aircraft carriers, to *kill thousands upon thousands of American sailors*. Make no mistake about it, *China's military might now threatens America and world peace*. If there is a crisis in that part of the world again, which there will be, we can predict that some day, unlike the last crisis when American aircraft carriers were able to become a peaceful element to bring moderation of judgment among the players who were in conflict, instead, *American aircraft carriers will find themselves vulnerable, and an American President will have to face the choice of risking the lives of all of those sailors on those aircraft carriers*.[39] (emphasis added)

Rohrabacher's statement hardly requires analysis. He repeatedly references the nondemocratic nature of China's government and draws a very direct connection between that government and his claim of a threat. The argument is not a strategic or economic one: Rohrabacher does not argue that China's weapons acquisitions pose a threat to U.S. trade interests or U.S. allies (aside from an implication at the end regarding Taiwan). Instead, Rohrabacher makes an identity-based securitizing move. China is a threat to the United States because of the nature of its government.

Public Response

Public opinion polling from the period suggests the securitizing move presented by members of Congress had an effect, but that securitization was not successful. In part this is because polling before the incident suggests China had already been securitized in the minds of many Americans. In February 2001, before the collision, 48 percent of respondents in a Gallup poll indicated they had a mostly (31 percent) or very (17 percent) unfavorable view of China.[40] A similar question in the same poll asked respondents to assign a value from −5 (most unfavorable) to +5 (most favorable) to their opinion of China. The result here was even stronger, with 51 percent indicating some level of negative opinion toward China.[41] These values correspond almost exactly to a Gallup poll run one year later. In that February 2002 poll, 49 percent of respondents

---

[39] Representative Dana Rohrabacher (R-CA) 2001.
[40] Gallup Organization 2001c.
[41] Gallup Organization 2001b.

indicated they had a mostly (37 percent) or very (12 percent) unfavorable opinion of China.[42] While favorability does not equate to conception of threat, the favorability level comes as close as the polling data allows to public threat construction.

During the period of the incident, opinion polling presents a mixed picture. A poll from April 1–4 shows a large majority of respondents (68 percent) indicating China presents an "extreme/somewhat threat" versus 32 percent responding China presents "Not much of a threat/no threat at all/not sure."[43] The same poll shows a spike in unfavorable perception of China's government to 61 percent holding a somewhat or very unfavorable impression.[44] These poll results suggest an increase in the number of people constructing China as a threat and may indicate congressional securitizing moves were successful. However, the polls contrast against an April 4–5 CBS News poll indicating 49 percent of respondents felt China was an ally (5 percent) or friendly but not an ally (44 percent).[45] To confuse matters further, the same CBS poll found that 48 percent of respondents held a "neutral" opinion of China.[46] Of those that did hold an opinion, 34 percent held an unfavorable impression while 13 percent held a favorable estimation of China. This result does not seem to square with the friend/enemy question from the survey; a plurality of respondents felt China was friendly or an ally, yet a plurality were agnostic toward the country.

An ABC News/*Washington Post* poll from April 5 shows yet another result, with a significant majority (57 percent) judging China as unfriendly (37 percent) or an enemy (20 percent).[47] An overwhelming majority (74 percent) agreed trade should be restricted if China did not return the crew and plane, suggesting congressional securitizing moves may have been successful here, since the Bush administration steadfastly refused to publically consider retaliatory action.[48] A plurality (48 percent) also felt the incident posed a serious threat to Sino-American relations.[49] In an April 6 Gallup poll, 55 percent of respondents considered the EP-3 crew hostages, also indicating congressional securitizing rhetoric may have been successful in constructing the situation.[50]

In the immediate aftermath of the incident (after the crew had been released), polls seemed to indicate an increase in unfavorable views of China. An April 20–22 Gallup/CNN/*USA Today* poll showed a large majority (69 percent)

---

[42] Gallup Organization 2002. It is worth noting that the second poll took place after the attacks of September 11, 2001.
[43] The Committee of 100 2001a.
[44] The Committee of 100 2001b.
[45] CBS News 2001b.
[46] CBS News 2001a.
[47] ABC News and *Washington Post* 2001c.
[48] ABC News and *Washington Post* 2001b. The question did not give the respondents a time horizon for restricting trade, that is, should trade be restricted if the crew and plane are not returned in X (days/weeks/months).
[49] ABC News and *Washington Post* 2001a.
[50] Gallup Organization 2001a.

saw China as unfriendly (44 percent) or an enemy (25 percent), a significant increase over similar questions asked during the first week of the incident.[51] This matches up well with a separate NBC News poll from April 21–23 in which 71 percent of respondents indicated they perceived China as an adversary.[52] These polls seem to suggest congressional securitizing moves were successful. Again complicating the picture, however, is a CBS News poll showing 44 percent of respondents viewing China negatively (34 percent as unfriendly, 11 percent as an enemy) while 49 percent viewed China positively (4 percent as an ally, 45 percent as friendly).[53] A May poll by the Pew Center largely supports the threat perceptions displayed in the Gallup/CNN/USA Today and NBC News polls. The poll showed an overwhelming majority of respondents (81 percent) considered the rise of China as a world power to be a major (51 percent) or minor (30 percent) threat to the United States.[54] Somewhat contradictory to the late April NBC poll, the Pew poll found that while 70 percent of respondents viewed China in a negative light, only 19 percent viewed China as an adversary while 51 percent felt China was a "serious problem."[55]

The picture painted by the polling numbers is far from clear. While there are indications that the congressional securitizing moves had an impact on public construction of the Chinese threat, these indications are not undisputed. Polls conducted at the same time asking similar questions produced significantly different results. In part, this hazy picture can be attributed to the nature of the incident, which may also account for the lack of clarity. The EP-3 collision and the ensuing negotiations over the crew release took place over a relatively short period of time, preventing strong feeling from cementing one way or another. Another factor was the congressional recess, cutting off the national platform for members seeking to make securitizing moves. Finally, the Bush administration did not present a strong desecuritizing narrative. Without the engagement narrative, the Bush administration was left with calls for patience and respect for diplomatic processes, hardly compelling discursive tools. These attributes of the situation may help explain the lack of coherence in the public opinion polling. As a consequence of this lack of coherence, while there are indications that the public responded to the securitizing move, the polling allows for only a tentative conclusion that securitizing moves had gained some traction with the public.

Conclusions

Drawing firm conclusions from this case is a much more challenging proposition than it was in the case of the Taiwan Strait Crisis. There was a significant effort

---

[51] CNN and *USA Today* 2001.
[52] NBC News and *Wall Street Journal* 2001.
[53] CBS News 2001c.
[54] Pew Research Center for the People and the Press 2001b.
[55] Pew Research Center for the People and the Press 2001a.

Collision Course: The 2001 Hainan Island EP-3 Incident

by members of Congress to securitize China. As expected, these efforts sourced the core of the threat to the nature of China's government. The desecuritizing narrative, however, does not meet with expectation. The Bush administration had jettisoned Clinton's engagement concept as a discursive tool. Its effort to desecuritize the situation relied on shared economic interests, calls for patience, and appeals to the diplomatic process. Bush did in one significant instance adopt an engagement-style argument, linking economic trade today with Chinese democracy tomorrow, but this did not represent a sustained counter-securitizing approach. Public opinion polling is not clear. While there are indications that congressional securitizing moves may have been effective, these are not definite. Thus, while the evidence in this case in general accords with the expectations generated by my analytical framework, they are not conclusive.

The situational nature of the EP-3 incident explains the difficulty in drawing conclusions. At eleven days, it took place over a relatively brief period. For over half that period, Congress was not in session, denying those who would securitize China their platform for doing so. These factors may also contribute to a more subtle security dynamic that outlasted the incident itself. This security dynamic would not be accounted for by securitization because it impacts policy below the level of public awareness.[56] For example, at the end of April, President Bush stated clearly that the United States had an obligation to defend Taiwan and would do "whatever it takes" to fulfill that commitment.[57] This represents a significant break from the prior U.S. policy of "strategic ambiguity." The security dynamic may have also played out in the missile defense debate in Congress. In May, Representative David Weldon (R-PA) argued that the United States needed missile defense as a precaution against Chinese or North Korean threats.[58] Similarly, Representative Neil Abercrombie (D-HI) linked China with North Korea and Russia in citing possible missile threats to the United States – and justifying the development of national missile defense.[59] Indeed, Senator Byron Dorgan (D-ND), in arguments against the missile defense system, emphasized that a weakness of the system was that it would not protect against Chinese or Russian missiles.[60] Echoing James Traficant's earlier comment, Representative Duncan Hunter linked China with North Korea as he specifically cited Chinese missile targeting as a cause for U.S. insecurity: "For example, China never signed that [Anti-Ballistic Missile] treaty. They are building ballistic missiles right now and aiming them at American cities and telling us, it is your obligation not to defend yourselves. North Korea now has recently tested a missile which, if we extrapolated its flight, would have enough stretch, enough distance to get to the United States, or at least parts of the United States."[61] Without belaboring

---

[56] In effect, there are no new focal points to draw public attention.
[57] Sanger 2001b.
[58] Representative David Weldon (R-PA) 2001.
[59] Representative Neil Abercrombie (D-HI) 2001.
[60] Senator Byron Dorgan (D-ND) 2001.
[61] Representative Duncan Hunter (R-CA) 2001.

the debate over missile defense, the point here is to highlight the prominence of China as a threat in that discussion. While there is no direct trace from the EP-3 incident – that is, no individuals indicated Chinese behavior during the incident justified missile defense – the prominence of China in the discussion less than a month later suggests the construction of China as a security threat may have gotten a boost from events during the first two weeks in April.

Democratic Identity and Security in Sino-American Relations

Taken together, the 1995–6 and 2001 cases strongly suggest that democratic identity plays an important role in how security policy is constructed. In both cases, the emphasis of policy makers on the lack of Chinese democracy accompanies efforts to securitize the relationship. The nondemocratic nature of China's governance, and the threat this posed to democracy, played a predominant role in the securitizing discourse. The reverse is also true, although less so in the 2001 case. When U.S. policy makers sought to desecuritize China – particularly in the 1995–6 case – they appealed to the policy of engagement, borrowing from future Chinese democratization to counter securitization of China in the present. The 2001 case proves a partial exception, with the concept of engagement playing a far less predominant role. The Bush presidential campaign had harshly criticized the outgoing Clinton administration on its engagement policy, making an appeal to the concept very difficult. Even so, during the latter stages of the incident, Bush once again appealed to engagement, suggesting the power of a counter-securitizing argument predicated on potential Chinese democracy. In both cases, there is significant evidence that the public did accept efforts to securitize China, although again this evident is weaker in the 2001 case. Regardless of the caveats, the importance of public democratic identity for security policy construction in the case of U.S.-China relations has been remarkably significant.

Unlike the relationship between the United States and India, the cases here suggest the U.S.-China relationship is a fragile one. From the American side, the lack of shared democratic identity gives securitizing actors powerful sociopolitical tools for securitizing China. While presidential administrations in the post–Cold War period have managed to fend off these securitizing moves, Chinese leaders – either by accident or by design – have terminated crises before securitization moves in the United States have achieved success. As nationalism gains strength in China, future Chinese leaders may not have the desire or ability to orchestrate crises as carefully. The potential for securitization will remain as long as China remains undemocratic, a factor that will no doubt weigh on relations between the countries. In short, my study suggests ample ground within the Sino-American relationship for the dire predictions of power transition theory to take root and bear (violent) fruit.

Conclusion

The Social Construction of Security

> Words matter. Words have consequences.
>
> –Senator Robert Byrd[1]

This book is predicated on a simple intuition: security is socially constructed and the words we use to talk about security play an important role in the construction of security. Drawing on securitization theory and social psychology, I argue that identity plays an important role in shaping what can and cannot be constructed as a security threat. By taking a social view of security, scholars can take a more holistic approach and in the process begin to systematically map how social, political, cultural, and economic conditions shape the construction of security. Mapping these boundary conditions of security can never be completed: as states and societies change, so will the conditions that constrain and facilitate securitization.

Of equal importance to the theoretical propositions are the case studies, which open a window into the fascinating process of security construction in the context of U.S. bilateral relations with India and China. Leaving aside the theoretical contributions, these cases provide important insight on two of the most significant relationships in the world today and for the foreseeable future. To summarize, democratic identity plays a critical role in efforts to construct India and China as threats as well as contravening efforts to foil securitizing moves. In the case of India, shared democracy overcame the prerogatives of the Cold War as well as strongly entrenched security concerns over the spread of nuclear weapons. With regard to China, powerful economic ties are not sufficient to keep relations with the United States out of the realm of security. Identity as a discursive tool for constructing threat is powerful indeed.

---

[1] Senator Byrd (D-WV) 2002.

Linking up the theory with the empirics, the cases demonstrate significant support for my theoretical expectations. To recap those expectations, I argue that democratic identity should play a prominent role in securitizing moves. If the external state is a democracy, political leaders will be unable to securitize it, and will often not even try. This does not mean some political actors will not make the attempt. To do so, political leaders will attempt to reconstruct the external democracy in nondemocratic terms. To counter these claims, political leaders who seek to prevent the securitization of the external democracy will emphasize shared democratic identity. Contestation should revolve around constructing the political nature of the external state because political actors are seeking to tap into the democratic prototype and the conceptions of security embodied therein. The same dynamic takes place with respect to nondemocratic external states. Those seeking to securitize the external state will emphasize that state's nondemocratic characteristics and identity, while those who seek to defuse the securitizing move will emphasize the external state's democratic characteristics.

The cases bear these expectations out. In 1971, Nixon and Kissinger clearly viewed India as a threat to U.S. interests both locally in the context of ally Pakistan's internal troubles and globally in the context of the struggle against communism, yet India remained desecuritized. As the crisis deepened, Nixon grew increasingly frosty toward India in public, eliminating references to Indian democracy that were common in the early days of the crisis before Indian involvement became significant. However, the Nixon administration's public securitizing efforts did not reflect the private security assessments of Nixon and Kissinger. In this respect, the 1971 case provides powerful support for the theory because it comes close to a "smoking gun" case – a situation where securitization (even war) would have occurred had the external state not been a democracy.[2] Nixon and Kissinger in their private conversations chafe at the restraints placed on their foreign policy-making ability by their belief that the public would not support a securitizing move against India because India was a democracy. In the 1971 case, political leaders who sought to counter Nixon's securitizing efforts relied heavily on Indian democracy in their countermove. For example, Senator Edward Kennedy repeatedly referred to the contrast between autocracy and democracy in the conflict, a distinction the Nixon administration did not make.

These dynamics would play out throughout the three Indo-American nuclear cases. In all three cases (although support from the 1974 case is not as strong as from the 1998 and 2006 cases), political leaders who sought to securitize India and its nuclear program downplayed Indian democracy, highlighted nondemocratic aspects of the Indian state, or linked India by implication with nondemocratic states that had been successfully securitized (i.e., Japan in World War II). Conversely, those who sought to keep relations with India within the realm of normal politics regularly emphasized India's status as a fellow democracy.

---

[2] I owe this point to Thomas Risse.

At no point, however, does public opinion polling suggest securitizing moves toward India were successful.

The Sino-American cases also provide significant support for my theoretical expectations. Support from the 1995–6 Taiwan Strait Crisis is particularly strong. Political leaders in Congress who sought to securitize China made China's lack of democracy a central point in their securitizing moves. Meanwhile, the Clinton administration and its allies in Congress regularly referred to the policy of engagement as a desecuritizing countermove, borrowing from future Chinese democratization to desecuritize China. The public opinion polling data suggests the securitizing moves were indeed successful – possibly prompting the U.S. deployment of two carrier battle groups to head off a more drastic response in Congress.

Support from the EP-3 incident, while significant, is not as strong as that provided by the Taiwan Strait Crisis. Congressional leaders, as in the Taiwan Strait Crisis, did make Chinese nondemocracy a prominent aspect of their securitizing moves; Congress was out of session for much of the crisis, denying a national platform to policy makers who sought to securitize China. The Bush administration clearly sought to keep the situation within the bounds of normal politics, but with a few notable exceptions did not rely on the Clinton administration's rhetorical strategy of engagement. The Bush administration's approach can be traced to President Bush's very recent and very clear repudiation of the Clinton administration's policy position regarding China, shifting the country from a "strategic partner" to a "strategic competitor." Denied the ability to borrow from future Chinese democracy, the Bush administration urged patience and respect for the authority of the executive branch to handle the situation.

Public opinion polling paints a very mixed picture, with different polls presenting contradictory results. In part, this may be due to the short duration of the incident, failing to allow opinions to congeal. That said, the evidence from the case is broadly supportive, particularly the securitizing moves of those in Congress. The support from the China cases also lines up well with other work I have done examining the securitization of Iran's nuclear program.[3]

Theoretical and Empirical Contributions

Before delving into the contributions of the approach laid out in this book, a few limiting caveats are in order. It is worth remembering that I do not claim to show why democratic states go to war. There are two points here. The first is that while securitization is necessary for war, it is not sufficient. Securitization can result in a range of policy outcomes, of which war is only one. This suggests greater work is called for on the factors that influence the policy response element of securitization.[4] The second is that the approach does not account

---

[3] Hayes 2009.
[4] Roe 2008.

for agency on the part of political actors in initiating securitizing moves. That is, while both China and Saudi Arabia are nondemocracies – a status that empowers political actors who seek to securitize them – the approach I outline here does not account for why a political leader might choose to securitize China but not Saudi Arabia. My framework addresses the constraints placed on policy options by the democratic public identity and the need for leaders in democracies to garner public support for major security policies. In the context of the democratic peace, it explains why democracies do not fight each other. In the context of nondemocracies, it outlines a powerful securitizing tool for policy makers who seek to make a securitizing move. Similarly, the approach does not speak to the day-to-day relations between democracies, where policy is made largely out of public view.

With these reservations accounted for, it is safe to move on to the contributions of this study. With perhaps the greatest appeal beyond the academy, the case studies speak to relationships of critical importance for academics, policy makers, and informed citizens. To a surprising degree, the U.S. relationship with India remains largely neglected by academics, the public, and even policy makers. Exemplary of this neglect of India in the United States is Strobe Talbott's revelation – in a chapter fittingly titled "The Lost Half Century" – that few inside the Clinton administration had any sense that India would test a nuclear weapon in 1998.[5] Indeed, according to Talbott, the State Department (including the secretary of state), the National Security Council staff, and the Department of Defense all first learned of the test from CNN. Thus, the cases here have value if for no other reason than that they contribute to a relatively small pool of empirical work on Indo-American relations. The cases go further than this, though. They demonstrate that U.S. relations with India rest on a fundamentally more stable foundation than do Sino-American relations, owing to shared identity. The identity basis for the instability of U.S. relations with China also emerges from the cases, contributing to the voluminous but typically power- or economic interests-based literature on the Sino-American dyad. In providing a social basis for understanding the security relationship, the cases provide important insights for managing the relationship in the future as well as deessentializing the role of security (e.g., blanket claims that China is or is not a threat to the United States) in the relationship.

Foremost among the theoretical contributions, this study and its findings suggest an important role for democratic identity in the processes that shape the formation of democratic security. In doing so, it provides a possible answer to the central puzzle of the democratic peace (why do democracies refrain from using force against each other). Through the categorization process, external democracies are included as part of the political self, and thus unlikely to use force to resolve conflicts. By focusing on the domestic-level mechanisms, the book also reconnects the democratic nature of the state back to the democratic

---

[5] Talbott 2004.

peace phenomenon. Through the use of securitization theory, the book sheds important insight on how security within democracies is constructed, in the process linking what happens within the state – where decisions of war and peace are made – to dynamics of international security. The research here also resituates the democratic peace within international security studies more generally. Rather than framing the phenomenon as an anomaly in international relations, my approach views it as a security (or lack thereof) regularity that may shed light on other aspects in international security. In particular, the combination of identity and securitization – with support from the cases – suggests a pathology of security within democracies. Democratic identity shapes securitizing moves with respect to democracies *and* nondemocracies. Moreover, a better understanding on how securitization processes take place within the interdemocratic context may generate insights, or at least potential avenues of exploration, on the relationship between identity and securitization in other types of states.

By taking this approach, this book addresses one of the central weaknesses of the democratic peace literature: the general neglect of the mechanisms that generate the phenomenon. As I argue elsewhere, large-N quantitative studies dominate the field.[6] While these studies have been invaluable in establishing the claim that the democratic peace phenomenon exists, by their very nature they are able to demonstrate only correlation, not causation. Not surprisingly, what effort these studies do make toward understanding and explaining the democratic peace focus on causes – norms and institutions – that can be quantified, either directly or by proxy. Yet, because the quantitative nature of the studies does not enable access to causal forces, the mechanisms behind the democratic peace remain shrouded in shadow. The end of the Cold War and the subsequent (at least rhetorical) inclusion of the democratic peace in U.S. foreign policy means the field, now more than ever, needs to develop a better understanding of the mechanisms within (and without) democracies that generate the observed peace. This study goes some way toward addressing that need.

By demonstrating that domestic dynamics play an important role in shaping international security outcomes, this monograph joins a growing chorus of academic voices calling for opening the state to inquiry and investigating the ways the domestic and the international influence each other. While parsimony is usually a virtue, it is not so when it sacrifices a realistic understanding of how and why phenomena emerge and play out. The emphasis on parsimony clearly comes from idealized models of inquiry in the physical sciences. Yet, as anyone familiar with the cutting edge of physics, chemistry, or biology can attest, parsimony is not the primary or even secondary concern. Returning to the issue of extant IR theory, it is not sufficient to understand international security primarily in terms of the distribution of military or economic capabilities isolated from the social and political contexts in which the capabilities are

---

[6] Hayes 2012.

found. The cases demonstrate – including during the Cold War when security was purportedly simpler than it is today – that approaches that do so have never been adequate for understanding international security.

The linkage of securitization with identity fuses norms (that inform democratic identity) and structure into a coherent, meaningful single approach rather than artificially separating them as many efforts at causal explanation do in the security literature (this is particularly the case in scholarship on the democratic peace). Securitization theory addresses the structure of democracies by highlighting the need of political leaders to gain public support for major security policies while democratic identity accounts for the role of democratic norms. Securitization coupled with identity also accounts for the dyadic nature of the democratic peace by linking peace to shared identity. At the same time, it explains one of the most troublesome complaints about the democratic peace – that democracies, notably the United States, have exercised the covert use of force against other (usually marginal) democracies.[7] Under this approach, we should expect political leaders disposed to use force against a fellow democracy to attempt to do so outside the public sphere. In doing so, they avoid desecuritizing narratives predicated on shared democracy, narratives that tap into the democratic identity of the public and thus thwarting the preferred security policy. Additionally, the political fallout in the event of discovery is tolerable because, in the case of marginal democracies, categorization becomes more contested and thus less likely to defuse claims of existential threat.

The advances here go beyond the traditional security literature. This book emphasizes that securitization should not be viewed as singular event, but rather as a process. In tracking public opinion polling responses over time, I also help shore up a weak point in securitization theory – the determination of audience acceptance of the securitizing move. More important, the central focus on the boundary conditions of security moves forward the conversation on the role of facilitating conditions in the securitization process, which are critical to understanding when and how securitization succeeds or fails. It also suggests security does not mean the same thing to different societies in different places and times. The research developed here indicates identity – in democracies democratic identity – is an important facilitator and limiter of securitization. By linking securitization theory and the social identity approach, this book begins to thicken securitization's analytical power by highlighting a set of tools – identity – political actors can use to make securitizing claims. It also contributes to understandings regarding ways social structures can act as boundary conditions on securitizing moves. While the Copenhagen School acknowledges constraints on securitizing moves, the approach here adds greater specificity. It also applies securitization theory in an empirical context, and in the process develops a methodology for the use of securitization theory, something to which the Copenhagen School devotes little attention. The work here also suggests greater

---

[7] Forsythe 1992; James and Mitchell 1995.

attention is called for in understanding how policy responses – a critical element of securitization – relate to the construction of threat. Several policy makers, in making their securitizing arguments, explicitly chose economic measures as the appropriate security policy response – not the use of force.

Significantly, the framework and evidence here also aids in establishing the external validity of the social identity approach. While the approach has significant laboratory verification, it's validity in the world outside the laboratory remains an open question. The cases clearly show that identity discourses and categorization are operative in the chaotic context of domestic politics and international relations, and should encourage further work on how social psychology can enrich our collective understanding of international relations. Drawing on social psychology also has the potential to improve constructivist discussions of identity by grounding them in an approach with solid experimental verification. Also beneficial is the linkage in this study between identity and speech act/discursive constructivism. Identity constructivism provides a context for understanding the constraints on the ability of individuals or groups to construct concepts like security in the political sphere. Speech act constructivism provides an avenue for measuring the influence and role of identity. Bringing these two types of constructivism together strengthens both.

The use of analogies in some of the securitizing discourse also suggests an important role for analogical reasoning outside the individual decision-maker context to which it has largely been constrained.[8] In the cases, there were several points when policy makers used analogies to communicate the construction of the external state as a threat. In the case of India, one policy maker referred to the Japanese attack on Pearl Harbor. Tiananmen Square served a similar purpose in the Chinese case. These examples suggest analogical reasoning occupies important causal niches outside the realm of elite foreign policy makers. By appealing to these historical events, securitizers seek to take advantage of analogical reasoning processes in the general public. The argument is, in effect, that the current event or situation is like the past events or situations, and likewise the current event or situation should be similarly securitized. Also intriguing is the apparent reluctance of desecuritizing actors to use analogies to make their cases, suggesting analogical reasoning – at least at the second image level – operates in ways significantly different from those theorized and observed at the individual level.

Policy Significance

The foremost policy contribution lies in the finding that the identity of the public plays an important role in the security policy process in democracies. For policy makers who seek to take advantage of the democratic peace, this finding should shift the perception of democracy away from a purely organizational

---

[8] Houghton 2001; Khong 1992.

view (legislatures, voting, separation of powers) to a more holistic conception. This reconceptualization indicates that policy makers seeking to pursue democracy promotion policies grounded in the use of force should reconsider. The role of identity suggests – if the democratic peace phenomenon is to spread – democracy needs to grow internally. This is not to say that external forces cannot play a role. Evidence that socialization into the global (liberal) culture can catalyze democratization suggests pathways for policy makers who would like to predicate policy on the democratic peace without endangering the identity dynamics that give rise to it.[9] However, Lynch's discussion of democratization in Asia also suggests how easily democratic identity can be undermined if democracy comes to be defined in opposition to, rather than in synergy with, national identity, as can be the case if it is seen as imposed from the outside rather than developed indigenously.[10]

In this context, the U.S. policy of spreading democracy through the use of force after the attacks of September 11, 2001 would be counterproductive. At the outset, it is worth asking how effective the use of force to impose democracy will be in imposing norms of nonviolent conflict resolution – critical to the operation of democracy – on the target society. More broadly, however, the U.S. policy generated a West versus Islam identity dynamic, pitting Western political systems of democracy against Islamic identities. The generation of this identity conflict does not bode well for the establishment of a democratic identity within the public because it forces an either/or identity decision – either the individual is a member of the Muslim identity/imagined community or the democratic identity/imagined community. While it is not impossible to overcome this dichotomy, creating it in the first place makes efforts to generate a public democratic identity increasingly difficult. Setting up the oppositional identity dynamic also presents the possibility that a hybrid regime that is not democratic by most measures – similar to that found in Iran – may arise as a compromise between the conflicting imagined communities. As evidenced by current controversy over Iran's nuclear program, such hybrid regimes would not further the zone of democratic peace.

The use of force, and unilateralism more generally, also has the potential to damage the existing democratic peace. Shared democratic identity blocks the existential threat argument. This is only possible because there is an expectation or assumption that the external democratic state will observe the same norms that inform the democratic identity of the home state. If the external democratic state does not observe these norms – for example, the unprovoked use of force, disregard for international institutions, and so forth – behavioral expectations

---

[9] D. Lynch 2006.
[10] Daniel Lynch attributes part of the success the PRC has had against democratization pressures to its linkage of democracy to Western domination. In Lynch's words, the PRC "rigorously micromanages the process [of global socialization] to prevent reconstitution at the level of collective identity" (2006, 13).

or assumptions are weakened. In effect, it becomes easier for securitizing actors to credibly claim the external democracy poses an existential threat.

The insight of this study on the mechanistic underpinning of the democratic peace also suggests important ways for defusing conflicts between democracies. Particularly in the case of militarized interstate disputes – where the use of force has been suggested – an emphasis on shared democracy both by desecuritizing actors within the participant states as well as by mediators may serve to undermine the arguments of securitizing actors pushing forceful responses. However, given the importance of public identity in shaping security policy, the emphasis on shared democracy must be made publicly, not in private to negotiating teams (although it may be beneficial there as well).

Moving Forward

A range of new questions arises from this study. Perhaps foremost is the question of how publics come to know social "facts" like which states are or are not democracies.[11] Certainly education and the media can be anticipated in the answer to the question. It remains, however, that the question calls for expansive inquiry. Another issue arising out of this study is the possibility that shared democratic identity may embolden democratic political actors to take more risks internationally than they might otherwise because they are confident other democracies, notably the United States, will not be able to mount successful securitizing moves.[12] Similarly, it may be possible that in jointly democratic dyads the weaker states may have more foreign policy options than they might otherwise because they are aware that force is not an (easily) viable option for political leaders in the stronger state.

The research can and should be extended to cases of transition. In doing so, the approach outlined here, or a derivative, may help explain outcomes like rivalry termination (which usually accompanies a political transition by one or both states). Another research opportunity can be found in testing the limits of shared identity. This can be done two ways. The first is to look at cases where one (or perhaps both) of the states are either recently or weakly democratic, that is, at the margins of the democratic community. How do mature democracies interact with these states in a security context? How do recently or weakly democratic states interact with each other in a security context? A different approach to this same question highlights states (possibly, but not necessarily jointly democratic) with strong alternative identities (i.e., religious, ethnic, class, etc.). The relationship between India and Pakistan is one such case, but there are others. An understanding of identity dynamics in these cases, particularly how these alternative identities interact with democratic identity, would be incredibly useful for understanding how securitization dynamics develop.

---

[11] I owe this point to Charli Carpenter.
[12] I owe this idea to Michael Doyle.

References

ABC News and Washington Post. 1996a. ABC. ABC News/*Washington Post* Poll, March 14–17, 1996: As You May Know, China Has Been Making Threatening Moves toward Taiwan, Which It Sees as a Breakaway Province, and the United States Has Increased Its Naval Presence in That Part of the World. Do You Approve or Disapprove of the Way (Bill) Clinton Is Handling the Situation Involving China and Taiwan?: The Roper Center for Public Opinion Research, University of Connecticut.
    1996b. ABC News/*Washington Post* Poll, March 14–17, 1996: Do You Think America's Vital Interests Are at Stake in the Situation Involving China and Taiwan?: The Roper Center for Public Opinion Research, University of Connecticut.
    2001a. ABC News/*Washington Post* Poll, April 5, 2001: As You May Know, a U.S. (United States) Spy Plane and a Chinese Military Aircraft Collided Last Saturday (March 31, 2001) and the U.S. Plane Had to Land on a Chinese Island, Where the Plane and Crew Remain. Do You Think This Incident Poses a Threat to US.-China Relations, or Not? (If Yes, Threat, Ask:) Would You Describe It as a Serious Threat or Not Serious?: The Roper Center for Public Opinion Research, University of Connecticut.
    2001b. ABC News/*Washington Post* Poll, April 5, 2001: In Order to Try to Recover the Plane (a U.S. Spy Plane and a Chinese Military Aircraft Collided Last Saturday (March 31, 2001) and the U.S. Plane Had to Land on a Chinese Island, Where the Plane and Crew Remain) and Crew, Do You Think the United States Should or Should Not…Move to Restrict U.S. (United States) Trade with China If the Crew and Plane Are Not Returned?: The Roper Center for Public Opinion Research, University of Connecticut.
    2001c. ABC News/*Washington Post* Poll, April 5, 2001: In Terms of Its Overall Relations with the United States, Do You Think of China as a Friendly Country or an Unfriendly Country?: The Roper Center for Public Opinion Research, University of Connecticut.
Abrams, Dominic, and Michael A. Hogg. 1990. Social Identification, Self-Categorization and Social Influence. *European Review of Social Psychology* 1: 195–228.

Acharya, Amitav. 2001. *Constructing a Security Community in Southeast Asia: ASEAN and the Problem of Regional Order, Politics in Asia Series*. London, New York: Routledge.
Adhikari, Gautham. 2004. India and America: Estranged No More. *Current History* 103(671): 158–65.
Adler, Emanuel. 1997. Seizing the Middle Ground: Constructivism in World Politics. *European Journal of International Relations* 3(3): 319–63.
Adler, Emanuel, and Michael N. Barnett. 1998. Security Communities. *Cambridge Studies in International Relations No. 62*: xiii, 462.
Ahlberg, Kristin L. 2007. "Machiavelli with a Heart": The Johnson Administration's Food for Peace Program in India, 1965–1966. *Diplomatic History* 31(4): 665–701.
Alker, Hayward R. 2006. On Securitization Politics as Contexted Texts and Talk. *Journal of International Relations and Development* 9(1): 70–80.
Anderson, Benedict. 1991. *Imagined Communities: Reflections on the Origin and Spread of Nationalism*. Revised ed. London, New York: Verso.
Aradau, Claudia. 2004. Security and the Democratic Scene: Desecuritization and Emancipation. *Journal of International Relations and Development* 7(4): 388–413.
Asal, Victor, and Kyle Beardsley. 2007. Proliferation and International Crisis Behavior. *Journal of Peace Research* 44(2): 139–55.
Associated Press. 1996a. Perry Voices Concern for Taiwan. In *New York Times*.
  1996b. World News Briefs; U.S. Warship Cruises China-Taiwan Passage. In *New York Times*.
Babst, D. V. 1972. A Force for Peace. *Industrial Research* 14(4): 55–8.
Bacon, Kenneth H. 1995a. DOD News Briefing: Mr. Kenneth H. Bacon, Atsd (Pa); August 1, 1995. Available from http://www.defenselink.mil/transcripts/transcript.aspx?transcriptid=156. (Accessed March 12, 2009).
  1995b. DOD News Briefing: Mr. Kenneth H. Bacon, Atsd (Pa); August 15, 1995. Available from http://www.defenselink.mil/transcripts/transcript.aspx?transcriptid=163. (Accessed March 12, 2009).
Baker, Peter. 2006. Bush Signs India Nuclear Law. In *Washington Post*.
Balzacq, Thierry. 2005. The Three Faces of Securitization: Political Agency, Audience and Context. *European Journal of International Relations* 11(2): 171–201.
Banerjee, Sanjoy. 1987. Explaining the American "Tilt" in the 1971 Bangladesh Crisis: A Late Dependency Approach. *International Studies Quarterly* 31(2): 201–16.
Barnett, Jon. 2003. Security and Climate Change. *Global Environmental Change* 13(1): 7–17.
BBC News. 1999. US Eases Sanctions on India. In *BBC News*.
Behnke, Andreas. 2006. No Way Out: Desecuritization, Emancipation and the Eternal Return of the Political – A Reply to Aradau. *Journal of International Relations and Development* 9(1): 62–9.
Bennet, James. 1998. Clinton Calls Tests a "Terrible Mistake" and Announces Sanctions against India. In *New York Times*, A13.
Berger, Samuel. 1994. Press Briefing by Deputy National Security Advisor Sandy Berger, Secretary of Treasury Lloyd Bentsen, Secretary of Commerce Ron Brown, U.S. Trade Representative Mickey Kantor, and Under Secretary of State for Economic

Affairs Joan Spero. In *The American Presidency Project*: The American Presidency Project.
Berger, Thomas U. 2000. Set for Stability? Prospects for Conflict and Cooperation in East Asia. *Review of International Studies* 26(03): 405–28.
——— 1996. Norms, Identity, and National Security in Germany and Japan. In *The Culture of National Security: Norms and Identity in World Politics*, edited by Peter J. Katzenstein, 317–56. New York: Columbia University Press.
——— 1998. *Cultures of Antimilitarism: National Security in Germany and Japan*. Baltimore, MD: Johns Hopkins University Press.
Bernstein, Richard, and Ross Munro. 1997a. *The Coming Conflict with China*. 1st ed. New York: A.A. Knopf: Distributed by Random House.
——— 1997b. China I: The Coming Conflict with America. *Foreign Affairs* 76(2): 18(15).
Bertsch, Gary K., Seema Gahlaut, and Anupam Srivastava. 1999. *Engaging India: U.S. Strategic Relations with the World's Largest Democracy*. New York: Routledge.
Bhaskar, Roy. 1975. *A Realist Theory of Science*. Leeds: Leeds Books.
Blair, Dennis C., and David B. Bonfili. 2006. The April 2001 EP-3 Incident: The U.S. Point of View. In *Managing Sino-American Crises: Case Studies and Analysis*, edited by Michael D. Swaine, Tuosheng Zhang, and Danielle F. S. Cohen, 377–90. Washington, DC, Baltimore, MD: Carnegie Endowment for International Peace, Hopkins Fulfillment Service distributor.
Blood, Archer K. 1971a. *Selective Genocide*. edited by United States Department of State: Office of the Historian, United States Department of State.
——— 1971b. *Specific Areas of Dissent with Current U.S. Policy toward East Pakistan*. edited by United States Department of State: Office of the Historian, United States Department of State.
Bollen, Kenneth A. 1980. Issues in the Comparative Measurement of Political Democracy. *American Sociological Review* 45(3): 370–90.
Booth, Ken. 1991. Security and Emancipation. *Review of International Studies* 17(4): 313–26.
——— 2005. *Critical Security Studies and World Politics*. Boulder, CO: Lynne Rienner.
——— 2007. *Theory of World Security*. Cambridge: Cambridge University Press.
Boucher, Richard A. 2006. The U.S.-India Friendship: Where We Were and Where We're Going. Available from http://www.state.gov/p/sca/rls/rm/2006/64230.htm. (Accessed May 22, 2006).
Brady, Henry E., David Collier, and Jason Seawright. 2004. Refocusing the Discussion of Methodology. In *Rethinking Social Inquiry: Diverse Tools, Shared Standards*, edited by Henry E. Brady and David Collier, 3–20. Lanham, MD: Rowman & Littlefield.
Brewer, M. B. 1999. The Psychology of Prejudice: Ingroup Love and Outgroup Hate? *Journal of Social Issues* 55(3): 429–44.
Broder, John M. 2009. Climate Change Seen as Threat to U.S. Security. In *New York Times*. New York: New York Times.
Brown, Harold, Joseph W. Prueher, and Adam Segal. 2003. *Chinese Military Power: Report of an Independent Task Force Sponsored by the Council on Foreign Relations Maurice R. Greenberg Center for Geostrategic Studies*. Washington, DC: Council on Foreign Relations.

Brown, James P. 1971. India's Desperate Mission. In *New York Times*.
Brown, Rupert. 2000. Social Identity Theory: Past Achievements, Current Problems and Future Challenges. *European Journal of Social Psychology* 30(6): 745–78.
Brzezinski, Zbigniew. 1998. Disruption without Disintegration. *Journal of Democracy* 9(1): 4–5.
Bueno de Mesquita, Bruce, James D. Morrow, Randolph M. Siverson, and Alastair Smith. 1999. An Institutional Explanation of the Democratic Peace. *American Political Science Review* 93(4): 791–807.
———. 2004. Testing Novel Implications from the Selectorate Theory of War. *World Politics* 56(3): 363–88.
Bumiller, Elisabeth, and Somini Sengupta. 2006. Bush and India Reach Pact That Allows Nuclear Sales. In *New York Times*.
Bunge, Mario. 1996. *Finding Philosophy in Social Science*. New Haven, CT: Yale University Press.
———. 2000. Systemism: The Alternative to Individualism and Holism. *Journal of Socio-Economics* 29(2): 147–57.
———. 2004. How Does It Work? The Search for Explanatory Mechanisms. *Philosophy of the Social Sciences* 34(2): 182–210.
Burns, John F. 1998. Fear of Arms Race. In *New York Times*, A1.
Burns, Nicholas. 1995a. U.S. Department of State 95/05/24 Daily Press Briefing. Available from http://dosfan.lib.uic.edu/ERC/briefing/daily_briefings/1995/9505/950524db.html. (Accessed March 11, 2009).
———. 1995b. U.S. Department of State 95/05/26 Daily Press Briefing. Available from http://dosfan.lib.uic.edu/ERC/briefing/daily_briefings/1995/9505/950526db.html. (Accessed March 11, 2009).
———. 1995c. U.S. Department of State 95/07/06 Daily Press Briefing. Available from http://dosfan.lib.uic.edu/ERC/briefing/daily_briefings/1995/9507/950706db.html. (Accessed March 13, 2009).
———. 1995d. U.S. Department of State 95/07/24 Daily Press Briefing. Available from http://dosfan.lib.uic.edu/ERC/briefing/daily_briefings/1995/9507/950724db.html. (Accessed March 13, 2009).
———. 1995e. U.S. Department of State 95/11/08 Daily Press Briefing. Available from http://dosfan.lib.uic.edu/ERC/briefing/daily_briefings/1995/9511/951108db.html. (Accessed March 13, 2009).
———. 1996a. U.S. Department of State 96/03/05 Daily Press Briefing. Available from http://dosfan.lib.uic.edu/ERC/briefing/daily_briefings/1996/9603/960305db.html. (Accessed March 14, 2009).
———. 1996b. U.S. Department of State 96/03/07 Daily Press Briefing. Available from http://dosfan.lib.uic.edu/ERC/briefing/daily_briefings/1996/9603/960307db.html. (Accessed March 14, 2009).
———. 1996c. U.S. Department of State 96/03/11 Daily Press Briefing. Available from http://dosfan.lib.uic.edu/ERC/briefing/daily_briefings/1996/9603/960308db.html. (Accessed March 14, 2009).
———. 2006. Ongoing Efforts to Implement the U.S.-India Civil Nuclear Agreement. Available from http://www.state.gov/r/pa/prs/ps/2006/63270.htm. (Accessed May 22, 2006).
———. 2007. America's Strategic Opportunity with India: The New U.S.-India Partnership. *Foreign Affairs* 86(6): 131.

Bush, George W. 2000. In Bush's Words: "Join Together in Making China a Normal Trading Partner." In *New York Times*.
  2001a. Remarks by the President at American Society of Newspaper Editors Annual Convention. Available from http://georgewbush-whitehouse.archives.gov/news/releases/2001/04/20010405-5.html. (Accessed March 22, 2009).
  2001b. Remarks Calling on China to Return the United States Military Crew and Surveillance Aircraft. In *The American Presidency Project*.
  2001c. Remarks Following Discussions with King Abdullah Ii of Jordan and an Exchange with Reporters. In *The American Presidency Project*.
  2001d. Remarks on Presenting the Malcolm Baldrige National Quality Awards in Crystal City, Virginia. In *The American Presidency Project*.
  2001e. Remarks Prior to a Cabinet Meeting and an Exchange with Reporters. In *The American Presidency Project*.
  2003. President Bush Discusses Freedom in Iraq and Middle East. Available from http://georgewbush-whitehouse.archives.gov/news/releases/2003/11/20031106-2.html (Accessed May 21, 2006).
  2005. President, Prime Minister of India Discuss Freedom and Democracy. Available from http://www.whitehouse.gov/news/releases/2005/07/20050718-1.html. (Accessed May 21, 2006).
  2006. Interview of the President by Doordarshan, India. Available from http://www.whitehouse.gov/news/releases/2006/02/20060224-5.html. (Accessed May 21, 2006).
Bush, George W., and Manmohan Singh. 2005. Joint Statement between President George W. Bush and Prime Minister Manmohan Singh. Available from http://www.whitehouse.gov/news/releases/2005/07/20050718-6.html. (Accessed August 1, 2008).
Buzan, Barry, and Lene Hansen. 2009. *The Evolution of International Security Studies*. Cambridge, New York: Cambridge University Press.
Buzan, Barry, and Ole Wæver. 1997. Slippery? Contradictory? Sociologically Untenable? The Copenhagen School Replies. *Review of International Studies* 23(02): 241–50.
  2003. *Regions and Powers: The Structure of International Security, Cambridge Studies in International Relations 91*. Cambridge: Cambridge University Press.
Buzan, Barry, Ole Wæver, and Jaap de Wilde. 1998. *Security: A New Framework for Analysis*. Boulder, CO: Lynne Rienner.
Callamari, Peter, and Derek Reveron. 2003. China's Use of Perception Management. *International Journal of Intelligence and CounterIntelligence* 16(1): 1–15.
Cameron, James E. 2004. A Three-Factor Model of Social Identity. *Self and Identity* 3(3): 239–62.
Campbell, David. 1998. *Writing Security: United States Foreign Policy and the Politics of Identity*. xiii, 289 p. 23 cm. Minneapolis: University of Minnesota Press.
Carpenter, Ted Galen. 2005. *America's Coming War with China: A Collision Course over Taiwan*. New York: Palgrave Macmillan.
Carter, Ashton B. 2006. America's New Strategic Partner. *Foreign Affairs* 85(4): 33.
Carter, Jimmy. 1978a. Diplomatic Relations between the United States and the People's Republic of China: Address to the Nation (December 15, 1978). In *Public Papers of the Presidents of the United States: Jimmy Carter, 1978*, 2264–6. Washington, DC: Office of the Federal Register National Archives and Records Administration: United States Government Printing Office.

1978b. Diplomatic Relations between the United States and the People's Republic of China: United States Statement (December 15, 1978). In *Public Papers of the Presidents of the United States: Jimmy Carter, 1978*, 2266. Washington, DC: Office of the Federal Register National Archives and Records Administration: United States Government Printing Office.

CBS News. 2001a. CBS News Poll, April 4–5, 2001: Are Your Feelings toward China Generally Favorable, Generally Unfavorable, or Neutral?: The Roper Center for Public Opinion Research, University of Connecticut.

2001b. CBS News Poll, April 4–5, 2001: Do You Consider China an Ally of the United States, Friendly but Not an Ally, Unfriendly, or an Enemy of the United States?: The Roper Center for Public Opinion Research, University of Connecticut.

2001c. CBS News Poll, April 23–5, 2001: Do You Consider China an Ally of the United States, Friendly but Not an Ally, Unfriendly, or an Enemy of the United States?: The Roper Center for Public Opinion Research, University of Connecticut.

Cederman, Lars-Erik, and Christopher Daase. 2003. Endogenizing Corporate Identities: The Next Step in Constructivist IR Theory. *European Journal of International Relations* 9(1): 5–35.

Chadda, Maya. 1986. India and the United States: Why Detente Won't Happen. *Asian Survey* 26(10): 1118–36.

Chan, Steve. 2002. Human Rights in China and the United States: Competing Visions and Discrepant Performances. *Human Rights Quarterly* 24(4): 1035–53.

Checkel, Jeffrey T. 1998. The Constructivist Turn in International Relations Theory. *World Politics* 50(2): 324–48.

1999. Norms, Institutions, and National Identity in Contemporary Europe. *International Studies Quarterly* 43(1): 84–114.

2006. Tracing Causal Mechanisms. *International Studies Review* 8(2): 362–70.

Chen, Jie, and Yang Zhong. 2008. Why Do People Vote in Semicompetitive Elections in China? *The Journal of Politics* 64(01): 178–97.

Cheng, Maria. 2002. The Standoff – What Is Unsaid? A Pragmatic Analysis of the Conditional Marker "If." *Discourse Society* 13(3): 309–17.

Childs, Marquis. 1974. The Growing Membership in the Nuclear Club. In *The Washington Post*, A23.

Chilton, Paul A. 2004. *Analysing Political Discourse: Theory and Practice*. London, New York: Routledge.

Choi, Seung-Whan. 2011. Re-Evaluating Capitalist and Democratic Peace Models. *International Studies Quarterly* 54(3).

Choi, Seung-Whan, and Patrick James. 2005. *Civil-Military Dynamics, Democracy, and International Conflict: A New Quest for International Peace*. 1st ed. Advances in Foreign Policy Analysis. New York: Palgrave Macmillan.

Christensen, Thomas J. 1996. *Useful Adversaries: Grand Strategy, Domestic Mobilization, and Sino-American Conflict, 1947–1958, Princeton Studies in International History and Politics*. Princeton, NJ: Chichester: Princeton University Press.

2001. Posing Problems without Catching Up: China's Rise and Challenges for U.S. Security Policy. *International Security* 25(4): 5–40.

2006. Fostering Stability or Creating a Monster? The Rise of China and U.S. Policy toward East Asia. *International Security* 31(1): 81–126.

Christopher, Warren. 1995. "U.S. National Interest in the Asia-Pacific Region." Address before the National Press Club, Washington, DC, July 28, 1995. Available from http://www.state.gov/www/regions/eap/950728.html. (Accessed March 13, 2009).

References

Clark, David H. 2003. Can Strategic Interaction Divert Diversionary Behavior? A Model of U.S. Conflict Propensity. *Journal of Politics* 65(4): 1013–39.

Clinton, William J. 1994a. 1994 State of the Union Address.

  1994b. The President's News Conference. In *The American Presidency Project*. The American Presidency Project.

  1998. Remarks by the President on U.S.-China Relations in the 21st Century. Available from http://clinton2.nara.gov/WH/New/html/19980611-18132.html. (Accessed June 1, 2006).

  1999a. Interview with Prime Minister Tony Blair of the United Kingdom by John King of the Cable News Network in Weston-under-Lizard, May 16, 1998. In *Public Papers of the Presidents of the United States: William J. Clinton, 1998*. Washington, DC: Office of the Federal Register National Archives and Records Administration: United States Government Printing Office.

  1999b. The President's Radio Address, May 16, 1998. In *Public Papers of the Presidents of the United States: William J. Clinton, 1998*. Washington, DC: Office of the Federal Register National Archives and Records Administration: United States Government Printing Office.

  1999c. Remarks Following Discussions with Chancellor Helmut Kohl of Germany and an Exchange with Reporters in Potsdam, Germany, May 13, 1998. In *Public Papers of the Presidents of the United States: William J. Clinton, 1998*. Washington, DC: Office of the Federal Register National Archives and Records Administration: United States Government Printing Office.

  2000. Letter to Congressional Leaders on the Continuation of the National Emergency Regarding Weapons of Mass Destruction, November 12, 1998. In *Public Papers of the Presidents of the United States: William J. Clinton, 1998*. Washington, DC: Office of the Federal Register National Archives and Records Administration: United States Government Printing Office.

CNA Corporation. 2007. National Security and the Threat of Climate Change – Report. Available from http://securityandclimate.cna.org/report/. (Accessed February 8, 2010).

CNN. 2001a. Disassembled U.S. Plane Could Head Home in Early July. In *CNN*.

  2001b. House Members Say Standoff Makes Arms Sales to Taiwan More Likely. In *CNN*.

CNN and USA Today. 2001. Gallup/CNN/*USA Today* Poll, April 20–2, 2001: For Each of the Following Countries, Please Say Whether You Consider It an Ally of the United States, Friendly, but Not an Ally, Unfriendly, or an Enemy of the United States. How About…China?:. The Roper Center for Public Opinion Research, University of Connecticut.

CNN, USA Today, and Gallup Organization. 1998. Gallup/CNN/*USA Today* Poll; June 5–7, 1998: I'm Going to Read a List of Countries, Some of Which Have and Some of Which Do Not Have Nuclear Weapons. As I Read Each One, Please Tell Me Whether You Think Possession of Nuclear Weapons by That Country Would Pose a Serious Threat to the United States or Not… India. The Roper Center for Public Opinion Research, University of Connecticut.

Collier, David, Jason Seawright, and Gerardo Munck. 2004. The Quest for Standards: King, Keohane, and Verba's *Designing Social Inquiry*. In *Rethinking Social Inquiry: Diverse Tools, Shared Standards*, edited by Henry E. Brady and David Collier, 21–50. Lanham, MD: Rowman & Littlefield.

Collingwood, R. G., and Jan Van der Dussen. 1994. *The Idea of History*. Rev. ed. Oxford: Oxford University Press.

Collins, Alan. 2005. Securitization, Frankenstein's Monster and Malaysian Education. *The Pacific Review* 18(4): 567–88.

Copeland, Dale C. 1996. Economic Interdependence and War: A Theory of Trade Expectations. *International Security* 20(4): 5–41.

Cortell, Andrew P., and James W. Davis, Jr. 1996. How Do International Institutions Matter? The Domestic Impact of International Rules and Norms. *International Studies Quarterly* 40(4): 451–78.

⎯⎯⎯. 2000. Understanding the Domestic Impact of International Norms: A Research Agenda. *International Studies Review* 2(1): 65–87.

Cowan, Edward. 1974. Blast by India Prompts High-Level U.S. Review of Aid. In *New York Times*, A2.

Crocker, Jennifer, and Riia Luhtanen. 1990. Collective Self-Esteem and Ingroup Bias. *Journal of Personality and Social Psychology* 58(1): 60–7.

Danilovic, Vesna, and Joe Clare. 2007. The Kantian Liberal Peace (Revisited). *American Journal of Political Science* 51(2): 397–414.

Davies, Glyn. 1996. U.S. Department of State 96/03/18 Daily Press Briefing. Available from http://dosfan.lib.uic.edu/ERC/briefing/daily_briefings/1996/9603/960318db.html. (Accessed March 14, 2009).

de Soysa, Indra, John R. Oneal, and Yong-Hee Park. 1997. Testing Power-Transition Theory Using Alternative Measures of National Capabilities. *Journal of Conflict Resolution* 41(4): 509–28.

Dessler, David. 1989. What's at Stake in the Agent-Structure Debate? *International Organization* 43(03): 441–73.

Dixon, William J., and Paul D. Senese. 2002. Democracy, Disputes, and Negotiated Settlements. *Journal of Conflict Resolution* 46(4): 547–71.

diZerega, Gus. 1995. Democracies and Peace: The Self-Organizing Foundation for the Democratic Peace. *The Review of Politics* 57(2): 279–308.

Donnelly, Eric. 2004. The United States-China EP-3 Incident: Legality and Realpolitik. *Journal of Conflict and Security Law* 9(1): 25–42.

Downs, Anthony. 1957. *An Economic Theory of Democracy*. New York: Harper.

Doyle, Arthur Conan, and Christopher Roden. 1993. *The Memoirs of Sherlock Holmes*. Oxford: Oxford University Press.

Dufton, Emily. 2012. The War on Drugs: How President Nixon Tied Addiction to Crime. In *The Atlantic*.

Dye, Lee. 1974. Plants Can Provide Weapons: Atoms for Peace May Supply Atoms for War, Experts Fear. In *Los Angeles Times*, A1.

Ebadi, Shirin. 2006. Online Newshour: Conversation | Ebadi Discusses U.S.-Iran Tension. Available from http://www.pbs.org/newshour/bb/politics/jan-june06/ebadi_05-05.html. (Accessed May 20, 2006).

Efird, Brian, Jacek Kugler, and Gaspare Genna. 2003. From War to Integration: Generalizing Power Transition Theory. *International Interactions* 29(4): 293–313.

Elbe, Stefan. 2006. Should HIV/AIDS Be Securitized? The Ethical Dilemmas of Linking HIV/AIDS and Security. *International Studies Quarterly* 50(1): 119–44.

Elman, Colin. 1996. Horses for Courses: Why Not Neorealist Theories of Foreign Policy? *Security Studies* 6(1): 7–53.

References

Ember, C. R., M. Ember, and B. Russett. 1992. Peace between Participatory Polities – A Cross-Cultural Test of the Democracies Rarely Fight Each Other Hypothesis. *World Politics* 44(4): 573–99.

Emmers, Ralf. 2003. ASEAN and the Securitization of Transnational Crime in Southeast Asia. *The Pacific Review* 16(3): 419–38.

Entman, Robert M. 2003. Cascading Activation: Contesting the White House's Frame after 9/11. *Political Communication* 20(4): 415–32.

2004. *Projections of Power: Framing News, Public Opinion, and U.S. Foreign Policy, Studies in Communication, Media, and Public Opinion*. Chicago, IL, London: University of Chicago Press.

Faison, Seth. 1995. Taiwan Reports Nearby Firing of 4 Test Missiles by China. In *New York Times*.

1996a. Tension in Taiwan: The Polemics; China Denounces U.S. "Interference" in Dispute with Taiwan. In *New York Times*.

1996b. U.S. Warship Pays a Visit to Shanghai. In *New York Times*.

Farnsworth, Clyde H. 1974. 1.4-Billion Pledged to India by West. In *New York Times*, A39.

Fleischer, Ari. 2001. Press Briefing by Ari Fleischer. Available from http://georgewbush-whitehouse.archives.gov/news/briefings/20010410.html. (Accessed March 24, 2009).

Floyd, Rita. 2007. Towards a Consequentialist Evaluation of Security: Bringing Together the Copenhagen and the Welsh Schools of Security Studies. *Review of International Studies* 33(02): 327–50.

Fordham, Benjamin O. 2005. Strategic Conflict Avoidance and the Diversionary Use of Force. *Journal of Politics* 67(1): 132–53.

Forsythe, D. P. 1992. Democracy, War, and Covert Action. *Journal of Peace Research* 29(4): 385–95.

Freeman, Chas W., Jr. 1996. Sino-American Relations: Back to Basics. *Foreign Policy* (104): 3–17.

Friedberg, Aaron L. 1993. Ripe for Rivalry: Prospects for Peace in a Multipolar Asia. *International Security* 18(3): 5–33.

2005. The Future of U.S.-China Relations: Is Conflict Inevitable? *International Security* 30(2): 7–45.

Friedman, Edward. 1997. Chinese Nationalism, Taiwan Autonomy and the Prospects of a Larger War. *Journal of Contemporary China* 6(14): 5–32.

Friedman, Thomas L. 1992. China Warns U.S. On Taiwan Jet Deal. In *New York Times*.

Frijda, Nico H., and Batja Mesquita. 2000. Beliefs through Emotions. In *Emotions and Beliefs: How Feelings Influence Thoughts*, edited by Nico H. Frijda, A. S. R. Manstead, and Sacha Bem, 45–77. Cambridge: Cambridge University Press.

Gaddis, John Lewis. 1986. The Long Peace: Elements of Stability in the Postwar International System. *International Security* 10(4): 99–142.

Gajwani, B. W. 1971. Civil War in Pakistan. In *New York Times*.

Gallucci, Robert L. 1994. Non-Proliferation and National Security. *Arms Control Today* 24(3): 13–16.

Gallup Organization. 1971. Hopes and Fears; April 2–5, 1971: In the Event a Nation Is Attacked by Communist Backed Forces There Are Several Things the U.S. Can

Do About It. As I Read the Name of Each Country, Tell Me What Action You Would Want to See Us Take If That Nation Is Actually Attacked – Send American Troops or Send Military Supplies but Not Send American Troops, or Refuse to Get Involved at All. How About India, What Action Would You Want to See Us Take If India Is Attacked?: The Roper Center for Public Opinion Research, University of Connecticut.

1973. Gallup Poll (Aipo), September 21–4, 1973: If Another World War Were to Break out, Do You Think Nuclear Bombs and Weapons Are Likely to Be Used, or Not?: The Roper Center for Public Opinion Research, University of Connecticut.

1995. Gallup Poll, August 11–14, 1995: Just Your Opinion, How Far Up or Down on a Ten Point Scale Would You Rate Each of the Following Nations in Terms of the Individual Freedom Granted to Its Citizens. A Ten Means the Highest Level of Personal Freedom and a One, the Lowest. You Can Choose Any Number from One to Ten…China: The Roper Center for Public Opinion Research, University of Connecticut.

1998a. Gallup Poll, June 5–7, 1998: I'm Going to Read a List of Countries, Some of Which Have and Some of Which Do Not Have Nuclear Weapons. As I Read Each One, Please Tell Me Whether You Think Possession of Nuclear Weapons by That Country Would Pose a Serious Threat to World Peace, or Not… India: The Roper Center for Public Opinion Research, University of Connecticut.

1998b. Gallup Poll, June 5–7, 1998: I'm Going to Read a List of Countries, Some of Which Have and Some of Which Do Not Have Nuclear Weapons. As I Read Each One, Please Tell Me Whether You Think Possession of Nuclear Weapons by That Country Would Pose a Serious Threat to World Peace, or Not…(Iraq, Iran, Pakistan, China): The Roper Center for Public Opinion Research, University of Connecticut.

1998c. Gallup Poll, June 5–7, 1998: Do You Think It Was a Good Thing or a Bad Thing That the Atomic Bomb Was Developed?: The Roper Center for Public Opinion Research, University of Connecticut.

2001a. Gallup Poll, April 6–8, 2001: As You May Know, a U.S. (United States) Navy Plane Was Involved in a Mid-Air Collision with a Chinese Plane and Had to Land in Chinese Territory. The Plane and Its 24 Crew Members Are Currently Being Held by China…Do You Consider the 24 U.S. Crew Members to Be Hostages of China or Has the Situation Not yet Reached the Point Where They Can Be Described as Hostages?: The Roper Center for Public Opinion Research, University of Connecticut.

2001b. Gallup Poll, February 1–4, 2001: I'd Like Your Overall Opinion of Some Foreign Countries. For Each One We'd Like You to Indicate Your Opinion on a Scale. If You Have a Favorable Opinion of That Country, Name a Number between Plus One and Plus Five – the Higher the Number, the More Favorable Your Opinion – with Plus Five Being the Most Favorable. If You Have an Unfavorable Opinion of That Country, Name a Number between Minus One and Minus Five – the Higher the Number the More Unfavorable Your Opinion – with Minus Five Being the Most Unfavorable. What Is Your Opinion Of…China…On This Scale?: The Roper Center for Public Opinion Research, University of Connecticut.

2001c. Gallup Poll, February 1–4, 2001: Is Your Overall Opinion Of…China…Very Favorable, Mostly Favorable, Mostly Unfavorable, or Very Unfavorable?: The Roper Center for Public Opinion Research, University of Connecticut.

2002. Gallup Poll, February 4–6, 2002: Is Your Overall Opinion Of…China…Very Favorable, Mostly Favorable, Mostly Unfavorable, or Very Unfavorable?: The Roper Center for Public Opinion Research, University of Connecticut.
Gallup Organization, CNN, and USA Today. 1995. Gallup/CNN/*USA Today* Poll, November 6–8, 1995: Which Country Do You Think Poses the Biggest Military Threat to Japan: China or North Korea?: The Roper Center for Public Opinion Research, University of Connecticut.
———. 1996a. Gallup/CNN/*USA Today* Poll, January 12–15, 1996: I'd Like You to Rate China on a Scale. If You Have a Favorable Opinion of China, Name a Number between Plus One and Plus Five – the Higher the Number, the More Favorable Your Opinion. If You Have an Unfavorable Opinion of China, Name a Number between Minus One and Minus Five – the Higher the Number the More Unfavorable Your Opinion: The Roper Center for Public Opinion Research, University of Connecticut.
———. 1996b. Gallup/CNN/*USA Today* Poll, March 8–10, 1996: I'd Like Your Overall Opinion of Some Foreign Countries. For Each One Please Indicate Your Opinion on a Scale. If You Have a Favorable Opinion of That Country, Name a Number between Plus One and Plus Five – the Higher the Number, the More Favorable Your Opinion. If You Have an Unfavorable Opinion of That Country, Name a Number between Minus One and Minus Five – the Higher the Number the More Unfavorable Your Opinion with Minus Five Being the Most Unfavorable. What Is Your Opinion Of…China…On This Scale?: The Roper Center for Public Opinion Research, University of Connecticut.
———. 1996c. Gallup/CNN/*USA Today* Poll, March 8–10, 1996: I'd Like Your Overall Opinion of Some Foreign Countries. For Each One Please Indicate Your Opinion on a Scale. If You Have a Favorable Opinion of That Country, Name a Number between Plus One and Plus Five – the Higher the Number, the More Favorable Your Opinion. If You Have an Unfavorable Opinion of That Country, Name a Number between Minus One and Minus Five – the Higher the Number the More Unfavorable Your Opinion with Minus Five Being the Most Unfavorable. What Is Your Opinion Of…Taiwan…On This Scale?: The Roper Center for Public Opinion Research, University of Connecticut.
———. 1996d. Gallup/CNN/*USA Today* Poll, March 15–17, 1996: If China Were to Attack Taiwan, Do You Think the United States Should Use Its Military Forces to Help Defend Taiwan, or Not?: The Roper Center for Public Opinion Research, University of Connecticut.
Ganguly, Sumit. 1999. India's Pathway to Pokhran II: The Prospects and Sources of New Delhi's Nuclear Weapons Program. *International Security* 23(4): 148–77.
Ganguly, Sumit, and Dinshaw Mistry. 2006. The Case for the U.S.-India Nuclear Agreement. *World Policy Journal* 23(2): 11–19.
Gartzke, Erik, and Quan Li. 2003. War, Peace, and the Invisible Hand: Positive Political Externalities of Economic Globalization. *International Studies Quarterly* 47(4): 561–86.
Garver, John W. 1997. *Face Off: China, the United States, and Taiwan's Democratization*. Seattle: University of Washington Press.
Gelb, Leslie H. 1974. Kissinger Reassures Soviets of Continued Mideast Role. In *New York Times*.
Geller, Daniel S. 1990. Nuclear Weapons, Deterrence, and Crisis Escalation. *The Journal of Conflict Resolution* 34(2): 291–310.

Gelpi, Christopher. 1997. Democratic Diversions: Governmental Structure and the Externalization of Domestic Conflict. *Journal of Conflict Resolution* 41(2): 255–82.
Giddens, Anthony. 1984. *The Constitution of Society: Outline of the Theory of Structuration*. Berkeley: University of California Press.
Gilboy, George, and Eric Heginbotham. 2001. China's Coming Transformation. *Foreign Affairs* 80(4): 26–39.
Gilley, Bruce. 2004. *China's Democratic Future: How It Will Happen and Where It Will Lead*. New York: Columbia University Press.
Gilpin, Robert. 1983. *War and Change in World Politics*. 1st paperback ed. Cambridge: Cambridge University Press.
Goertz, Gary, and Paul F. Diehl. 1992. Toward a Theory of International Norms: Some Conceptual and Measurement Issues. *The Journal of Conflict Resolution* 36(4): 634–64.
Greenhouse, Steven. 1995. Aides to Clinton Say He Will Defy Beijing and Issue Visa to Taiwan's President. In *New York Times*.
Gries, Peter Hays. 2001. Tears of Rage: Chinese Nationalism and the Belgrade Embassy Bombing. *The China Journal* 46: 25–43.
  2005. Social Psychology and the Identity-Conflict Debate: Is a "China Threat" Inevitable? *European Journal of International Relations* 11(2): 235–65.
Gries, Peter Hays, and Kaiping Peng. 2002. Culture Clash? Apologies East and West. *Journal of Contemporary China* 11(30): 173–8.
Guihong, Zhang. 2005. US-India Strategic Partnership: Implications for China. *International Studies* 42(3–4): 277–93.
Gwertzman, Bernard. 1971a. Firm Soviet Backing of India Is Said to Irk Nixon. In *New York Times*.
  1971b. Goldwater Identifies Kissinger as "Sources." In *New York Times*.
  1971c. U.S. Cuts Economic Aid to India. In *New York Times*.
  1971d. U.S. Says India Attacked after Concessions by Foe. In *New York Times*.
  1972. Packard Opposed Kissinger on India. In *New York Times*.
  1974. Ford and Kissinger Warn Exorbitant Prices of Oil Imperil World's Economy. In *New York Times*.
Haendel, Dan. 1977. *The Process of Priority Formulation: U.S. Foreign Policy in the Indo-Pakistani War of 1971*. Westview Replica Edition. Boulder, CO: Westview Press.
Hall, Rodney Bruce. 1999. *National Collective Identity: Social Constructs and International Systems*. New York: Columbia University Press.
Hansen, Lene. 2000. The Little Mermaids Silent Security Dilemma and the Absence of Gender in the Copenhagen School. *Millennium: Journal of International Studies* 29: 285–306.
Hansen, Lene, and Helen Nissenbaum. 2009. Digital Disaster, Cyber Security, and the Copenhagen School. *International Studies Quarterly* 53(4): 1155–75.
Harding, Harry. 1992. *A Fragile Relationship: The United States and China since 1972*. Washington, DC: Brookings Institution.
  1998. The Halting Advance of Pluralism. *Journal of Democracy* 9(1): 11–17.
Harré, Rom, and Edward H. Madden. 1975. *Causal Powers: A Theory of Natural Necessity*. Oxford: Blackwell.

References

Harris Interactive. 2005. Harris Poll, August 9–16, 2005: Do You Feel That…India Is a Close Ally of the U.S. (United States), Is Friendly but Not a Close Ally, Is Not Friendly but Not an Enemy, or Is Unfriendly and Is an Enemy of the U.S.?: The Roper Center for Public Opinion Research, University of Connecticut.

2006. Harris Poll, July 5–11, 2006: Do You Feel That…India Is a Close Ally of the U.S. (United States), Is Friendly but Not a Close Ally, Is Not Friendly but Not an Enemy, or Is Unfriendly and Is an Enemy of the U.S.?: The Roper Center for Public Opinion Research, University of Connecticut.

Hathaway, Robert M. 2002. The US-India Courtship: From Clinton to Bush. *Journal of Strategic Studies* 25(4): 6–31.

Hayes, Jarrod. 2009. Identity and Securitization in the Democratic Peace: The United States and the Divergence of Response to India and Iran's Nuclear Programs. *International Studies Quarterly* 53(4): 977–99.

2012. The Democratic Peace and the New Evolution of an Old Idea. *European Journal of International Relations* 18(4): 767–91.

Herman, Robert G. 1996. Identity, Norms, and National Security: The Soviet Foreign Policy Revolution and the End of the Cold War. In *The Culture of National Security: Norms and Identity in World Politics*, edited by Peter J. Katzenstein, 271–316. New York: Columbia University Press.

Hickey, Dennis van Vranken. 1998. The Taiwan Strait Crisis of 1996: Implications for US Security Policy. *Journal of Contemporary China* 7(19): 405–19.

Higgott, R. 2004. US Foreign Policy and the "Securitization" of Economic Globalization. *International Politics* 41: 147–75.

Hogg, Michael A. 2000. Subjective Uncertainty Reduction through Self-Categorization: A Motivational Theory of Social Identity Processes. *European Review of Social Psychology* 11: 223–55.

2001. A Social Identity Theory of Leadership. *Personality and Social Psychology Review* 5(3): 184–200.

2003. Social Categorization, Depersonalization, and Group Behavior. In *Blackwell Handbook of Social Psychology: Group Processes*, edited by Michael A. Hogg and Scott Tindale, 56–85. Oxford: Blackwell.

2006. Social Identity Theory. In *Contemporary Social Psychological Theories*, edited by Peter J. Burke, 111–36. Stanford, CA: Stanford Social Sciences.

Hogg, Michael A., and Dominic Abrams. 1993. Towards a Single-Process Uncertainty-Reduction Model of Social Motivation in Groups. In *Group Motivation: Social Psychological Perspectives*, edited by Dominic Abrams and Michael A. Hogg, 173–90. London: Harvester Wheatsheaf.

Hogg, Michael A., **Dominic Abrams**, Sabine Otten, and **Steve Hinkle**. 2004. The Social Identity Perspective. *Small Group Research* 35(3): 246–76.

Hollis, Martin, and Steve Smith. 1990. *Explaining and Understanding International Relations*. Oxford: Clarendon Press.

Hopf, Ted. 1998. The Promise of Constructivism in International Relations Theory. *International Security* 23(1): 171–200.

2002. *Social Construction of International Politics: Identities & Foreign Policies, Moscow, 1955 and 1999*. Ithaca, NY: Cornell University Press.

2010. The Logic of Habit in International Relations. *European Journal of International Relations* 16(4): 539–61.

2012. *Reconstructing the Cold War the Early Years, 1945–1958*. Oxford: Oxford University Press.

Houghton, David Patrick. 2001. *US Foreign Policy and the Iran Hostage Crisis*. Cambridge, New York: Cambridge University Press.

Houweling, Henk, and Jan G. Siccama. 1988. Power Transitions as a Cause of War. *Journal of Conflict Resolution* 32(1): 87–102.

Hughes, Thomas L. 1969. Ayub Seeks Talks with the Opposition on the Political Crisis, edited by United States Department of State: Office of the Historian, United States Department of State.

Hutchings, Kimberly. 2001. The Nature of Critique in Critical International Relations Theory. In *Critical Theory and World Politics*, edited by Richard Wyn Jones, 79–90. Boulder, CO: Lynne Rienner.

Hyde, Henry. 2001. Cnn Evans, Novak, Hunt & Shields: Congressman Hyde Discusses U.S.-China Standoff. In *CNN Transcripts*.

Hymans, Jacques E. C. 2002. Applying Social Identity Theory to the Study of International Politics: A Caution and an Agenda. At *International Studies Association Annual Convention*. New Orleans.

International Institute for Strategic Studies. 2012. Chapter Six: Asia. *The Military Balance* 112(1): 205–302.

Jahn, Egbert, Pierre Lemaitre, and Ole Wæver. 1987. European Security: Problems of Research on Non-Military Aspects. *Copenhagen Papers* 1: 75.

James, Patrick. 2002. Systemism and International Relations: Toward a Reassessment of Realism. In *Realism and Institutionalism in International Studies*, edited by Michael Brecher and Frank P. Harvey: University of Michigan Press.

James, Patrick, and Glenn E. Mitchell. 1995. Targets of Covert Pressure – The Hidden Victims of the Democratic Peace. *International Interactions* 21(1): 85–107.

James, Patrick, and John R. Oneal. 1991. The Influence of Domestic and International Politics on the President's Use of Force. *Journal of Conflict Resolution* 35(2): 307–32.

Jha, Nalini Kant. 1994. Reviving U.S.-India Friendship in a Changing International Order. *Asian Survey* 34(12): 1035–46.

John, A. Tures. 2002. The Dearth of Jointly Dyadic Democratic Interventions. *International Studies Quarterly* 46(4): 579–89.

Johnston, Alastair I. 1995. *Cultural Realism: Strategic Culture and Grand Strategy in Chinese History, Princeton Studies in International History and Politics*. Princeton, NJ: Princeton University Press.

2003. Is China a Status Quo Power? *International Security* 27(4): 5–56.

Johnston, Alastair I., and Robert S. Ross. 1999. *Engaging China: The Management of an Emerging Power, Politics in Asia Series*. London: Routledge.

Jones, Jeffrey M. 2006. Americans Rate Iran Most Negatively of 22 Countries. Available from http://www.gallup.com/poll/21604/Americans-Rate-Iran-Most-Negatively-Countries.aspx. (Accessed April 15, 2008).

Jones, Richard Wyn. 1999. *Security, Strategy, and Critical Theory*. Boulder, CO: Lynne Rienner.

2001. *Critical Theory and World Politics*. Boulder, CO: Lynne Rienner.

Kagan, Robert. 2012. *The World America Made*. 1st ed. New York: Alfred A. Knopf.

Kahl, Colin H. 1999. Constructing a Separate Peace: Constructivism, Collective Liberal Identity, and Democratic Peace. *Security Studies* 8(2–3): 94–144.

Kaplan, Robert D. 2005. How We Would Fight China. In *The Atlantic*.
Kapur, S. Paul, and Sumit Ganguly. 2007. The Transformation of U.S.-India Relations: An Explanation for the Rapprochement and Prospects for the Future. *Asian Survey* 47(4): 642–56.
Katzenstein, Peter J. 1996. *The Culture of National Security: Norms and Identity in World Politics, New Directions in World Politics*. New York: Columbia University Press.
Katzenstein, Peter J., and Nobuo Okawara. 1993. *Japan's National Security: Structures, Norms and Policy Responses in a Changing World, Cornell East Asia Series*. Ithaca, NY: East Asia Program, Cornell University.
Keohane, Robert O. 1984. *After Hegemony: Cooperation and Discord in the World Political Economy*. Princeton, NJ: Princeton University Press.
  1988. International Institutions: Two Approaches. *International Studies Quarterly* 32(4): 379–96.
Keohane, Robert O., and Lisa L. Martin. 1995. The Promise of Institutionalist Theory. *International Security* 20(1): 39–51.
Khan, Roedad. 1999. *The American Papers: Secret and Confidential India-Pakistan-Bangladesh Documents, 1965–1973*. Karachi, Pakistan, New York: Oxford University Press.
Khong, Yuen Foong. 1992. *Analogies at War: Korea, Munich, Dien Bien Phu, and the Vietnam Decisions of 1965*. Princeton, NJ: Princeton University Press.
Kicinger, Anna. 2004. *International Migration as a Non-Traditional Security Threat and the EU Responses to This Phenomenon*. Central European Forum For Migration Research.
Kier, Elizabeth. 1997. *Imagining War: French and British Military Doctrine between the Wars*. Princeton, NJ: Princeton University Press.
Kim, Samuel S. 1998. Chinese Foreign Policy in Theory and Practice. In *China and the World: Chinese Foreign Policy Faces the New Millennium*, edited by Samuel S. Kim. Boulder, CO: Westview Press.
Kim, Woosang. 1992. Power Transitions and Great Power War from Westphalia to Waterloo. *World Politics* 45(1): 153–72.
Kinsella, David, and Jugdep S. Chima. 2001. Symbols of Statehood: Military Industrialization and Public Discourse in India. *Review of International Studies* 27: 353–73.
Knopf, Jeffrey W. 1998. *Domestic Society and International Cooperation: The Impact of Protest on US Arms Control Policy*. Cambridge: Cambridge University Press.
Krause, Keith. 1998. Critical Theory and Security Studies: The Research Programme of "Critical Security Studies." *Cooperation and Conflict* 33(3): 298–333.
Krause, Keith, and Michael C. Williams. 1997a. *Critical Security Studies: Concepts and Cases*. London: UCL Press.
  1997b. From Strategy to Security: Foundations of Critical Security Studies. In *Critical Security Studies: Concepts and Cases*, edited by Keith Krause and Michael C. Williams, 33–59. London: UCL Press.
Krebs, Ronald R., and Patrick Thaddeus Jackson. 2007. Twisting Tongues and Twisting Arms: The Power of Political Rhetoric. *European Journal of International Relations* 13(1): 35–66.

Kugler, Jacek, and Douglas Lemke. 1996. *Parity and War: Evaluations and Extensions of the War Ledger*. Ann Arbor: University of Michigan Press.

Kupchan, Charles. 2012. The Decline of the West: Why America Must Prepare for the End of Dominance. In *The Atlantic*.

Kux, Dennis. 1994. *India and the United States: Estranged Democracies 1941–1991*. New Delhi, London: Sage.

   2002. A Remarkable Turnaround: U.S.-India Relations. *Foreign Service Journal* 79.

Lake, Anthony. 1994. Press Briefing by National Security Advisor Tony Lake, Assistant Secretary of State for Human Rights John Shattuck, Assistant Secretary of State for Asian and Pacific Affairs Winston Lord and Assistant to the President for Economic Policy Bob Rubin. In *The American Presidency Project*: The American Presidency Project.

Lampton, David M. 2001. *Same Bed, Different Dreams: Managing U.S.-China Relations, 1989–2000*. Berkeley: University of California Press.

Laustsen, C. B., and O. Wæver. 2000. In Defence of Religion: Sacred Referent Objects for Securitization. *Millennium: Journal of International Studies* 29: 705–39.

Lebow, Richard Ned. 2010. *Why Nations Fight: Past and Future Motives for War*. New York, Cambridge: Cambridge University Press.

Lemke, Douglas, and Ronald L. Tammen. 2003. Power Transition Theory and the Rise of China. *International Interactions* 29(4): 269–71.

Levine, Steven I. 1998. Sino-American Relations: Practicing Damage Control. In *China and the World: Chinese Foreign Policy Faces the New Millennium*, edited by Samuel S. Kim, 91–113. Boulder, CO: Westview Press.

Levy, Jack S. 1987. Declining Power and the Preventive Motivation for War. *World Politics* 40(1): 82–107.

   1988. Domestic Politics and War. *Journal of Interdisciplinary History* 18(4): 653–73.

Levy, Michael A., and Charles D. Ferguson. 2006. U.S.-India Nuclear Cooperation: A Strategy for Moving Forward. Council on Foreign Relations.

Lewis, Anthony. 1971. The Wringing of Hands. In *New York Times*.

Li, Lianjiang. 2002. The Politics of Introducing Direct Township Elections in China. *The China Quarterly* 171(-1): 704–23.

   2003. The Empowering Effect of Village Elections in China. *Asian Survey* 43(4): 648–62.

Lipson, Charles. 2003. *Reliable Partners: How Democracies Have Made a Separate Peace*. Princeton, NJ: Princeton University Press.

Lomas, Peter. 2005. Anthropomorphism, Personification and Ethics: A Reply to Alexander Wendt. *Review of International Studies* 31(02): 349–55.

Lord, Winston. 1995. U.S. Department of State 95/05/30 Daily Press Briefing. Available from http://dosfan.lib.uic.edu/ERC/briefing/daily_briefings/1995/9505/950530db.html. (Accessed March 11, 2009).

Los Angeles Times. 1974. India Detonates 1st Nuclear Shot for "Technology." *Los Angeles Times*.

Louis Harris and Associates. 1971. Harris Survey, October, 1971: For Each Woman on the List, Tell Me If You Respect Her a Great Deal, Somewhat, or Not at All... Indira Gandhi, Prime Minister of India: The Roper Center for Public Opinion Research, University of Connecticut.

References

1972a. Harris Survey, December 28, 1971–January 4, 1972: How Would You Rate President Nixon on His Handling of the War between India and Pakistan – Excellent, Pretty Good, Only Fair, or Poor?: The Roper Center for Public Opinion Research, University of Connecticut.

1972b. Harris Survey, December 28, 1971–January 4, 1972: In the Recent War between India and Pakistan, Did You Feel More in Sympathy with India or with Pakistan?: The Roper Center for Public Opinion Research, University of Connecticut.

1974a. Harris Survey, July 31–August 2, 1974: Now, Let Me Read You Some Statements About the Situation on Nuclear Development. For Each, Tell Me If You Tend to Agree or Disagree…If Too Many Countries Get a Nuclear Capability, Some Irresponsible Country Is Bound to Set Off a Bomb That Could Blow up the Earth in World War III: The Roper Center for Public Opinion Research, University of Connecticut.

1974b. Harris Survey, July 31–August 2, 1974: Would You Approve or Disapprove of the U.S. Giving Nuclear Reactors and Nuclear Assistance To…(Australia, Israel, Japan, West Germany)?: The Roper Center for Public Opinion Research, University of Connecticut.

Harris Poll, August 31–September 3, 1995: Do You Feel That…China…Is a Close Ally of the U.S. (United States), Is Friendly but Not a Close Ally, Is Not Friendly but Not an Enemy, or Is an Enemy of the U.S.?: The Roper Center for Public Opinion Research, University of Connecticut.

1995b. Harris Poll, August 31–September 3, 1995: Do You Feel That…Taiwan…Is a Close Ally of the U.S. (United States), Is Friendly but Not a Close Ally, Is Not Friendly but Not an Enemy, or Is an Enemy of the U.S.?: The Roper Center for Public Opinion Research, University of Connecticut.

1996a. Harris Poll, February 22–9, 1996: China Is Threatening to Hold Military Exercises Off the Coast of Taiwan in an Attempt to Influence Taiwan's First Democratic Presidential Election in March. Should the United States Send an Aircraft Carrier to the Taiwan Straits to Try to Decrease China's Influence on Taiwan's Election, or Not?: The Roper Center for Public Opinion Research, University of Connecticut.

1996b. Harris Poll, February 22–9, 1996: From What You Know, or Have Heard or Read, Do You Feel That Taiwan Should Eventually Be Reunified with Mainland China under Any Circumstances or Do You Feel China and Taiwan Should Be Reunified Only If the Taiwanese Want to Be Reunified, or Should It Never Be Reunified?: The Roper Center for Public Opinion Research, University of Connecticut.

1996c. Harris Poll, February 22–9, 1996: If Mainland China Tried to Invade Taiwan Militarily, Should America Fight to Defend Taiwan against China, or Not?: The Roper Center for Public Opinion Research, University of Connecticut.

1996d. Harris Poll, February 22–9, 1996: Supporting Taiwan's Bid to Become a Member of the United Nations Might Well Anger China. Should the United States Support Taiwan's U.N. Bid, or Not?: The Roper Center for Public Opinion Research, University of Connecticut.

Lynch, Daniel C. 2006. *Rising China and Asian Democratization: Socialization to "Global Culture" in the Political Transformations of Thailand, China, and Taiwan*, East-West Center Series on Contemporary Issues in Asia and the Pacific. Stanford, CA: Stanford University Press.

2007. Envisioning China's Political Future: Elite Responses to Democracy as a Global Constitutive Norm. *International Studies Quarterly* 51(3): 701–22.

Lynch, Marc. 2002. Why Engage? China and the Logic of Communicative Engagement. *European Journal of International Relations* 8(2): 187–230.

Mahoney, James, and Gary Goertz. 2004. The Possibility Principle: Choosing Negative Cases in Comparative Research. *American Political Science Review* 98(4): 653–69.

Manicas, Peter T. 2006. *A Realist Philosophy of Social Science: Explanation and Understanding*. Cambridge: Cambridge University Press.

Mann, Jim. 1999. *About Face: A History of America's Curious Relationship with China from Nixon to Clinton*. 1st ed. New York: Alfred Knopf: Distributed by Random House.

Maoz, Zeev, and Nasrin Abdolali. 1989. Regime Types and International Conflict, 1816–1976. *Journal of Conflict Resolution* 33(1): 3–35.

Maoz, Zeev, and Bruce M. Russett. 1993. Normative and Structural Causes of Democratic Peace, 1946–1986. *American Political Science Review* 87(3): 624–38.

Marder, Murrey. 1974. U.S. Shifts View of India Role. In *The Washington Post*.

Marwah, Onkar. 1977. India's Nuclear and Space Programs: Intent and Policy. *International Security* 2(2): 96–121.

McCardle, Dorothy. 1974. Discussing India's Nuclear Capability. In *The Washington Post*.

McClellan, Scott. 2001. Press Briefing by Scott Mcclellan. Available from http://georgewbush-whitehouse.archives.gov/news/briefings/20010402.html. (Accessed March 24, 2009).

McCurdy, Jack. 1974. Scholars' Opinions Bode Ill for Nixon's Place in History. In *Los Angeles Times*.

McCurry, Mike. 1995. Press Briefing by Assistant Secretary of State for East Asian and Pacific Affairs Winston Lord and Director of Asian Affairs Robert Suettinger. Available from http://clinton6.nara.gov/1995/10/1995-10-24-briefing-by-winston-lord-and-bob-suettinger-nyc.html. (Accessed March 12, 2009).

McDonald, Matt. 2008. Securitization and the Construction of Security. *European Journal of International Relations* 14(4): 563–87.

McGarty, Craig. 1999. *Categorization in Social Psychology*. Thousand Oaks, CA: Sage.

McMahon, Robert J. 1994. *The Cold War on the Periphery: The United States, India, and Pakistan*. New York: Columbia University Press.

McSweeney, Bill. 1996. Identity and Security: Buzan and the Copenhagen School. *Review of International Studies* 22(1): 81–93.

1999. *Security, Identity and Interests: A Sociology of International Relations, Cambridge Studies in International Relations*. Cambridge, New York: Cambridge University Press.

Mead, Walter Russell. 2012. The Myth of American Decline. In *The Wall Street Journal*.

Mearsheimer, John J. 1990. Back to the Future: Instability in Europe after the Cold War. *International Security* 15(1): 5–56.

Mehta, Pratap Bhanu. 1998. India: The Nuclear Politics of Self-Esteem. *Current History* 97(623): 403.

Mercer, Jonathan. 1995. Anarchy and Identity. *International Organization* 49(2): 229–52.

Meyer, John W., John Boli, and George M. Thomas. 1987. Ontology and Rationalization in the Western Cultural Account. In *Institutional Structure: Constituting State, Society, and the Individual*, edited by George M. Thomas, John W. Meyer, Francisco O. Ramirez, and John Boli. Newbury Park: Sage.

Middleton, Drew. 1974. Who's Next in Atom Club? In *New York Times*.

Mitchell, Sara McLaughlin. 2002. A Kantian System? Democracy and Third-Party Conflict Resolution. *American Journal of Political Science* 46(4): 749–59.

Mitzen, Jennifer. 2006. Ontological Security in World Politics: State Identity and the Security Dilemma. *European Journal of International Relations* 12(3): 341–70.

Moore, David W. 2001. Americans Divided in Feelings About China. Available from http://www.gallup.com/poll/1837/Americans-Divided-Feelings-About-China.aspx. (Accessed April 15, 2008).

2004. Iran or North Korea More of a Threat? It Depends. Available from http://www.gallup.com/poll/14362/Iran-North-Korea-More-Threat-Depends.aspx. (Accessed April 14, 2008).

2005. "Axis of Evil" Countries Seen as America's Greatest Enemies. Available from http://www.gallup.com/poll/15022/Axis-Evil-Countries-Seen-Americas-Greatest-Enemies.aspx. (Accessed April 15, 2008).

Moravcsik, Andrew. 1997. Taking Preferences Seriously: A Liberal Theory of International Politics. *International Organization* 51(4): 513–53.

Morgan, Dan. 1974. India Used Own Material, U.S. Feels. In *The Washington Post*.

Morozov, Viatcheslav. 2002. Resisting Entropy, Discarding Human Rights: Romantic Realism and Securitization of Identity in Russia. *Cooperation and Conflict* 37(4): 409–29.

Mousseau, M., and Y. H. Shi. 1999. A Test for Reverse Causality in the Democratic Peace Relationship. *Journal of Peace Research* 36(6): 639–63.

Müller, Harald. 1993. The Internationalization of Principles, Norms and Rules by Governments: The Case of Security Regimes. In *Regime Theory and International Relations*, edited by Volker Rittberger. Oxford: Clarendon Press.

Müller, Harald, and Jonas Wolff. 2006. Many Data, Little Explanation. In *Democratic Wars: Looking at the Dark Side of Democratic Peace*, edited by Anna Geis, Lothar Brock, and Harald Müller, 41–73. Basingstoke: Palgrave Macmillan.

Nathan, Andrew J. 1996. China's Goals in the Taiwan Strait. *The China Journal* (36): 87–93.

1999. Forward. In *Across the Taiwan Strait: Mainland China, Taiwan, and the 1995–1996 Crisis*, edited by Suisheng Zhao, vii–x. New York, London: Routledge.

2003. Authoritarian Resilience. *Journal of Democracy* 14(1): 6–17.

Nathan, Andrew J., and Robert S. Ross. 1997. *The Great Wall and the Empty Fortress: China's Search for Security*. New York, London: W.W. Norton.

National Security Council. 1971. Contingency Study on Pakistan – East Pakistan Secession (Nssm-118), edited by United States Department of State: Office of the Historian, United States Department of State.

Naughton, James M. 1971. Nixon May Review Trip Unless Soviet Curbs India. In *New York Times*.

NBC News and Wall Street Journal. 1995a. NBC News/*Wall Street Journal* Poll, June 2–6, 1995: Which One of the Following Do You Think Is the Most Serious Foreign Policy Issue Facing the United States Today...Economic Instability in Mexico, Trade Relations with Japan, Relations with China, North Korea's Nuclear Program, the

War in Bosnia, or Relations between Israel and the Arab Nations?: The Roper Center for Public Opinion Research, University of Connecticut.

1995b. NBC News/*Wall Street Journal* Poll, September 16–19, 1995: Which One of the Following Do You Think Is the Most Serious Foreign Policy Issue Facing the United States Today…Economic Instability in Mexico, Trade Relations with Japan, Relations with China, North Korea's Nuclear Program, the War in Bosnia, or Relations between Israel and the Arab Nations?: The Roper Center for Public Opinion Research, University of Connecticut.

2001. NBC News/*Wall Street Journal* Poll, April 20–2, 2001: Today, in General Do You Think of China as More of an Ally or More of an Adversary?: The Roper Center for Public Opinion Research, University of Connecticut.

NBC News, Wall Street Journal, and Hart and McInturff Research. 2006. NBC News/*Wall Street Journal* Poll, March 10–13, 2006: I'm Going to Read You a Number of Actions and Positions That George W. Bush and His Administration Have Taken over the Past Few Years. For Each One, Please Tell Me Whether You Strongly Support That Action or Position, Somewhat Support It, Somewhat Oppose It, or Strongly Oppose It…Signing a Pact with India That Allows India to Buy Technologies from the United States to Develop Its Non-Military Nuclear Energy Program: The Roper Center for Public Opinion Research, University of Connecticut.

New York Times. 1971a. Abetting Repression. In *New York Times*.

1971b. Aid to Democratic India. In *New York Times*.

1971c. An Internal Matter? In *New York Times*.

1971d. McGovern Says India Was Justified in Action. In *New York Times*.

1971e. Transcript of the President's News Conference on Foreign and Domestic Matters. In *New York Times*.

1972. Kissinger Parley Excerpts. In *New York Times*.

1974a. Detente with India. In *New York Times*.

1974b. India's Nuclear Threat. In *New York Times*.

1974c. Kissinger Bids India Join in Curbing Atomic Arms. In *New York Times*.

1974d. On to Armageddon. In *New York Times*.

1974e. Setback Is Seen for Arms Parley. In *New York Times*.

1974f. U.S. Sees "Adverse Impact." In *New York Times*.

1992. The 1992 Campaign, Transcript of First TV Debate among Bush, Clinton, and Perot. In *New York Times*.

1995a. China Warns U.S. Over Taiwan Visitor. In *New York Times*.

1995b. World News Briefs; China Plans War Games Off Coast near Taiwan. In *New York Times*.

Nixon, Richard M. 1971a. The President's News Conference of August 4, 1971. In *Public Papers of the Presidents of the United States: Richard Nixon, 1971*, 849–50. Washington, DC: Office of the Federal Register National Archives and Records Administration: United States Government Printing Office.

1971b. Remarks of Welcome to Prime Minister Indira Gandhi of India, November 4, 1971. In *Public Papers of the Presidents of the United States: Richard Nixon, 1971*, 1079–80. Washington, DC: Office of the Federal Register National Archives and Records Administration: United States Government Printing Office.

1971c. Statement About Additional Funds for Humanitarian Relief and Refugee Rehabilitation in South Asia, October 1, 1971. In *Public Papers of the Presidents of the United States: Richard Nixon, 1971*, 1017–18. Washington, DC: Office of

the Federal Register National Archives and Records Administration: United States Government Printing Office.
   1972. Third Annual Report to the Congress on United States Foreign Policy, February 9, 1972. In *Public Papers of the Presidents of the United States: Richard Nixon, 1972*, 194–346. Washington, DC: Office of the Federal Register National Archives and Records Administration: United States Government Printing Office.
Noorani, A. G. 1981. Indo-U.S. Nuclear Relations. *Asian Survey* 21(4): 399–416.
Nunes, João. 2012. Reclaiming the Political: Emancipation and Critique in Security Studies. *Security Dialogue* 43(4): 345–61.
Oakes, Penelope. 1996. The Categorization Process: Cognition and the Group in the Social Psychology of Stereotyping. In *Social Groups and Identities: Developing the Legacy of Henri Tajfel*, edited by W. Peter Robinson, 65–94. Oxford: Butterworth-Heinemann.
O'Brien, Kevin J., and Lianjiang Li. 2000. Accommodating "Democracy" in a One-Party State: Introducing Village Elections in China. *China Quarterly* 162: 465–89.
OECD. (2010). SITC Revision 3. http://www.oecd-ilibrary.org/trade/data/international-trade-by-commodity-statistics/sitc-revision-3_data-00054-en.
Office of the Prime Minister. 1998. Press Conference Given by Tony Blair, President Clinton and President Santer. Available from http://www.pm.gov.uk/output/Page1164.asp. (Accessed May 28, 2006).
Ollapally, Deepa, and Raja Ramanna. 1995. U.S.-India Tensions – Misperceptions on Nuclear Proliferation. *Foreign Affairs* 74: 13.
Oneal, John R., and Bruce M. Russet. 1997. The Classical Liberals Were Right: Democracy, Interdependence, and Conflict, 1950–1985. *International Studies Quarterly* 41(2): 267–94.
Oneal, John R., Bruce Russett, and Michael L. Berbaum. 2003. Causes of Peace: Democracy, Interdependence, and International Organizations, 1885–1992. *International Studies Quarterly* 47(3): 371–93.
Onuf, Nicholas Greenwood. 1989. *World of Our Making: Rules and Rule in Social Theory and International Relations*. Columbia: University of South Carolina Press.
Oren, Ido. 1995. The Subjectivity of the Democratic Peace – Changing US Perceptions of Imperial Germany. *International Security* 20(2): 147–84.
Organski, A. F. K. 1958. *World Politics*. New York: Knopf.
   1968. *World Politics*. 2nd ed. New York: Knopf.
Organski, A. F. K., and Jacek Kugler. 1980. *The War Ledger*. Chicago, IL: University of Chicago Press.
O'Toole, Thomas. 1974. Experts Fear India's a-Blast May Trigger New Rivalries. In *The Washington Post*.
Owen, John M. 1994. How Liberalism Produces Democratic Peace. *International Security* 19(2): 87–125.
   1997. *Liberal Peace, Liberal War: American Politics and International Security*. Ithaca, NY: Cornell University Press.
Papayoanou, Paul A. 1999. *Power Ties: Economic Interdependence, Balancing, and War*. Ann Arbor: University of Michigan Press.
Peoples, Columba, and Nick Vaughan-Williams. 2010. *Critical Security Studies: An Introduction*. Milton Park, Abingdon, Oxon, England, New York: Routledge.
Perkovich, George. 1998. Nuclear Proliferation. *Foreign Policy*(112): 12–23.

2002. *India's Nuclear Bomb: The Impact on Global Proliferation*. New Delhi: Oxford University Press.
Perlez, Jane, and David E. Sanger. 2001. Collision with China: The Overview; Bush Aides Saying Some Hope Is Seen to End Standoff. In *New York Times*.
Perry, William H. 1995. U.S. Strategy: Engage China, Not Contain It. Available from http://www.defenselink.mil/speeches/speech.aspx?speechid=1023. (Accessed March 12, 2009).
Perry, William J. 1996. DOD News Briefing: Secretary of Defense William J. Perry; March 18, 1996. Available from http://www.defenselink.mil/transcripts/transcript.aspx?transcriptid=446. (Accessed March 12, 2009).
Pew Research Center for the People & the Press. 2001a. Pew News Interest Index Poll, May 11–20, 2001: All Things Considered, Which of These Descriptions Comes Closest to Your View of China Today? Do You Think China Is...An Adversary, a Serious Problem, but Not an Adversary, or Not Much of a Problem?: The Roper Center for Public Opinion Research, University of Connecticut.
2001b. Pew Research Center for the People & the Press Foreign Threats Poll, May 11–20, 2001: I'd Like Your Opinion About Some Possible International Concerns for the US (United States). Do You Think That... China's Emergence as a World Power Is a Major Threat, a Minor Threat, or Not a Threat to the Well Being of the United States?: The Roper Center for Public Opinion Research, University of Connecticut.
Pew Research Center for the People & the Press, and Council on Foreign Relations. 2005. Pew Research Center for the People & the Press/Council on Foreign Relations Poll, October 12–24, 2005: As Far as You Know, Does...India Now Have Nuclear Weapons, or Not?: The Roper Center for Public Opinion Research, University of Connecticut.
Pinsker, R. 2003. Drawing a Line in the Taiwan Strait: Strategic Ambiguity and Its Discontents. *Australian Journal of International Affairs* 57: 353–68.
Prueher, Joseph W. 2001. Collision with China; Envoy's Letter to Beijing. In *New York Times*.
Putnam, Robert D. 1988. Diplomacy and Domestic Politics: The Logic of Two-Level Games. *International Organization* 42(3): 427–60.
Quigley, Craig R. 2001a. DOD News Briefing – Rear Admiral Craig R. Quigley, Dasd Pa; April 3, 2001. Available from http://www.defenselink.mil/transcripts/transcript.aspx?transcriptid=1032. (Accessed March 24, 2009).
2001b. DOD News Briefing – Rear Admiral Craig R. Quigley, Dasd Pa; April 10, 2001. Available from http://www.defenselink.mil/transcripts/transcript.aspx?transcriptid=1056. (Accessed March 24, 2009).
Rajamony, Venu. 2002. India-China-US Triangle: A Soft Balance of Power System in the Making. In *CSIS Occasional Report*. Washington, DC: Center for Strategic and International Studies.
Rathbun, Brian C. 2004. *Partisan Interventions: European Party Politics and Peace Enforcement in the Balkans*. Ithaca, NY, London: Cornell University Press.
Ray, James Lee. 1995. *Democracy and International Conflict: An Evaluation of the Democratic Peace Proposition*. Columbia: University of South Carolina Press.
Reagan, Ronald. 1982. United States-China Joint Communiqué on United States Arms Sales to Taiwan (August 17, 1982). In *Public Papers of the Presidents of the United States: Ronald Reagan, 1982*, 1052–3. Washington, DC: Office of the

References

Federal Register National Archives and Records Administration: United States Government Printing Office.
Reid, Scott A., and Michael A. Hogg. 2005. Uncertainty Reduction, Self-Enhancement, and Ingroup Identification. *Personality and Social Psychology Bulletin* 31: 804–17.
Representative Neil Abercrombie (D-HI). 2001. *United States Missile Defense, United States House of Representatives*, H1668–H69: U.S. Government Printing Office.
Representative Sherrod Brown (D-OH). 1996. *China Threatens Taiwan, United States House of Representatives*, E88: U.S. Government Printing Office.
Representative Dan Burton (R-IN). 1998. India Considers Sanctions a Blessing – Indian Villagers Report Side-Effects from Nuclear Tests. E1123–E25: Washington, DC: United States Government Printing Office.
Representative Christopher Cox (R-CA). 1996a. H.Con.Res.148: A Concurrent Resolution Expressing the Sense of Congress Regarding Missile Tests and Military Exercises by the People's Republic of China, United States House of Representatives, H2342: U.S. Government Printing Office.
　1996b. United States Must Be Clear about Its Position Regarding Democracy in Taiwan, edited by United States House of Representatives, H2327: U.S. Government Printing Office.
Representative Jo Ann Davis (R-VA). 2001. Our Servicemen and Women in China, United States House of Representatives, H1467: U.S. Government Printing Office.
Representative Peter Deutsch (D-FL). 1996. *Sense of Congress Regarding United States Support of Taiwan, edited by United States House of Representatives*, H2347: U.S. Government Printing Office.
Representative Cornelius Gallagher (D-NJ). 1971. The Situation on the Indian Subcontinent. 45545: Washington, DC: United States Government Printing Office.
Representative Elton Gallegly (R-CA). 1995. Supporting Taiwan, United States House of Representatives E1957: U.S. Government Printing Office.
Representative Benjamin Gilman (R-NY). 1996. Sense of Congress Regarding United States Support of Taiwan, United States House of Representatives, H2342–H50: U.S. Government Printing Office.
Representative John Hayworth (R-AZ). 2001. Brandon Funk of Show Low, Arizona, Being Held by the PRC, United States House of Representatives, H1467: U.S. Government Printing Office.
Representative Stephen Horn (R-CA). 1996. Think Twice, Communist China, before You Use Force against Taiwan, United States House of Representatives, H1202–H04: U.S. Government Printing Office.
Representative Duncan Hunter (R-CA). 2001. In Support of a Missile Defense Shield for America, United States House of Representatives, H1831–H32: U.S. Government Printing Office.
Representative Peter T. King (R-NY). 1995. *The United States Must Stand with Taiwan, United States House of Representatives*, E1790–E91: U.S. Government Printing Office.
Representative Bradford Morse (R-MA). 1971. *The Subcontinent – A World Responsibility.* 44355: Washington, DC: United States Government Printing Office.

Representative George Nethercutt (R-WA). 1996. Sense of Congress Regarding United States Support of Taiwan, United States House of Representatives, H2347: U.S. Government Printing Office.
Representative Joseph Pitts (R-PA). 2001. China Is at Fault, United States House of Representatives, H1413–14: U.S. Government Printing Office.
Representative Bob Price (R-TX). 1974. *India's Test of a Nuclear Explosive*. 16192–4: Washington, DC: United States Government Printing Office.
Representative Dana Rohrabacher (R-CA). 1996. Sense of Congress Regarding United States Support of Taiwan, United States House of Representatives, H2344: U.S. Government Printing Office.
2001. Wake up, America: Engagement with China Has Failed, United States House of Representatives, H1564–H49: U.S. Government Printing Office.
Representative Toby Roth (R-WI). 1996. Sense of Congress Regarding United States Support of Taiwan, United States House of Representatives, H2345: U.S. Government Printing Office.
Representative Brad Sherman (D-CA). 2001. Americans Held Hostage, Day Four, United States House of Representatives, H1478: U.S. Government Printing Office.
Representative Christopher Smith (R-NJ). 2001. Urging Introduction of U.N. Resolution Calling Upon the People's Republic of China to End Its Human Rights Violations in China and Tibet, United States House of Representatives, H1371: U.S. Government Printing Office.
Representative Gerald Solomon (R-NY). 1996a. China and Taiwan: The Obvious Differences, United States House of Representatives, E32: U.S. Government Printing Office.
1996b. Sense of Congress Regarding United States Support of Taiwan, United States House of Representatives, H2344: U.S. Government Printing Office.
Representative Clifford Sterns (R-FL). 2001. China: Friend or Foe?, United States House of Representatives, H1354: U.S. Government Printing Office.
Representative James Traficant (D-OH). 2001. China Testing American Resolve, United States House of Representatives, H1414: U.S. Government Printing Office.
Representative Enid Waldholtz (R-UT). 1996. Sense of Congress Regarding United States Support of Taiwan, United States House of Representatives, H2345: U.S. Government Printing Office.
Representative David Weldon (R-PA). 2001. Defense of America's Homeland, United States House of Representatives, H1842–H45: U.S. Government Printing Office.
Representative Heather Wilson (R-NM). 2001. Detention of 24 Crew Members in China, United States House of Representatives, H1465: U.S. Government Printing Office.
Reston, James. 1974. The Nuclear Nightmare. In *New York Times*.
Reuters. 1996. World News Briefs; China Announces Tests of Missiles near Taiwan. In *New York Times*.
Reuveny, Raphael, and Quan Li. 2003. The Joint Democracy-Dyadic Conflict Nexus: A Simultaneous Equations Model. *International Studies Quarterly* 47(3): 325–46.
Risse-Kappen, Thomas. 1995. Democratic Peace – Warlike Democracies?: A Social Constructivist Interpretation of the Liberal Argument. *European Journal of International Relations* 1(4): 491.
Roe, Paul. 2008. Actor, Audience(S) and Emergency Measures: Securitization and the UK's Decision to Invade Iraq. *Security Dialogue* 39(6): 615–35.

Rohrabacher, Dana. 2001. Hastert Questions "Appropriateness" of Congressional Trips to China. In *CNN*.
Roper Organization. 1975a. Roper Report 75-2, January 11-25, 1975: The United States Has Formed Ties of Varying Degrees with Different Nations in the World. Here Is a List of a Few Countries. Would You Read Down That List and Tell Me for Each Country What You Think Would Be Best for Us in the Long Run – to Strengthen Our Ties with Them, or to Continue Things About as They Are, or to Lessen Our Commitments to Them?...India: The Roper Center for Public Opinion Research, University of Connecticut.
   1975b. Roper Report 75-6, June 14-21, 1975: There Are Many Problems Facing Our Nation Today. But at Certain Times Some Things Are More Important Than Others, and Need More Attention from Our Federal Government Than Others. I'd Like to Know for Each of the Things on This List Whether You Think It Is Something the Government Should Be Making a Major Effort on Now, or Something the Government Should Be Making Some Effort on Now, or Something Not Needing Any Particular Government Effort Now... Trying to Seek Agreements with Other Nations to Limit Nuclear Weapons: The Roper Center for Public Opinion Research, University of Connecticut.
Rosenthal, Elisabeth, and David E. Sanger. 2001. U.S. Plane in China after It Collides with Chinese Jet. In *New York Times*.
Rosenthal, Jack. 1972. Anderson Ready for Battle with Government, but Appears Unlikely to Get One. In *New York Times*.
Ross, Robert S. 1995. *Negotiating Cooperation: The United States and China, 1969-1989*. Stanford, CA: Stanford University Press.
   1997. China II: Beijing as a Conservative Power. *Foreign Affairs* 76(2): 33.
   2000. The 1995-96 Taiwan Strait Confrontation: Coercion, Credibility, and the Use of Force. *International Security* 25(2): 87-123.
Roth, Ariel Ilan. 2007. Nuclear Weapons in Neo-Realist Theory. *International Studies Review* 9(3): 369-84.
Rousseau, David L. 2006. *Identifying Threats and Threatening Identities: The Social Construction of Realism and Liberalism*. Stanford, CA: Stanford University Press.
Roy, Denny. 1996. The "China Threat" Issue: Major Arguments. *Asian Survey* 36(8): 758-71.
Rubin, Robert. 1994. Press Briefing by National Security Advisor Tony Lake, Assistant Secretary of State for Human Rights John Shattuck, Assistant Secretary of State for Asian and Pacific Affairs Winston Lord, and Assistant to the President for Economic Policy Bob Rubin. In *The American Presidency Project*: The American Presidency Project.
Rubinoff, Arthur G. 2005. The Diaspora as a Factor in U.S.-India Relations. *Asian Affairs, an American Review* 32(3): 169-87.
Rummel, Rudolph J. 1975. *Understanding Conflict and War*. 5 vols. Vol. 4. Beverly Hills, NY: Sage Publications; distributed by Halsted Press.
Rush, Kenneth. 1974. 162. Telegram Tosec 794/104621 from the Department of State to the Mission to the International Atomic Energy Agency, May 18, 1974, 2238z. In *Foreign Relations, 1969-1976, Volume E-8, Documents on South Asia, 1973-1976*: United States Department of State.
Russett, Bruce M. 1993. *Grasping the Democratic Peace: Principles for a Post-Cold War World*. Princeton, NJ: Princeton University Press.

Russett, Bruce M., and John R. Oneal. 2001. *Triangulating Peace: Democracy, Interdependence, and International Organizations.* New York: Norton.
Saad, Lydia. 2000. Americans Agree That Mideast Is Vitally Important to U.S. Interests. Available from http://www.gallup.com/poll/2821/Americans-Agree-Mideast-Vitally-Important-To-US-Interests.aspx. (Accessed April 15, 2008).
 2008. Americans Most and Least Favored Nations. Available from http://www.gallup.com/poll/104734/Americans-Most-Least-Favored-Nations.aspx. (Accessed April 15, 2008).
Sagan, Scott D. 1996. Why Do States Build Nuclear Weapons?: Three Models in Search of a Bomb. *International Security* 21(3): 54–86.
Sagan, Scott D., and Kenneth N. Waltz. 1995. *The Spread of Nuclear Weapons: A Debate.* 1st ed. New York: W.W. Norton.
 2003. *The Spread of Nuclear Weapons: A Debate Renewed.* 2nd ed. New York: W.W. Norton & Co.
Sagar, Rahul. 2004. What's in a Name? India and America in the Twenty-First Century. *Survival* 46(3): 115–35.
Sahadi, Jeanne. 2012. Why Debt Is a Threat to National Security. In *CNNMoney*.
Salliday, Robert. 1998. Pelosi on China: A Voice in the Global Wilderness? In *San Francisco Chronicle*.
Sanger, David E. 2001a. Collision with China: The Overview; Bush Is Demanding a "Prompt Return of Plane and Crew." In *New York Times*.
 2001b. U.S. Would Defend Taiwan Bush Says. In *New York Times*.
Sanger, David E., and Jane Perlez. 2001. U.S. Sends Beijing Formal Statement Expressing Regret. In *New York Times*.
Sathasivam, Kanishkan. 2005. *Uneasy Neighbors: India, Pakistan and US Foreign Policy*, edited by Tom Lansford and Jack Kalpakian, *Us Foreign Policy and Conflict in the Islamic World*. Burlington, VT: Ashgate.
Saunders, Harold H. 1969a. *Memorandum of Conversation*, edited by United States Department of State: *Office of the Historian*, United States Department of State.
 1969b. *Memorandum of Conversations: New Delhi Advisers Meeting*, edited by United States Department of State: *Office of the Historian*, United States Department of State.
 1969c. *Memorandum of Conversation*, edited by United States Department of State: *Office of the Historian*, United States Department of State.
Schafer, Mark, and Stephen G. Walker. 2006. Democratic Leaders and the Democratic Peace: The Operational Codes of Tony Blair and Bill Clinton. *International Studies Quarterly* 50(3): 561–83.
Schaffer, Teresita C. 2002. Building a New Partnership with India. *Washington Quarterly* 25(2): 31–44.
Schimmelfennig, Frank. 2001. The Community Trap: Liberal Norms, Rhetorical Action, and the Eastern Enlargement of the European Union. *International Organization* 55(01): 47–80.
Schmidt, Vivien A. 2008. Discursive Institutionalism: The Explanatory Power of Ideas and Discourse. *Annual Review of Political Science* 11(1): 303–26.
 2010. Taking Ideas and Discourse Seriously: Explaining Change through Discursive Institutionalism as the Fourth "New Institutionalism." *European Political Science Review* 2(01): 1–25.

Schmitt, Carl. 1928. *Die Diktatur: Von Den Anfängen Des Modernen Souveränitätsgedankens Bis Zum Proletarischen Klassenkampf.* 2. Aufl., mit einem Anhang: Die Diktatur des Reichspr-asidenten nach Art. 48 der Weimarer Verfassung. ed. München: Duncker & Humblot.

2007. *The Concept of the Political.* Translated by George Schwab. Expanded ed. Chicago, IL: University of Chicago Press.

Schrafstetter, Susanna. 2002. Preventing the Smiling Buddha: British-Indian Nuclear Relations and the Commonwealth Nuclear Force, 1964–68. *Journal of Strategic Studies* 25: 87–108.

Schumpeter, Joseph Alois. 1942. *Capitalism, Socialism, and Democracy.* New York: Harper.

Schweller, Randall L., and Xiaoyu Pu. 2011. After Unipolarity: China's Visions of International Order in an Era of U.S. Decline. *International Security* 36(1): 41–72.

Sciolino, Elaine. 1995. In Warning to U.S., China Cracks Down on 2 Dissidents. In *New York Times*.

1996. China, Vying with Taiwan, Explores Public Relations. In *New York Times*.

Scobell, Andrew. 2000. Show of Force: Chinese Soldiers, Statesmen, and the 1995–1996 Taiwan Strait Crisis. *Political Science Quarterly* 115(2): 227–46.

Senator Joseph Biden (D-DE). 2006. *Henry J. Hyde United States and India Nuclear Cooperation Promotion Act of 2006-Conference Report.* S11822–S25: Washington, DC: United States Government Printing Office.

Senator Sam Brownback (R-KS). 1998. *National Defense Authorization Act of 1999.* S6863–S67: Washington, DC: United States Government Printing Office.

Senator Harry F. Byrd, Jr. (I-VA). 1974. *U.S. Participation in the International Development Association.* 16079–96: Washington, DC: United States Government Printing Office.

Senator Robert Byrd (D-WV). 2002. *War on Terrorism.* S700–S08: Washington, DC: United States Government Printing Office.

Senator Frank Church (D-ID). 1971. *War between India and Pakistan and the Ineptitude of U.S. Policy.* 44849–50: Washington, DC: United States Government Printing Office.

Senator Byron Dorgan (D-ND). 2001. *National Missile Defense System, United States Senate,* S4051–S52: U.S. Government Printing Office.

Senator Tom Harkin (D-IA). 1998. *India's Nuclear Tests.* S4680–S82: Washington, DC: United States Government Printing Office.

Senator Fred Harris (D-OK). 1971. *A New Low in American Diplomacy.* 44834–35: Washington, DC: United States Government Printing Office.

Senator Hubert Humphrey (D-MN). 1974. *U.S. Participation in the International Development Association.* 16079–96: Washington, DC: United States Government Printing Office.

Senator Ted Kennedy (D-MA). 1971. *U.S. Policy toward the Crisis in South Asia.* 45124–6: Washington, DC: United States Government Printing Office.

1974. *India and a Comprehensive Test Ban.* 16020–24: Washington, DC: United States Government Printing Office.

Senator Connie Mack (R-FL). 1998. *India-China.* S6357–S59: Washington, DC: United States Government Printing Office.

Senator Frank Murkowski (R-AK). 1996. Senate Concurrent Resolution 43 – Relative to the People's Republic of China, United States Senate, S1605–S06: U.S. Government Printing Office.

Senator Sam Nunn (D-GA). 1996. The Relationship between the United States and China, edited by United States Senate, S1285–S89: U.S. Government Printing Office.

Senator Paul Simon (D-IL). 1996. China, Taiwan, and the United States, United States Senate, S1634–S36: U.S. Government Printing Office.

Senator Arlen Specter (R-PA). 2007. Recent Trip to India, Syria, and Israel. S536–S45: Washington, DC: United States Government Printing Office.

Shambaugh, David. 1994. Growing Strong: China's Challenge to Asian Security. *Survival* 36(2): 43–59.

Shanker, Thom, and Mark Mazzetti. 2009. China and U.S. Clash on Naval Fracas. In *New York Times*.

Shattuck, John. 1994. Press Briefing by National Security Advisor Tony Lake, Assistant Secretary of State for Human Rights John Shattuck, Assistant Secretary of State for Asian and Pacific Affairs Winston Lord, and Assistant to the President for Economic Policy Bob Rubin. In *The American Presidency Project: The American Presidency Project*.

1996. U.S. Department of State 96/03/06 Daily Press Briefing. Available from http://dosfan.lib.uic.edu/ERC/briefing/daily_briefings/1996/9603/960306db.html. (Accessed March 14, 2009).

Shi, Tianjian. 1999. Village Committee Elections in China: Institutionalist Tactics for Democracy. *World Politics* 51(3): 385–412.

Simons, Lewis M. 1974. India Explodes A-Device, Cites "Peaceful Use." In *The Washington Post*.

Singh, S. Nihal. 1983. Can the U.S. and India Be Real Friends? *Asian Survey* 23(9): 1011–24.

Sisson, Richard, and Leo E. Rose. 1990. *War and Secession: Pakistan, India, and the Creation of Bangladesh*. Berkeley: University of California Press.

Slingerland, Edward, Eric M. Blanchard, and Lyn Boyd-Judson. 2007. Collision with China: Conceptual Metaphor Analysis, Somatic Marking, and the EP-3 Incident. *International Studies Quarterly* 51(1): 53–77.

Small, Melvin, and J. David Singer. 1976. The War-Proneness of Democratic Regimes. *Jerusalem Journal of International Relations* 1(1): 50–69.

Smith, Craig S. 2001. Collision with China: Looking Homeward; China Releases U.S. Plane Crew 11 Days after Midair Collision. In *New York Times*.

Smith, Hedrick. 1971. Moscow Assails U.S. Step. In *New York Times*.

Smith, Terence. 1971. U.S. Will Grant No New Permits for Indian Arms. In *New York Times*.

Strang, David, and John W. Meyer. 1993. Institutional Conditions for Diffusion. *Theory and Society* 22(4): 487–511.

Stritzel, Holger. 2007. Towards a Theory of Securitization: Copenhagen and Beyond. *European Journal of International Relations* 13(3): 357–83.

Szulc, Tad. 1971. Enterprise Is Flagship. In *New York Times*.

Tajfel, Henri. 1978. Social Categorization, Social Identity and Social Comparison. In *Differentiation between Social Groups: Studies in the Social Psychology of*

References

Intergroup Relations, edited by Henri Tajfel, 61–76. New York: Academic Press Inc.

Tajfel, Henri, M. G. Billig, R. P. Bundy, and Claude Flament. 1971. Social Categorization and Intergroup Behavior. *European Journal of Social Psychology* 1: 149–78.

Tajfel, Henri, and John Turner. 1979. An Integrative Theory of Intergroup Conflict. In *The Social Psychology of Intergroup Relations*, edited by William G. Austin and Stephen Worchel, 33–47. Monterey, CA: Brooks/Cole Publishing.

Talbott, Strobe. 1999. Dealing with the Bomb in South Asia. *Foreign Affairs* 78(2): 110–22.

2004. *Engaging India: Diplomacy, Democracy, and the Bomb*. Washington, DC: Brookings Institution Press.

Tammen, Ronald L. 2008. The Organski Legacy: A Fifty-Year Research Program. *International Interactions* 34(4): 314–32.

Tammen, Ronald L., and Jacek Kugler. 2006. Power Transition and China-US Conflicts. *The Chinese Journal of International Politics* 1(1): 35–55.

Taureck, Rita. 2006. Securitization Theory and Securitization Studies. *Journal of International Relations and Development* 9(1): 53–61.

Tempest, Rone. 1995. China TV Cautions Voters in Taiwan. In *Los Angeles Times*. Los Angeles.

The Committee of 100. 2001a. Attitudes toward Chinese-Americans & Asian-Americans Survey, March 1–14, 2001: I'd Like You to Think About Various Countries Which May Present a Future Threat to the US (United States) – Perhaps Ten Years in the Future. For Each One, Please Tell Me If Each Country Is an Extreme Threat, Somewhat of a Threat, Not Much of a Threat, or No Threat at All?... China: The Roper Center for Public Opinion Research, University of Connecticut.

2001b. Attitudes toward Chinese-Americans & Asian-Americans Survey, March 1–14, 2001: What Is Your Impression of the Government Of...China? As of Today, Is It Very Favorable, Somewhat Favorable, Somewhat Unfavorable, or Very Unfavorable?: The Roper Center for Public Opinion Research, University of Connecticut.

The Washington Post. 1974a. U.S. Dismayed at Blast, Soviet Union Uncritical. In *The Washington Post*.

1974b. Uranium for India. In *The Washington Post*.

Thornton, John L. 2008. Long Time Coming: The Prospects for Democracy in China. *Foreign Affairs* 87(1): 2–22.

Thornton, Thomas P. 1992. U.S.-India Relations in the Nixon and Ford Years. In *The Hope and the Reality: U.S.-India Relations from Roosevelt to Reagan*, edited by Harold A. Gould and Sumit Ganguly, 91–120. Oxford: Westview Press.

Tilly, Charles. 2001. Mechanisms in Political Processes. *Annual Review of Political Science* 4(1): 21–41.

Timberg, Thomas A. 1998. The Impact of Indian Economic Liberalization on US-India Relations. *SAIS Review* 18(1): 123–36.

Times Mirror. 1995a. News Interest Index Poll, August 17–20, 1995: Do You Think the U.S. (United States) Should Try to Promote Democracy in China, Even If It Risks Worsening Relations with China? Or, Do You Think the U.S. Should Not Get Involved in China's Domestic Affairs, Even If It Means over-Looking Human

Rights Abuses?: The Roper Center for Public Opinion Research, University of Connecticut.

1995b. News Interest Index Poll, August 17–20, 1995: What Is Your Impression: These Days Are Relations between the U.S. (United States) and China Improving, Getting Worse, or Staying About the Same?: The Roper Center for Public Opinion Research, University of Connecticut.

Trumbull, Robert. 1974. Canada Says India's Blast Violated Use of Atom Aid. In *New York Times*.

Tuosheng, Zhang. 2006. The Sino-American Aircraft Collision: Lessons for Crisis Management. In *Managing Sino-American Crises: Case Studies and Analysis*, edited by Michael D. Swaine, Tuosheng Zhang, and Danielle F. S. Cohen, 391–422. Washington, DC, Baltimore, MD: Carnegie Endowment for International Peace; Hopkins Fulfillment Service distributor.

Turner, John C., Michael A. Hogg, Penelope J. Oakes, Stephen D. Reicher, and Margaret S. Wetherell. 1987. *Rediscovering the Social Group: A Self-Categorization Theory*. Oxford, New York: Basil Blackwell.

Tyler, Patrick E. 1995a. China Demands U.S. Cancel Visit by Taiwan's President. In *New York Times*.

1995b. China War Games Viewed as a Tactic to Press Taiwan. In *New York Times*.

1995c. China-U.S. Ties Warm a Bit as China-Taiwan Relations Chill. In *New York Times*.

1995d. Sound and Fury in East Asia. In *New York Times*.

1995e. Taiwan President Throws His Hat in a Powder Keg. In *New York Times*.

1996a. As China Threatens Taiwan, It Makes Sure U.S. Listens. In *New York Times*.

1996b. Beijing Steps up Military Pressure on Taiwan Leader. In *New York Times*.

1996c. China Hints at a Timetable to Take Control of Taiwan. In *New York Times*.

1996d. China Says Maneuvers Will Last through Taiwan's Elections. In *New York Times*.

1996e. China Signaling U.S. That It Will Not Invade Taiwan. In *New York Times*.

1996f. China Warns U.S. To Stay out of Taiwan Feud. In *New York Times*.

1996g. Taiwan's Leader Wins Its Election and a Mandate. In *New York Times*.

1996h. War Games Off Taiwan to Expand, Beijing Says. In *New York Times*.

United Nations. 2010. United States 1971 Total Commodity Trade SITC as Reported (Import, Export).

United States Central Intelligence Agency. 1971. SNIE 32–71: Prospects for Pakistan, edited by United States Department of State: Office of the Historian, United States Department of State.

United States Congress. 1979. Taiwan Relations Act, Public Law 96–8. United States Department of State, Bureau of International Information Programs.

1995. Major Actions on House Concurrent Resolution 53 Thomas.

United States Department of State. 1971a. Conversation among President Nixon, the President's Assistant for National Security Affairs (Kissinger), and Attorney General Mitchell, Washington, DC, December 8, 1971, 4:20–5:01 P.M., edited by United States Department of State: Office of the Historian, United States Department of State.

1971b. Conversation among President Nixon, the President's Assistant for National Security Affairs (Kissinger), and the Ambassador to India (Keating), Washington,

DC, June 15, 1971, 5:13–5:40 P.M., edited by United States Department of State: Office of the Historian, United States Department of State.

1971c. Conversation among President Nixon, the President's Assistant for National Security Affairs (Kissinger), and the Ambassador to Pakistan (Farland), Washington, DC, July 28, 1971, 4:21–4:54 P.M., edited by United States Department of State: Office of the Historian, United States Department of State.

1971d. Conversation among President Nixon, the President's Assistant for National Security Affairs (Kissinger), and the Pakistani Foreign Secretary (Sultan Khan), November 15, 1971, 4:31–4:39 P.M., edited by United States Department of State: Office of the Historian, United States Department of State.

1971e. Conversation among President Nixon, the President's Assistant for National Security Affairs (Kissinger), and the President's Chief of Staff (Haldeman), Washington, DC, November 5, 1971, 8:15–9:00 A.M. Foreign Relations, 1969–76, Volume E-7, Documents on South Asia, 1969–72.

1971f. Conversation among President Nixon, the President's Assistant for National Security Affairs (Kissinger), and the President's Deputy Assistant for National Security Affairs (Haig), Washington, DC, December 12, 1971, 8:45–9:42 A.M., edited by United States Department of State: Office of the Historian, United States Department of State.

1971g. Conversation among President Nixon, the President's Assistant for National Security Affairs (Kissinger), the British Foreign Secretary (Douglas-Home), and the British Ambassador (Cromer), Washington, DC, September 30, 1971, 4:10–5:31 P.M., edited by United States Department of State: Office of the Historian, United States Department of State.

1971h. Conversation between President Nixon and His Assistant for National Security Affairs (Kissinger), Washington, DC, December 9, 1971, 12:44–1:27 P.M., edited by United States Department of State: Office of the Historian, United States Department of State.

1971i. Conversation between President Nixon and His Assistant for National Security Affairs (Kissinger), Washington, DC, June 4, 1971, 9:42–9:51 A.M., edited by United States Department of State: Office of the Historian, United States Department of State.

1971j. Conversation between President Nixon and His Assistant for National Security Affairs (Kissinger), Washington, DC, May 26, 1971, 10:38–10:44 A.M.: Office of the Historian, United States Department of State.

1971k. Minutes of Senior Review Group Meeting. Foreign Relations of the United States.

1971l. Minutes of Washington Special Actions Group Meeting. Foreign Relations of the United States.

1971m. Pakistan-American Relations ** a Reassessment, edited by United States Department of State: Office of the Historian, United States Department of State.

1971n. Transcript of Telephone Conversation between President Nixon and His Assistant for National Security Affairs (Kissinger). Foreign Relations of the United States.

1971o. Transcript of Telephone Conversation between Secretary of State Rogers and the President's Assistant for National Security Affairs (Kissinger), Washington, DC, December 23, 1971, 8 P.M., edited by United States Department of State: Office of the Historian, United States Department of State.

1971p. Transcript of Telephone Conversation between Secretary of State Rogers and the President's Assistant for National Security Affairs (Kissinger), Washington, DC, November 23, 1971, 10:55 A.M., edited by United States Department of State: Office of the Historian, United States Department of State.

1971q. Transcript of Telephone Conversation between Secretary of the Treasury Connally and the President's Assistant for National Security Affairs (Kissinger), Washington, DC, December 5, 1971. edited by United States Department of State: Office of the Historian, United States Department of State.

1971r. Transcript of Telephone Conversation between the President's Assistant for National Security Affairs (Kissinger) and the Pakistani Ambassador (Raza), Washington, DC, December 8, 1971, 2:47 P.M., edited by United States Department of State: Office of the Historian, United States Department of State.

1972. Joint Statement Following Discussions with Leaders of the People's Republic of China, edited by United States Department of State, 812–16: Office of the Historian, United States Department of State.

1974a. 164. Memorandum of Conversation, Washington, DC, May 23, 1974, 10:30 A.M., edited by United States Department of State: United States Department of State.

1974b. 166. Memorandum of Conversation, Washington, DC, June 3, 1974. United States Department of State.

1974c. 170. Memorandum from the Secretary of State Kissinger to President Nixon, Washington, DC, July 23, 1974, edited by United States Department of State.

1982. The "Six Assurances" to Taiwan. In *Taiwan Documents Project*.

United States Department of State Office of the Historian. 2008. Foreign Relations, 1969–76, Volume E-7, Documents on South Asia, 1969–72, Docs 122–97. Available from http://www.state.gov/r/pa/ho/frus/nixon/e7/48213.htm. (Accessed May 23, 2008).

United States Department of the Treasury. 2012. Major Foreign Holders of Treasury Securities. Available from http://www.treasury.gov/resource-center/data-chart-center/tic/Documents/mfh.txt. (Accessed May 15, 2012).

United States Embassy to Iran. 1969. Secretary's Lahore Meeting with President Yahya, edited by United States Department of State: Office of the Historian, United States Department of State.

United States Embassy to Pakistan. 1969. Admiral Ahsan's Call on Under Secretary, edited by United States Department of State: Office of the Historian, United States Department of State.

United States Library of Congress. 2001. Cosponsors: H.R. 1467 to Withdraw Nondiscriminatory Treatment (Normal Trade Relations Treatment) from the People's Republic of China. Available from http://thomas.loc.gov/cgi-bin/bdquery/z?d107:HR01467:@@@P. (Accessed March 26, 2009).

United States Office of the President. 1970a. Memorandum of Conversation: Meeting between President and Pakistan President Yahya. Foreign Relations of the United States.

1970b. Transcript of Telephone Conversation between the President's Assistant for National Security Affairs (Kissinger) and the President's Assistant (Haldeman), edited by United States Department of State: Office of the Historian, United States Department of State.

2005. Joint Statement between President George W. Bush and Prime Minister Manmohan Singh. Available from http://georgewbush-whitehouse.archives.gov/news/releases/2005/07/20050718-6.html. (Accessed May 11, 2012).

2006. Press Gaggle by Secretary of State Rice and National Security Advisor Hadley. Available from http://www.whitehouse.gov/news/releases/2006/02/20060228-7.html. (Accessed May 20, 2006).

Valencia, Mark J., and Ji Guoxing. 2002. The "North Korean" Ship and U.S. Spy Plane Incidents: Similarities, Differences, and Lessons Learned. *Asian Survey* 42(5): 723–32.

Van Hollen, Christopher. 1980. The Tilt Policy Revisited: Nixon-Kissinger Geopolitics and South Asia. *Asian Survey* 20(4): 339–61.

Vaughn, P. Shannon. 2000. Norms Are What States Make of Them: The Political Psychology of Norm Violation. *International Studies Quarterly* 44(2): 293–316.

Von Clausewitz, Carl. 1976. *On War*. Translated by Michael Howard and Peter Paret. Princeton, NJ: Princeton University Press.

Vuori, Juha A. 2008. Illocutionary Logic and Strands of Securitization: Applying the Theory of Securitization to the Study of Non-Democratic Political Orders. *European Journal of International Relations* 14(1): 65–99.

Wæver, Ole, Barry Buzan, Morten Kelstrup, and Pierre Lemaitre. 1993. *Identity, Migration, and the New Security Agenda in Europe*. New York: St. Martin's Press.

Walker, William. 1998. International Nuclear Relations after the Indian and Pakistani Test Explosions. *International Affairs* 74(3): 505–28.

Walt, Stephen M. 1987. *The Origins of Alliances*. Ithaca, NY: Cornell University Press.

———. 1991. The Renaissance of Security Studies. *International Studies Quarterly* 35(2): 211–39.

Waltz, Kenneth N. 1979. *Theory of International Politics*. Reading, MA: Addison-Wesley Publishing Company.

———. 1990. Nuclear Myths and Political Realities. *American Political Science Review* 84(3): 731–45.

Weinraub, Bernard. 1974a. India Becomes 6th Nation to Set Off Nuclear Device. In *New York Times*.

———. 1974b. New Role Abroad Is Likely for India. In *New York Times*.

———. 1974c. U.S. Grain Pledge to India Reported in Kissinger Visit. In *New York Times*, 1.

Welles, Benjamin. 1971a. Divided Attention from Mrs. Gandhi's Hosts. In *New York Times*.

———. 1971b. Mrs. Gandhi Meets Nixon, Asks Pressure on Pakistan. In *New York Times*.

———. 1971c. U.S. Cancels Remaining Export Licenses for Shipment of Military Goods to India. In *New York Times*.

———. 1971d. U.S. Says Indians Bear Main Blame. In *New York Times*.

———. 1972. Anti-India Remark Is Laid to Kissinger. In *New York Times*.

Wendt, Alexander. 1992. Anarchy Is What States Make of It: The Social Construction of Power Politics. *International Organization* 46(2): 391–425.

———. 1994. Collective Identity Formation and the International State. *American Political Science Review* 88(2): 384–97.

———. 1999. Social Theory of International Politics. *Cambridge Studies in International Relations* (67.): xv, 429 p.

Widmaier, Wesley W. 2005. The Democratic Peace Is What States Make of It: A Constructivist Analysis of the US-Indian "Near-Miss" in the 1971 South Asian Crisis. *European Journal of International Relations* 11(3): 431–55.

Wight, Colin. 2004. State Agency: Social Action without Human Activity? *Review of International Studies* 30(02): 269–80.

Williams, Michael C. 1998. Identity and the Politics of Security. *European Journal of International Relations* 4(2): 204–25.

  2001. The Discipline of the Democratic Peace: Kant, Liberalism and the Social Construction of Security Communities. *European Journal of International Relations* 7(4): 525–53.

World Bank. 2012. World Development Indicators. Available from http://data.worldbank.org/data-catalog/world-development-indicators. (Accessed May 15, 2012).

Xinbo, Wu. 2007. Understanding Chinese and U.S. Crisis Behavior. *Washington Quarterly* 31(1): 61–76.

Yang, Carter M. 2001. GOP Divided on China Standoff. In *ABC News*.

Yee, Albert S. 2004. Semantic Ambiguity and Joint Deflections in the Hainan Negotiations *China: An International Journal* 2(1): 53–82.

Zakaria, Fareed. 2008. *The Post-American World*. New York: Norton.

Index

analogy, 71, 90, 129, 135–6
  reluctance of desecuritizing actors to use, 165
  in securitizing discourse, 165
Anderson, Jack, 68, 71, 77
audience. *See* public audience
Awami League party of East Pakistan, 54, 58, 68, 71, 73
Aziz Ahmed (Pakistani Foreign Minister), 81

Bacon, Kenneth (Defense Department spokesman), 123–4
Balzacq, Thierry, 17
Bangladesh War and Bay of Bengal crisis (1971), 12, 42, 47, 49, 52, 55–8, 96, *See also* U.S.-India relations
  Congressional challenges to Nixon policy via India democracy, 71–2
  diplomacy and, 56
  Entrerprise deployment by Nixon and, 49, 55
  historical overview of, 54–5
  Kissinger rape metaphor and, 63
  Kissinger's fear of public backlash from *Enterprise* deployment, 70–1
  lack of public attention to, 74, 75, 78
  New York Times on Nixon's policy during, 73–5
  Nixon Administration self-censorship and policy secrecy and, 74–5
  Nixon and Kissinger's lack of concern over atrocities in, 60–1
  Nixon's public Indian democracy rhetoric and, 61–3
  Nixon's public reframing of Indian democracy and, 53, 63–7, 160
  public opinion polls on India during, 75–7
  public opinion polls on Nixon's handling of, 75–6
  public refusal to 68–71 *See* India as threat during
Biden, Joseph (U.S. Senator), 93
boundary conditions and security construction. *See* socio-political boundary conditions of security
Bunge, Mario, 39–41
Burns, Nicholas (State Department spokesman), 121–2
Burton, Dan (U.S. Representative), 90
Bush Administration. 79, *See also* Congressional securitizing moves and threat construction; desecuritization of China; desecuritization of Indian nuclear program; EP-3 incident (2001); nuclear technology deal (2005–2006)
Bush, George W. (U.S. President), 16

carrier battle groups (CBG), 55, 70, 77–8, 99, 115, 132, 161, *See also Enterprise, Independence; Nimitz*
  Bay of Bengal and, 49
  Clinton Administration deployment of to Taiwan Strait, 140
  public opinion on sending of, 140
Cascading Activation, 28
case selection, 41–5

203

categorization, 28, 164, 165
  cultural congruence and, 28
  external democracies and, 162
causal mechanisms, 39, 41
  democratic peace and, 163
Childs, Marquis, 83
Chilton, Paul, 45
China. 28, *See also* Congressional securitizing moves and threat construction; desecuritization of China; EP-3 incident (2001); Taiwan Strait Crisis (1995–96); U.S.-China relations
  economy of, 100
  elections as non-existent in, 99
  as future world dominant power, 8
  military and nuclear program of, 100
  political relevance of, 100
  rogue nation label, 146
  versus Cuba in U.S. discourse, 132–3
Christiansen, Thomas J., 107
Christopher, Warren (U.S. Secretary of State), 122–3
Church, Frank (U.S. Senator), 72
climate change, 20
Clinton Administration,
  See also Congressional securitizing moves and threat construction; desecuritization of China; desecuritization of Indian nuclear program; nuclear tests (1998); Taiwan Strait Crisis (1995–96)
  avoidance of the authoritarian nature of China's government, 122
  carrier group deployment to Taiwan Strait by, 115, 140
  Indian nuclear tests and, 87, 162
  MFN-human rights policy failure and, 117–18
  sanctions on India and Pakistan by, 79
  visa to Taiwanese President Lee Teng-hui and, 113
Clinton, Bill (U.S. President)
  Indian nuclear tests and, 87–9
Cold War, 6, 39, 51, 52, 141, 159, 163, 164
  U.S.-India relations during, 48, 51
Comprehensive Test Ban Treaty, 51, 85
Congress
  challenge to Nixon attempt to securitize India during Bangladesh War, 71–2
  missile defense debate in, 157
  reaction to peaceful nuclear explosion by, 85
  support of desecuritization in, 149
  support of Nixon's securitization of India by, 67

Congressional securitizing moves and threat construction, 44, 161
  during EP-3 incident, 146–8, 149–51, 157
  House Concurrent Resolution 148 and, 134–7
  ideology and belief systems in, 141
  nondemocratic governance of China and, 124–6, 128–30, 133–7, 140, 141, 146–8, 149–51, 153–4, 161
  shared democracy with Taiwan and, 124–6, 133–7, 140
constructivism, 14, 17, 20, 23, 37, 45, 92
  identity and speech act, 165
  societal constructivism, 10
  U.S.-China relations and, 107
  U.S.-India relations and, 50, 52
context, in security outcomes, 4
Copenhagen School securitization theory, 10, 14–23, 37, *See also* securitization theory
  in empirical context, 38
  external facilitating conditions and, 17–18
  regionalism and multisectorality and, 14
  securitization as ahistorical in, 17
  three main texts of, 14
corporate identity, 27, 28, 31, 32, 33, 35, 36, 38
  democratic identity and, 32
Cox, Christopher (U.S. Representative), 136
Cuba
  U.S. sanctions against, 132
  versus China in U.S. discourse, 132–3
cultural congruence, 28, 29, 30, 33
cyber security, 20

democratic identity, 6, 12, 13, 33, 36, 45, 72, 140; *See also* identity; shared democratic identity; social identity approach (SIA)
  as boundary condition, 20
  corporate identity and, 32, 33
  democratic peace and, 166
  desecuritization moves with democratic external states and, 53
  desecuritization moves with nondemocratic external states and, 108
  as facilitator and limiter of securitization, 164
  Nixon and Kissinger as unbound by, 60
  norms and expectations in social identity approach and, 32–3
  as participatory identity, 33
  as policy constraint, 53, 71, 78, 108, 159, 162

Index

securitization moves with democratic external states and, 39, 53, 160
securitization moves with nondemocratic external states and, 39, 108, 160, 161, 162
threat construction and, 19, 32, 36, 70, 71, 74, 93, 95, 140, 159
as shaper of securitizing moves in democracies and nondemocracies, 163
as shaper of security policy of democratic political leaders, 7, 31–2, 34, 35, 36, 37, 52, 53, 78, 96, 165
undermining of, 166
democratic norms, 32, 33, 36, 39
democratic identity and, 31
democratic peace, 1, 2, 13, 31, 39, 92, 162, 163, 165
becomes a subset of broader security dynamics rather than a special condition, 13
force as damaging to, 166
internal growth of democracy and, 166
international security studies and, 163
linking peace to shared identity, 164
near misses of, 49
neglect of causal mechanisms of in literature of, 163
oppositional identity dynamic in, 166
as subset of state security processes, 38
democratic political behavior. *See* negotiation and compromise reconciliation
democratic states
covert force against other democracies and, 38
covert force between, 38–9
developing democratic states, 47
public as securitization audience in, 34–5
relations between, 35
U.S. policy of spreading democracy by force post-9/11 and, 166
Department of Defense, 44, 145
depersonalization, 26
desecuritization of China (Bush Administration), 161,
See also Congressional securitizing moves and threat construction
Congressional support of in EP-3 incident, 149
emphasis on unusual nature of EP-3 situation and, 144–6
emphasis on utilitarian benefits of U.S.-China relationship and, 148–9, 151

future democracy discourse and engagement policy and, 151–3, 157, 158
shared economic interests, patience, and diplomacy vs. engagement and, 157
desecuritization of China (Clinton Administration), 161,
See also Congressional securitizing moves and threat construction
future democracy discourse and engagement policy and, 121–4, 126–7, 130–3, 141, 158, 161
desecuritization of Indian nuclear program (Bush Administration)
focus on trust and shared democracy and, 91–4
desecuritization of Indian nuclear program (Clinton Administration)
focus on Indian democracy by Clinton and, 87–9
focus on Indian democracy in Congress, 89–90
public acceptance of, 91
desecuritization of Indian nuclear program (Nixon Administration), 81–3
Congress and, 85
Kissinger's lack of reference to Indian democracy and, 85
diplomacy, 152–3
Bay of Bengal (1971) and, 56
Indian nuclear weapons test (1998) and, 91
discourse, 10, 11, 28–31, 44, 141, 144,
See also threat construction
analogy in, 129, 165
of Congress members opposed to securitization, 149
discursive constructivism, 165
identity and, 28, 165
discursive fit, 28, 29, 30, 36
discursive institutionalism, 30, 36
domestic dynamics, 35, 37, 52
international security and, 162, 163
international system and, 4–5
socio-political boundary conditions of security and, 4
domestic salience, 29, 30

East Pakistan. *See* Awami League party of East PakistanBangladeshBangladesh War and Bay of Bengal crisis (1971)
economic interdependence, 101, 102
Enterprise (CBG), 12, 55, 68, 75, 77–8

EP-3 incident (2001), 12, 42, 99, 108, 161
  Congressional securitizing moves and threat construction and, 2–4, 149–51
  Congressional support for desecuritization, 149
  desecuritization attempt by Bush Administration during, 144–6, 148–9, 151–3
  historical overview and literature on, 143–4
  missile defense debate in Congress and, 157
  public opinion polls on, 154–6, 161
Executive Branch, 44, 149, 161
  China policy as preserve of, 141
existential threat, 1, 3, 15, 33, 64, 108, 123, 125, 164
  boundary conditions of, 19, 36
  public acceptance of, 53, 108
  shared democratic identity and, 34, 166
  in social identity, 36

Fleischer, Ari (White House spokesman), 148–9, 151
force, 166, 167, *See also* carrier battle groups (CBG), war
  Bangladesh War as interdemocratic, 56
  covert force against other democracies, 35, 38–9
  covert force against other democracies by U.S., 164
  as damaging to democratic peace, 166
  by democracies against other democracies, 38
  U.S. against India, 49
  U.S. policy of spreading democracy post-September 11, 2001 by, 166

Gallagher, Cornelius (U.S. Representative), 72
Gallegly, Elton (U.S. Representative), 126
Gandhi, Indira (Indian Prime Minister), 47, 48, 59, 62, 72, 79
  public opinion polls on, 76
Gelpi, Christopher, 97
Glenn Amendment, 88
group membership, 25–8, 31
  self-esteem hypothesis and, 27

Hall, Rodney Bruce, 23
Harkin, Tom (U.S. Senator), 90
Harris, Fred (U.S. Senator), 72
hegemonic stability theory, 8
Helms-Burton Act, 132
Hogg, Michael, 25, 27

Hopf, Ted, 10, 23–4, 28, 30, 45
Horn, Stephen (U.S. Representative), 128–9
House Concurrent Resolution 148, 134–7
human rights, 105, 117–19
Hyde, Henry (International Relations Committee Chair), 152

identity, 7, 23, *See also* democratic identity, shared democratic identity; social identity approach (SIA)
  constructivism and, 165
  discourse and, 28, 165
  as facilitating and inhibiting on security, 1
  oppositional, 166
  in securitization, 35
  securitization theory and, 11
  security policy formation in democratic states and, 35
  security processes and, 2
  as state-centric in International Relations scholarship, 23, 24, 25
Independence (CBG), 115, 132, *See also* carrier battle groups (CBG), Taiwan Strait Crisis (1995–96)
India., *See also* Bangladesh War and Bay of Bengal crisis (1971); Congressional securitizing moves and threat construction; desecuritization of Indian nuclear program; Indian nuclear program; nuclear technology deal (2005–2006); nuclear tests (1998); peaceful nuclear explosion (PNE, 1974); securitization of India (Nixon Administration); U.S.-India relations
  as democracy, 47, 73
  economy of, 100
  military of, 100
India and the United States: Estranged Democracies (Kux), 50
Indian nuclear program, 47, 49, 80–1, 83, *See also* desecuritization of Indian nuclear program, nuclear technology deal (2005–2006), nuclear tests (1998), peaceful nuclear explosion (PNE, 1974)
  as case study of shared democratic identity, 96–8, 159–61
  desecuritization of, 6, 80, 95
  gap in between 1974 and 1988, 86–7
  muted response of U.S. to, 52
  structural realism approach to, 80
  subcontinent dominance of due to, 79, 80

Index

India-Pakistan relations, 47, 167,
  See also Bangladesh War and Bay of
  Bengal crisis (1971)
International Atomic Energy Agency
  (IAEA), 6, 48
international norms, 29
International Relations literature
  identity in, 23
  material factors assumption in security
    threats in, 2
  norms and structure as disaggregated
    in, 37
  on U.S.-China relations, 102–8
  on U.S.-India relations, 50–2
Iran, 80, 128
Iranian nuclear program, 3, 161
Iraq, U.S. invasion of, 16, 17

Johnson, Lyndon B. (U.S. President), 48, 51

Kahl, Colin H., 45
Kennedy, Edward (U.S. Senator), 71, 160
  on nuclear proliferation, 85
King, Peter (U.S. Representative), 124–6
Kissinger, Henry (U.S. Secretary of State), 95
  fear of public backlash from *Enterprise*
    deployment of, 70–1
  Indian peaceful nuclear explosion
    and, 81–3
  natural disaster in East Pakistan
    and, 57
  rape metaphor of during Bangladesh
    War, 63
Korean War, 103, 107
Krause, Keith, 10
Kux, Dennis, 50–1

Lee Teng-hui (Taiwanese President), 113,
  114–15
Lewis, Anthony, 74

Mack, Connie (U.S. Senator), 89–90
material-based security approaches
  Cold War and, 6
McClellan, Scott (White House spokesman),
  145
McDonald, Matt, 18
Morse, Bradford (U.S. Representative), 68
motivated bias, 142
Müller, Harald, 29, 38
Murkowski, Frank (U.S. Senator), 133
Mutual Defense Treaty, 109

National Defense Authorization Act for Fiscal
  Year 1999, 90
national imagined community, 23, 31, 32, 53
negotiation and compromise, 31, 32
  in U.S.-Indian relations, 98
neoliberal institutional models, 10, 49, 52
  India nuclear programs and, 52
  U.S.-China relations and, 101–2
  U.S.-India relations and, 56
neorealism, 55, 56
  India nuclear program and, 52, 80
  U.S.-China relations and, 101–2
New York Times, 73, 145
  as data source, 44, 75
  on Nixon administration reaction
    to PNE, 82
  on Nixon's policy during Bangladesh
    War, 73–5
  on peaceful nuclear explosion, 84
Nimitz (CBG), 114, 115, 132, See also carrier
  battle groups (CBG); Taiwan Strait Crisis
  (1995–96)
Nixon Administration. 12, See also Bangladesh
  War and Bay of Bengal crisis;
  Congressional securitizing moves and
  threat construction; desecuritization of
  China; desecuritization of Indian nuclear
  program; Kissinger, Henry (U.S. Secretary
  of State); peaceful nuclear explosion
  (PNE, 1974); securitization of India
  (Nixon Administration)
  animosity towards Indira Gandhi of, 59
  democratic norms and identity and, 60
  Enterprise deployment to Bay of Bengal
    (1971), 49, 55
  fear of public backlash from *Enterprise*
    deployment of, 70–1
  India as threat and, 59–60, 78, 79, 97
  lack of concern over atrocities in Bangladesh
    War and, 60–1
  public and social construction of democracy
    in foreign policy making of, 55–8
  self-censorship and policy secrecy and, 74–5
  support of military government of Khan
    and, 58
  Watergate scandal and, 96–7
nondemocracies, 36, 94, 162, See also China
  democratic security processes with, 39, 99,
    100, 102
  threat perception and, 84, 91
nondemocratic political behavior, 33
  of Yahya Khan (Pakistani President), 61

Non-Proliferation Treaty (NPT), 6, 80, 84
   India and, 52
   peaceful nuclear explosion and, 48
normal politics, 85, 91, 98
norms, 29, 166
   disaggregation of in IR literature, 37
   security policy formation in democratic states and, 35
   structure and, 37
North Korea, 80, 94, 128, 138
nuclear technology deal (2005–2006), 12, 49, 91–5
   historical overview of, 79
   public acceptance and, 53
   public opinion polls on, 94
   trust and shared democracy emphasis in, 91–4
nuclear tests (1998), 12, 49
   Clinton's desecuritization of through focus on Indian democracy, 87–9
   historical overview of, 79
   ignorance of Clinton Administration on, 162
   public acceptance and, 53
   public opinion polls on, 91
   securitization attempts and, 90
nuclear weapons and proliferation, 42, 80–1, *See also* Indian nuclear program; nuclear technology deal (2005–2006); nuclear tests (1998); peaceful nuclear explosion (PNE, 1974)
   Edward Kennedy speech on, 85
   Kissinger speech on, 83
   organizations and, 6
   public opinion polling on, 91
   socio-political context of, 3
   as a top foreign policy concern in polls, 80
Nunn, Sam (U.S. Senator), 130

ontological security, 7, 19
Oren, Ido, 97

Pakistan, 43, 58, 64, 65, 66, 70, 88–9, 91, *See also* Awami League party of East Pakistan; Bangladesh War and Bay of Bengal crisis (1971)
   Condoleeza Rice on, 93
   nuclear program of, 49
   nuclear response of to India's PNE, 79
   U.S. sanctions against, 91
parsimony, 163
peace. , *See also* democratic peace
   public opinion polling on India's threat to, 91
   U.S.-India relations and, 47
peaceful nuclear explosion (PNE, 1974), 12, 48, 49, 81–7, 95–7
   Congressional reaction to, 85
   historical overview, 79
   New York Times on, 84
   public acceptance and, 53
   public opinion polling on, 86
   Watergate scandal and, 96–7
Permanent Normal Trade Relations (PNTR), 148
Perry, William (Secretary of Defense), 126–7
Pitts, Joseph (U.S. representative), 150–1
power transition theory, 7, 8, 9
   ambiguity in, 8
   U.S.-China relations and, 158
Price, Robert (U.S. Representative), 85
public audience. 2, 3, 4, 7, 11, 12, 15–16, 45, 53, *See also* public opinion polls
   acceptance of securitizing moves by, 44, 53, 108, 164
   in authoritarian states, 34–5, 36
   Bangladesh War and, 74, 75, 78
   in democracies, 33, 34–5, 36, 37, 42
   democratic leaders accountability to, 34
   Indian securitization attempts by Nixon Administration and, 68–71, 97
   Nixon's public Indian democracy rhetoric during Bangladesh War and, 61–3
   Taiwan Strait Crisis and, 120, 137–40
   in U.S.-China relations, 105–6
   unsuccessful securitizing moves and, 38
public opinion polls, 75
   audience acceptance of securitizing moves and, 44, 164
   nuclear weapons as top concern and, 80
   on EP-3 incident, 154–6, 161
   on India, 94–5
   on India during Bangladesh War (1971), 75–7
   on Indian nuclear deal (2005–2006), 94
   on Indian nuclear tests (1998), 91
   on involvement in a hypothetical communist attack against India, 76
   on Nixon's handling of Bangladesh War, 75–6
   on peaceful nuclear explosion by India (1974), 86
   on public perception of India and Indira Gandhi (1971), 76

Index

on Taiwan Strait Crisis (1995–96), 137–40, 161
securitizing moves toward India and, 161

Quigley, Craig (Department of Defense spokesman), 153

reconciliation, 32
Republicans in Congress, 141–2
Rice, Condoleeza, 93
rising powers, 7–10, 98
  case studies of U.S. security relations with, 10
  conflict with, 7, 8, 9
  defined, 7
  nuclear weapons and, 52
  social construction of security in policy decisions and, 9
  status quo concept in, 9
rivalry termination, 6, 167
Rohrabacher, Dana (U.S. Representative), 136, 149, 153–4

Saudi Arabia, 36, 162
scientific realism, 39
securitization of India (Nixon Administration), 74
  Congressional and Senatorial challenges to via India democracy, 71–2
  public refusal to 68–71 *See* India as threat and
  reframing of Indian democracy and, 53, 63–7
  silence of *Enterprise* deployment as indicator of unsuccessful, 77–8
securitization theory, 13, 45,
  See also Copenhagen School securitization theory
  as analytical tool, 22
  dyadic dynamics mechanisms in, 38
  in empirical context, 37
  external facilitating conditions and, 17–18
  identity and, 11, 37
  policy response element of, 161
  public audience acceptance of securitizing moves and, 42, 53, 108, 164
  social identity approach and, 35, 37, 164
  war and, 161
securitizing moves, 15–16, 33, 35, 37, 38, 42, 43, *See also* Congressional securitizing moves and threat construction, democratic identity; desecuritization of China; desecuritization of Indian nuclear program; securitization of India (Nixon Administration); socio-political boundary conditions of security; threat construction
  agency of political actors in, 162
  defined, 14
  with democratic external states, 39, 53, 160
  existential threats and shared democracy and, 34
  with nondemocratic external states, 39, 160, 162
  self-categorization and, 36
  temporal framing in, 20, 21–2, 42
securitizing moves, public acceptance of. *See* public audience
security as socio-political construction, 2–4, 13, 19, *See also* socio-political boundary conditions of security; threat construction
  language of security and, 159
  Nixon Administration and, 55–8
  security relations between states and, 3
  threat construction and, 159
security space, 4, 6
  democratic identity and, 6
  political social identity and, 23
security speech act. *See* discourse; securitizing moves
self-categorization, 25–8, 33, 35, 36
  corporate identity and, 27
September 11, 2001
  spreading democracy by force after, 166
  threat construction after, 4
shared democratic identity, 49, 64
  as defuser of conflict between democracies, 167
  desecuritizing narratives and, 164
  existential threats and, 34, 166
  increased risk taking by democratic leaders due to, 167
  Indian nuclear program case studies and, 96–8, 159–61
  India's peaceful nuclear explosion and, 82, 83, 85, 86, 97
  lack of in U.S.-China relations, 158, 162
  need for public emphasis on, 167
  nuclear technology deal and, 91–4
  as policy constraint, 97, 98, 164
  political leaders emphasis on to prevent securitization, 160
  security construction by U.S. leaders and, 108
  testing limits of as research opportunity, 167

shared democratic identity (cont.)
  threat construction and, 12
  U.S. with Taiwan, 120, 124–6, 133–7, 140
  U.S.-India relations and, 47, 159
  unsuccessful securitization of India during Bangladesh War and, 68–71, 74, 77, 78
Simon, Paul (U.S. Senator), 129
Sino-American relations. See U.S.-China relations
Smith, Christopher (U.S. Representative), 147
Social Categorization Theory, 25
social identity approach (SIA), 13, 25, 32–3
  corporate identity and, 28
  external validity of, 38, 165
  group membership and social behavior and, 25
  International Relations and, 38
  scholarship on discursive fit, 30
  securitization theory and, 35, 37, 164
  security space definition and, 31
  self-categorization and ingroup ties and affect, 25–8
  self-esteem as a motivator for group behavior, 27
  theoretical and empirical basis of identity in securitization and, 35
socio-political boundary conditions
  of security, 5, 6, 19, 31, 32, 35, 36, 37, 159, 164
  as broad framework for securitization, 36
  desecuritization and, 6
  domestic and international level interaction and, 4–5
  existential value of objects and, 19
  temporal framing in, 20, 21–2, 42
Solomon, Gerald (U.S. Representative), 135
South Korea, 3
Soviet Union, linking of India to by U.S. Nixon Administration, 59, 65, 66, 75, 77
Specter, Arlen (U.S. Senator), 94
status quo concept, 9
Sterns, Clifford (U.S. Representative), 147–8
structural realism, 10, 27
  Bay of Bengal and, 55
  nuclear proliferation and, 80
  possibility of war between India and U.S. and, 48
systemism, 39–41

Taiwan. 42, 103, 105, See also Taiwan Strait Crisis (1995–96), U.S.-Taiwan relations
  Presidential elections in, 114–15

Taiwan Strait Crisis (1995–96), 12, 42, 99, 103, 104, 108, 140–2, 161
  Chinese military build-up and U.S. response, 113–15
  Clinton Administration policy of engagement to further human rights and democratization of China and, 117–19
  engagement vs. securitization, 119–37
  future democracy discourse and engagement policy desecuritization moves in, 121–4, 141
  granting of visa to Lee Teng-hui Taiwanese, 113
  House Concurrent Resolution 148 and, 134–7
  literature on, 115–17
  public opinion polls on, 161
  public response to, 137–40
  shared democratic identity and, 124–6, 133–7
  Taiwanese Presidential elections and, 113
  threat construction in, 108, 117
Tajfel, Henri, 25, 26
Talbott, Strobe, 162
threat construction, 65, 165,
  See also Congressional securitizing moves and threat construction, desecuritization of China, desecuritization of Indian nuclear program, securitization of India (Nixon Administration)
  against China during EP-3 incident, 149–51, 158
  analogies in, 90
  boundary conditions for successful, 19
  boundary conditions of, 5
  democratic identity and, 1, 19, 32, 33, 36, 53, 70, 71, 74, 93, 95, 159
  economic identity of a fellow democracy and, 97
  governance type centrality in, 136
  identity and, 159
  ideology and belief systems in, 107, 141
  of India by Nixon and Kissinger, 59–60, 68, 78, 79, 97
  of India vs. nondemocratic states, 84, 91
  Indian democracy versus Chinese authoritarianism, 85, 89, 94
  material factor assumption in, 2
  motivated bias and, 142
  nondemocratic governance of China and, 12, 108, 146–8, 153–4, 157, 158
  private rationales behind vs. public presentation of, 53, 108

Index

public acceptance of, 108
rising powers and, 9, 10
after September 11, 2001, 4
shared democratic identity with India and, 68–71
shared democratic identity with Taiwan and, 137, 140
in U.S.-China relations, 108
use of analogies in, 165
Tiananmen Square, 28, 105, 106, 122, 133, 165
public awareness of, 141
Traficant, James (U.S. Representative), 150

U.S.-China relations, 11, 41–4, 99–102, 103, 109, 143, 148–9, *See also* Congressional securitizing moves and threat construction; desecuritization of China, EP-3 incident (2001); Taiwan Strait Crisis (1995–96)
as case study of democratic security with nondemocracies and, 99, 100, 102
constructivism and, 107
economic interdependence and, 43, 101–5
election of Lee Teng-hui and, 114–15
Executive Branch and, 141
future potential international conflict and, 8
global stability and, 100
ideology in, 107, 141
instability of, 158, 162
Korean War and, 103
lack of shared democratic identity in security construction and, 158, 162
literature and scholarship on, 102–8
neoliberal and neorealism models and, 101–2
power transition theory and, 158
public audience in U.S.-China relations scholarship, 105–6
Taiwan and, 109–13
threat as constructed vs. objective reality and, 108
visa to Lee Teng-hui and (Taiwanese President) and, 113
vs. U.S.-India relations, 43, 100
U.S.-India relations, 11, 41–4, 47, 49, 79–81, *See also* Bangladesh War and Bay of Bengal crisis (1971); desecuritization of Indian nuclear program; Indian nuclear program; nuclear technology deal (2005–2006); nuclear tests (1998); peaceful nuclear explosion (PNE, 1974); securitization of India (Nixon Administration)
Bangladesh War and, 56
as case study of shared democratic identity, 47, 49, 159
cultural differences and, 48
during Cold War, 48, 51
economic interdependence and, 49, 50
Indian democracy as a critical factor in, 72
linking of India to Soviet Union by Nixon Administration and, 65, 66, 75, 77
literature and scholarship on, 50–2
neglect of in academia, public and by policymakers, 162
negotiation and compromise in, 98
potential war between, 48
shared democracy as positive sign for future, 98
social construction of democracy of Nixon and Kissinger and, 55–8
trade figures and, 49
U.S. policy towards Indian droughts of 1965 and 1966 and, 48
vs. U.S.-China relations, 43, 100
world peace and, 47
U.S.-Pakistan relations, 48, 51, 63, 75, 91, *See also* Bangladesh War and Bay of Bengal crisis (1971)
U.S.-Taiwan relations., *See also* Taiwan Strait Crisis (1995–96)
economic relations and, 102
historical overview of, 109–13
uncertainty reduction, 27
undemocratic identity, 33
United Nations, 64

Vietnam, 24, 75, 103

war, 42
between democracies, 48, 161
power transitions and, 8
Watergate scandal, 60, 96–7
Welsh School, 11
Wendt, Alexander, 5, 10
Widmaier, Wesley, 24, 57, 97
Williams, Michael C., 10

Yahya Khan (Pakistani President), 54, 60, 61, 62, 67, 69, 71, 73, 74
Nixon Administration support of, 58

Zulfikar Ali Bhutto (Pakistani Prime Minister), 82